CLIO THE ROMANTIC MUSE

CLIO
THE ROMANTIC MUSE

HISTORICIZING THE
FACULTIES IN GERMANY

Theodore Ziolkowski

CORNELL UNIVERSITY PRESS

Ithaca and London

First published 2004 by Cornell University Press

Printed in the United States of America

Library of Congress Cataloging-in-Publication Data

Ziolkowski, Theodore.
  Clio the Romantic muse : historicizing the faculties in Germany / Theodore
Ziolkowski.—1st ed.
    p.   cm.
  Includes bibliographical references and index.
  ISBN 0-8014-4202-8 (alk. paper)
    1. Historiography—Germany—History—18th century.   2. Historiog-
raphy—Germany—History—19th century.   3. Germany—Historiography.
4. Germany—Intellectual life—18th century.   5. Germany—Intellectual
life—19th century.   I. Title.
D13.5.G3 Z56 2004
901—dc22
                                                                        2003020137

Cornell University Press strives to use environmentally responsible suppliers and
materials to the fullest extent possible in the publishing of its books. Such materials
include vegetable-based, low-VOC inks and acid-free papers that are recycled, totally
chlorine-free, or partly composed of nonwood fibers. For further information,
visit our website at www.cornellpress.cornell.edu.

Cloth printing

10 9 8 7 6 5 4 3 2 1

For Charles and Emily Gillispie

CONTENTS

PREFACE

In 1987 I opened a review article titled "Varieties of Experiencing Religion" with the claim that "Clio is arguably the Romantic muse"; the idea underlying that image has occupied my mind ever since. That the nineteenth century paid particular reverence to history is a commonplace of intellectual history. Hajo Holburn maintained in his *History of Modern Germany 1648–1840* that "In the discovery of history, which has added a new dimension to Western thought, the Germany of the first half of the nineteenth century made its most original intellectual contribution to the modern world" (527). G. P. Gooch, Friedrich Meinecke, Ernst Troeltsch, Heinrich von Srbik, Ernst Breisach, and other historians of historiography have amply documented that statement as far as the professional historians of the period are concerned. But it is not sufficiently appreciated, I believe, how profoundly Clio, the muse of history, permeated *every* aspect of thought during the Romantic era: philosophy, theology, law, natural science, medicine, and all other fields of intellectual endeavor.

By "Romantic" I do not mean to imply any specific and rigorous definition or to enter into the lively terminological debate carried on for almost a century by scholars, especially in Germany and the United States. I use the term simply as a code word to designate the social, cultural, and intellectual life in German-speaking lands between the French Revolution and the years following the defeat of Napoleon at Waterloo. Indeed, several of the most important and typical works of the period were written by thinkers whose membership in any narrowly defined "Romanticism" is widely disputed—Hegel, Savigny, even the later Schleiermacher.

It is well understood by thoughtful students of the period that "Romanticism" is not merely a literary or aesthetic movement but, rather, a general climate of opinion touching every realm of intellectual endeavor.

This premise underlies such works as Ricarda Huch's remarkable introduction to German Romanticism (1899–1902), Paul Kluckhohn's survey of Romantic ideas (1930), the mid-century Tübingen lecture cycle edited by Theodor Steinbüchel (1948), and the more recent interdisciplinary symposium edited by Richard Brinkmann (1978). However, those works rarely deal with history and often give little more than a nod to such fields as theology and law. As the significance of interdisciplinarity becomes increasingly evident to scholars in every field, projects have tended at least initially to focus on single individuals, as in the recent interdisciplinary collections revolving around Goethe: e.g., *Johann Wolfgang Goethe: L'Un, l'Autre et le Tout,* edited by Jean-Marie Valentin ; or *Goethe und die Verzeitlichung der Natur,* edited by Peter Matussek.

The following chapters, in contrast, are based on three assumptions. The first is that a new sense of history initiated what Thomas Kuhn in *The Structure of Scientific Revolution* called a "paradigm shift," or what Michel Foucault in *The Order of Things* designated as a new *episteme* in European intellectual life. This diachronic argument is accompanied by a second assumption: that the new "paradigm" or *episteme* can be assayed most thoroughly and systematically if it is disaggregated into the four faculties that, according to the then prevailing theory, encompassed synchronically the world of knowledge: philosophy, theology, law, and medicine. It is the third assumption, finally, that the process of this shift as disaggregated into the faculties can be most clearly traced by considering the intellectual development of specific leaders in each field and the genesis of their foundational works, a process often ignored in more general histories of ideas or historiography. To that extent, this enterprise constitutes a chapter in German *Wissenschaftsgeschichte*—the history of scholarship, science, and the universities—as well as in intellectual biography.

Hence this book is not concerned with what is often understood under German Romanticism—the literature, art, and music of the period. Rather, it deals with its intellectual context and with several academic works of the period between Hegel's *Phenomenology of the Spirit* (1807) and the first volume of Savigny's *History of Roman Law in the Middle Ages* (1815), which had a far-reaching impact on European thought of the nineteenth and twentieth centuries. Indeed, the leading literary figures are mentioned only to the extent that they were associated with the thinkers (e.g., Hölderlin as the friend of Schelling and Hegel, or Brentano as the brother-in-law of Savigny) or that they were themselves engaged intellectually with various fields (e.g., Goethe's studies of morphology).

In the course of teaching a graduate seminar on Romanticism for more than thirty years at Princeton University, I became convinced that German Romanticism cannot be understood without at least a general familiarity with the various fields in which many of the leading writers were professionally engaged—as doctors, lawyers, pastors, scientists, university professors, and otherwise. This is what I set out to demonstrate in my earlier book *German Romanticism and Its Institutions* (1990). Going a step beyond the institutions to the intellectual disciplines informing them, and the thinkers who reshaped those disciplines in the early nineteenth century, this book focuses on the four faculties and the phenomenon of historicization, which governs the Romantic "paradigm" or *episteme*. To the extent that it deals systematically with the faculties of philosophy, theology, law, and medicine/biology, it differs from other works approaching Romanticism from an interdisciplinary point of view (e.g., Brinkmann's symposium or the Goethe collections cited above). And to the extent that it focuses on the theme of historicizing within those faculties it differs from the historiographic works that are concerned principally with developments in the field of history itself (e.g., Gooch, Meinecke, Troeltsch, Srbik, Breisach).

Over a century ago, Wilhelm Dilthey opened his *Life of Schleiermacher* with the claim that Kant's philosophy can be fully comprehended without any consideration of his person and life, but that "Schleiermacher's significance, his world-view, and his works require for any basic understanding a biographical presentation." To the extent that this book applies Dilthey's claim to the other principal thinkers that it treats, it is methodologically akin to Robert J. Richards's recent *Romantic Conception of Life,* which deals broadly with "science and philosophy in the age of Goethe." Richards perfectly expresses my view that "we catch ideas in the making only when we understand rather intimately the character—the attitudes, the intellectual beliefs, the emotional reactions—of the thinkers in question" (5).

Interdisciplinary undertakings of this scope are often left to conferences or symposia or lecture cycles involving specialists from various fields. Nevertheless, the individual scholar has certain advantages. First, he can provide a sustained focus that is often lacking in conference papers—in this case, on the theme of historicization in the four faculties. Second, he can offer a consistent methodological approach from field to field and from chapter to chapter—a focus that, in this case, involves the attempt to show biographically how and why the representative leaders in their fields were led to a sense of history. Third, he can—indeed, he must because he is dealing with such varied disciplines—present the material in a manner accessible to the non-specialist. Finally, while I have relied gratefully on the standard histories of the various disciplines and the biographies of the principal figures, a synchronic treatment can generate surprising insights and thematic commonalities that may not emerge in more specialized approaches.

As I was making my final revisions, Robert J. Richards sent me his newly published *Romantic Conception of Life,* in which I quickly recognized a kindred spirit. I am indebted to him for the intellectual stimulation that his book provided as I completed my work, and specifically his chapter on medicine and biology. As a referee for Cornell University Press, Karl Ameriks brought to my manuscript an unusual breadth and depth of learning in the intellectual culture of Germany during the age of Romanticism; his suggestions have appreciably sharpened my argument, especially in the chapter on philosophy. Bernhard Kendler is a true author's editor—steadily supportive and challenging when necessary. I am grateful to Herman Rapaport for his incisive comments and the thoughtful attention that he devoted to my manuscript; and I admire the professional skill with which Susan Barnett and Teresa Jesionowski of Cornell University Press handled the many technical and administrative matters associated with publication. The dedication, finally, attests to my family's friendship of almost forty years with one of the world's most distinguished historians of science and his muse-in-residence.

Theodore Ziolkowski

Princeton, New Jersey

CLIO THE ROMANTIC MUSE

One

ᕲᕡ

HISTORY

FROM DECORATION
TO DISCIPLINE

The Sense of History

O N 18 September 1806 the newly promoted professor *extraordinarius* Georg Wilhelm Friedrich Hegel delivered his final lecture of the summer semester and, though he did not yet know it, his last lecture altogether at the University of Jena, concluding his course on phenomenology of the spirit with the exhortation:

> This, gentlemen, is speculative philosophy, as far as I have come in my elaboration of it. Consider it as a beginning of philosophizing, which you will continue. We are standing in an important epoch, a fermentation where spirit has made a leap and moved beyond its previous form to assume a new one. The entire body of earlier ideas, concepts, the boundaries of the world, are dissolved and, like a dream vision, collapse upon themselves. The spirit is preparing to emerge anew. It is the principal task of philosophy to welcome its appearance and to acknowledge it, while others, impotently resisting, cling to the past, and the majority mindlessly make up the mass of its apparition. But philosophy, recognizing it as the Eternal, must pay tribute.[1]

Hegel, who would soon leave Jena to become editor of a political newspaper in Bamberg, was addressing his students at a crucial moment in German and European history. Six weeks earlier, on 6 August 1806, Francis II had abdicated as ruler of the Holy Roman Empire, bringing to its igno-minious end an institution that, while long ailing, had nonetheless sur-vived for a millennium—since the crowning of Charlemagne by Pope Leo III on Christmas day in the year 800—as an often dominant force in Eu-ropean politics. Only four weeks later, on October 14, Napoleon's forces would defeat the armies of Prussia in the battle of Jena, sending King Friedrich Wilhelm III into a humiliating exile in the eastern marches and reducing the kingdom of Prussia—which since its establishment in 1701 and under the long reign of Frederick the Great had come to be regarded as the ideal enlightened monarchy—to half its size and power.

During the ten years following the Treaty of Basel (1795), Prussia and its North German neighbors had enjoyed a relatively peaceful neutrality while Napoleon waged his wars in other parts of Europe. From this state of timeless tranquillity thinkers like Kant and Herder cultivated their vi-sions of eternal peace, poets like Hölderlin and Novalis imagined a Europe led spiritually by Germany, and philosophers like Fichte and Schelling con-structed their systems of transcendental idealism. But in 1806 Prussia and the rest of Germany were plunged violently from transcendental timeless-ness into history. Hegel, writing on the eve of the battle of Jena, reported that he had seen Napoleon—"this world-soul" (Weltseele)—riding out from Jena for recognizance: "It is a wonderful sensation to see such an in-dividual, here concentrated on a single point and sitting on horseback, who embraces the entire world and dominates it."[2]

Of course, the sense of history had not been absent in eighteenth-cen-tury Europe, as scholars from Wilhelm Dilthey to Peter Gay have empha-sized.[3] Already in 1770 David Hume wrote confidently from Scotland: "I believe this is the historical Age and this the historical Nation."[4] Such mag-isterial works as Hume's own History of Great Britain (1754–62), Voltaire's Age of Louis XIV (Le siècle de Louis XIV, 1751), Gibbon's Decline and Fall of the Roman Empire (1776–88), and Frederick the Great's History of My Times (Histoire de mon temps, 1746) attest overwhelmingly to that claim. The principal contributions of these historians were the secularization of a history that had previously been religiously eschatological and an expan-sion of its vision to encompass cultural history. But to the extent that their history ignored vast periods and areas; that it was highly judgmental, eval-uating the past by the author's enlightened values or according to what was assumed to be an unchanging natural law; and that it was largely unsys-tematic, being guided by no larger organizing principles—to that extent it fell far short of the standards of modern historiography.

In Germany—and notably in Hanoverian Göttingen with its close ties to England—the situation was similar. The new University of Göttingen, established in 1737, could boast of a proud succession of competent historians, albeit none of European stature: Johann Christoph Gatterer, August Ludwig von Schlözer, Ludwig Timotheus Spittler, and Arnold Ludwig Hermann Heeren, among others.[5] In their capacity as propaedeutic educators for the faculties of law and theology, they applied themselves to detailed source studies and editions, to physical geography, and to *Statistik*, the sociological depiction of political entities and states deemed necessary for the training of future cameralists.[6] The favored mode was *Universal-Historie,* a highly selective account of world history according to a progressive pattern that led unerringly to the enlightened present in its movement from superstition to reason: e.g., Isaak Iselin's *Philosophical Conjectures on the History of Humankind* (*Versuch philosophischer Muthmaßungen über die Geschichte der Menschheit,* 1764).

Outside the universities a totally new and different pre-Romantic conception of history opposed to this Enlightenment version was being proclaimed by the earliest members of what has been called "the great pleiad of heroes who introduced the concept of historical development into the consideration of the world and thus laid the foundation of German culture."[7] The thirty-year-old theologian Johann Gottfried Herder (1744–1803) took on not only the German *Universal-Historiker* but also Voltaire, Montesquieu, Gibbon, Hume, and others in a short treatise entitled *Yet Another Philosophy of History for the Education of Humankind* (*Auch eine Philosophie der Geschichte zur Bildung der Menschheit,* 1774) with the ironic subtitle: "contribution to many contributions of the century." Herder is generally credited with having laid the foundation with this work for the historicism that dominated the nineteenth century.[8] The term "philosophy of history" had already been coined by Voltaire in his *Philosophie de l'histoire* (1765), and a philosophical approach to history had been introduced by the Swiss historian Iselin in his *Philosophical Conjectures on the History of Humankind* (1764). But Herder's small book, based on his earlier studies of the development of language and the historical relativity of poetic styles and genres, belongs among the earliest representatives of the systematic philosophy of history.[9]

It was Herder's ambition to refute the underlying thesis of *Universal-Historie*—that humankind in the eighteenth century had attained a new Golden Age through reason—and to overcome the Enlightenment disdain for earlier ages.[10] Herder argued that humankind moves through history in stages of genetic development, each of which is valuable in itself. The Orient represents humankind in its childhood, and its despotism is no more than the paternal authority required by the child. While ancient Egypt and Phoenicia show us humankind during its boyhood school years, Greece exemplifies its youth and Rome its manhood. What foolishness, cries Herder, to judge any stage in this history by the standards of a different age, for every culture constitutes "that to which God, climate, time, and stage of the world-age were able to shape it."[11] He accuses Hume, Voltaire, and Robertson of wishing to model all centuries after the unique form of their own age.[12] No people can remain forever at one level of development; each has "its period of growth, of blossoming and of decrease."[13] As Herder pithily summarized in one of the most frequently cited sentences: "every nation has its center of happiness within itself, just as every sphere has its center of gravity."[14]

Humankind reached an initial climax with Roman civilization and then disintegrated. (Herder's praise of Greece over Rome is consistent with what E. M. Butler labeled "the tyranny of Greece over Germany" that dominated the decades following Winckelmann.) But rather than blaming Christianity for this decline, as Voltaire and others had done, Herder sees in that religion the "mainspring" ("Triebfeder") of the new process that began with the Middle Ages and extended through the Renaissance to the Enlightenment[15]—not simply repeating the process as it first occurred in the Orient and around the Mediterranean, but going through analogous stages of growth according to the utterly different circumstances of Northern Europe (section 2). Herder concludes his essay (section 3) not with a glorification of the Enlightenment as a new Golden Age, but rather with a series of devastating critiques of every aspect of social and intellectual life in a contemporary society that has lost all virtue and all sense of religion. "Liberty, fraternity, and equality, as they are now sprouting up everywhere—they have brought about evil in a thousand abuses, and will continue to do so."[16]

Herder did not believe that he had written an adequate philosophy of history, for the time was not yet ripe for such an ambitious undertaking. He regarded his work simply as a corrective. As for *"Philosophy of humankind and its true history,"* he confidently believed, "no one but a priest of God will someday write it."[17] Only from the heights of revelation would it be possible to expose "God's order in the human race." In such a philosophy of history, "the noblest history of nature becomes theology." That was the grand project that Herder, himself a theologian and thus a "priest of God," undertook ten years later in his *Ideas toward à Philosophy of the History of Humankind* (*Ideen zur Philosophie der Geschichte der Menschheit,* 1784–91).[18] That *magnum opus,* which for boldness of ambition finds its closest analogy in Hegel's *Phenomenology of the Spirit* and is based on similarly voracious reading in all the sciences of his day, begins not with the earliest human culture, as did *Yet Another Philosophy,* but in the heavens— "Our earth is a star among stars"—because the earth received its shape and composition from powers permeating the entire universe. It proceeds from the organization of the heavens (bk. 1) to the place of man among the plants and animals of the earth (bks. 2–3) and the organization of human reason and intellect (bks. 4–5). Herder spends many more pages (bks. 6–10) discussing the human senses, the development of language, and the most ancient vestiges of anthropological pre-history before he arrives at recorded civilization, which he traces from the Far East (bk. 11) by way of the Near East (bk. 12), Greece (bk. 13), and Rome (bk.14) to an initial summary of stages of culture. The last part (bks. 16–20) deals with the various Northern European peoples, the development of Christianity, the Germanic tribes and the Holy Roman Empire, and the mediation of culture by the Arabs. Since a planned fifth part was never written, the vast fragment ends with the early Renaissance and the age of invention and exploration in Europe.

Herder's *Ideas* was still largely a product of the eighteenth century, focused as it was on the evolution of the physical universe, the development of the earth, and the influence of geographical conditions on the life of nations.[19] But in his concept, alien to other contemporary historians, of the autonomous value of each phase and form of human history, Herder set forth a principle that was to govern future philosophies of history.[20] The modernity of his project is evident in his conception of history not merely as the record of human events but as man's conscious reflection on his nature as a historical being. To that extent this youthful work represents perhaps the earliest premonition of the emerging sense of history in Europe.[21] For the moment, however, Herder's view was rejected by Kant and other academics, and *Universal-Historie* continued to prevail in the schools and universities.[22] The public consciousness had not yet been awakened to the new sense of history.

Three Revolutions

The fall of the Holy Roman Empire and the collapse of Prussia at the battle of Jena were symptoms, not causes. Several powerful factors accounted for the belief in new beginnings and the sense of history that began to permeate German thought during the decade from 1806 to 1815. Most conspicuous among these were the French Revolution and its aftermath, which shook the political foundations of Europe and prompted German intellectuals to reexamine the assumptions and priorities that had dominated the preceding century. It is of course true that the French Revolution itself was the outcome of political and social upheavals that had already shaken the courtly-aristocratic absolutism of the past and opened the way for the middle-class society of the nineteenth century; however, the Revolution was the cataclysmic event that fulfilled and symbolized those changes.

As French and German émigrés were swept across the Rhine before the tides of the Revolution in France, many young thinkers in Germany turned to the past in an effort to understand the present, regarding the Revolution according to Lord Acton as "an alien episode, the error of an age, a disease to be treated by the investigation of its origin."[23] Jacques Droz echoed this thought when he observed that "the excesses that the Revolution had stirred up in France, the crimes that it provoked, the indifference and the despotism into which it degenerated—all this permitted German thinkers to condemn the immorality of the French nation, its impotence to found liberty on a solid basis."[24] And Donald R. Kelley paraphrased it wittily in terms of public opinion: "France seemed to have violated the deepest traditions of European society: 1789 betrayed social order, 1792 betrayed political conventions, 1794 betrayed human values, and 1804 . . . betrayed everything, especially the future of the family of European nations."[25] The reaction is not an uncommon one—the turn to history in response to cataclysmic events of the present. In 1939, composing the preface to volume four of his vast *Study of History*, Arnold Toynbee pointed to the dates of its composition (1933–39) as "painfully appropriate" to the "breakdown" and "disintegration" that constitute its central themes, and he recalled the example of Saint Augustine writing *De Civitate Dei* following the turmoil produced by the Visigothic sack of Rome in 410.

In Germany the shock of the French Revolution and the revolutionary wars produced yet another effect: a new appreciation of German history and culture. In the late summer of 1807, returning from Tilsit where he had witnessed the humiliating truce imposed on Friedrich Wilhelm III of Prussia by Napoleon, the twenty-one-year-old crown prince of Bavaria spent several weeks inspecting the art treasures of Berlin. It was then and there, in the capital city now occupied by French troops and with the royal family in exile in remote Königsberg, that the future Ludwig I conceived the idea of a temple of honor featuring busts of famous Germans.[26] The handsome neo-classical temple set picturesquely above the Danube near Regensburg, and called Walhalla at the suggestion of the Swiss historian Johannes von Müller, was built in the years from 1830 to 1842 by the architect Leo von Klenze as a national monument.

The French Revolution with its consequences was the most important factor, but only one among several other important ones. We know from the writings of Wordsworth, Blake, Carlyle, and others how profoundly the mines, furnaces, and "dark Satanic mills" of the Industrial Revolution stirred the imagination of the English Romantics. In the postscript to *Waverley* (1814; chap. 72) Sir Walter Scott described the transformations that had taken place in Scotland since the insurrection of 1745. "The gradual influx of wealth, and extension of commerce, have since united to render the present people of Scotland a class of beings as different from their grandfathers, as the existing English are from those of Queen Elizabeth's time." It was this sense of social transformation produced by the varied effects of modernization—industrialization, urbanization, and commercialization—that prompted Scott to undertake his portrayal of life "Sixty Years Since."

While Germany lagged considerably behind England in its industrialization, it was by no means immune to the effects of the growing wealth of an industrial and commercial bourgeoisie. Among the hundreds of German principalities, Prussia was the leader.[27] Since the late seventeenth century, Prussia, long the most liberal state in Europe, had welcomed immigrants who brought their abilities into the growing state—the Huguenots with their silk and textile skills, Bohemian craftsmen, Jewish merchants whose trade provided the nobility with goods from afar. To be sure, mechanization was slow. In what has been called "the pre-Homeric Age of industrial Germany," the first modern steam-engine was not set up until 1788 in Prussian Silesia.[28] The first cotton-spinning mill was established in 1794 near Düsseldorf, and that same year a coke-blast furnace was built at Gleiwitz by an engineer brought in from Scotland.[29]

Precisely because of their novelty, these early tentative manifestations of industrialization attracted the attention of young Romantic intellectuals, many of whom pursued the currently fashionable study of mining at the renowned mining academy in the Saxon town of Freiberg, which attracted students from countries extending from the United States to Russia.[30] On the Whitsuntide excursion that Ludwig Tieck and Wilhelm Wackenroder made in 1793—an event often cited to mark the beginning of the Romantic movement in Germany—the two students visited iron mines in Upper Franconia and reported the event in ecstatic letters to their parents.[31] Elsewhere Wackenroder recorded his impressions of pencil and needle factories, of mirror-polishing mills, of manufactories for metal buttons, and other proto-industrial enterprises.

Other, more unsettling manifestations of the post-revolutionary era could soon be perceived.[32] It produced a social mobility that, while still limited, nonetheless enabled enterprising individuals to move beyond the class or estate to which they had previously been bound by traditions existing since the Middle Ages. This new mobility was symbolized by the Prussian reforms of the early nineteenth century: the opening of the civil service to capable individuals recruited from other countries, regardless of class or background. The territorial redistribution following the edict of 1803 (*Reichsdeputationshauptschluß*) completely reorganized the Holy Roman Empire by incorporating scores of previously independent municipalities and principalities, including more than a hundred imperial estates, into a much smaller group of larger states. The liberation of the peasants on the royal domains in Prussia from 1799 to 1805 brought about an extensive agrarian reform by freeing land for thousands of new freehold farms; but it also resulted in unemployment on the land and contributed to the new urban proletariat as peasants made their way into Berlin, seeking jobs in the new mills and factories.

More sinister effects soon made themselves felt, notably in Tieck's and Wackenroder's hometown. Berlin, numbering around the turn of the century some 150,000 inhabitants and at that size the largest city in Germany and sixth-largest in Europe, had already begun to experience the problems of urbanization.[33] The proto-industrial city employed almost a third of its population, 50,000 workers, in its various textile mills. In 1803, fourteen hundred persons worked in the great municipal warehouse—the largest early industrial enterprise in Berlin and Europe's largest cloth factory. Indeed, with an eye to its textile mills, its gold and silver works, its leather and tobacco plants, its sugar refineries, its breweries and distilleries, one contemporary observer called Berlin "in the most literal sense a factory town."[34]

While these workers lived under deplorable circumstances (which later appalled the young Karl Marx), the conditions surrounding the 13,500 soldiers and their families in the vast barracks on the outskirts of the city were scarcely better. The city boasted some 10,000 registered beggars, a group that had swollen after Prussia's calamitous defeat at the battle at Jena, along with a notoriously lively commerce in over fifty houses of prostitution. The moral degradation corresponded to the filth in the poorly illuminated streets with their open gutters. The widely praised promenade Unter den Linden with its elegant buildings amounted to a Potemkin village, behind whose handsome façades a largely miserable urban populace eked out their pitiful existence. Small wonder that German intellectuals, and especially those in Berlin, were challenged to come to grips historically with this new reality. (Early literary evidence of the Romantic critique of the Industrial Revolution can be seen, for instance, in Friedrich Schlegel's rejection of the Storm-and-Stress hero Prometheus in the "Idyll on Idleness" in his novel *Lucinde* [1799].)[35]

Both the French Revolution and the Industrial Revolution contributed to an intensified awareness of time itself. The revolutionaries in France promoted this awareness by the new calendar that they put in place in 1793— a calendar intended to locate their Revolution in history as something utterly novel. In addition, as the economic historian David S. Landes has pointed out, the discipline required by factories and their machines created "a new breed of worker, broken to the inexorable demands of the clock."[36] In its diversity of technological improvement, he continues, "the Industrial Revolution marked a major turning point in man's history."

It should not be forgotten, finally, that in Germany, more so than in other European countries, the turn of the century was marked by great excitement, notably the controversy between the "Ninety-Niners" and the "Nullists" about its proper date, and by innumerable celebrations. "There can scarcely have been any other event that stirred up every contemporary without exception and stimulated everyone to reflection," concluded the scholar who anthologized scores of poems and plays written for the occasion.[37] Meditations on the turn of the century naturally inspired thoughts about history. The theologian Friedrich Schleiermacher concluded his *On Religion* (*Über die Religion,* 1799) with a peroration to the new age. "What is not to be expected from a time that is so obviously the boundary between two different orders of things!"[38]

The French Revolution and the Industrial Revolution were accompanied by an additional cluster of factors that, together, could be called the Epistemological Revolution. I mean by this the sense that the traditional sustaining systems of meaning had collapsed and needed to be replaced by new ones. Most conspicuous among these was the collapse of metaphysics produced by Kant's "Copernican Revolution" in philosophy, which shifted epistemological emphasis from external reality to human consciousness with its categories, and thus posed the problem of subject and object, Self and Other, that obsessed his successors—and, concomitantly, brought about a revaluation of the entire history of philosophy. Second, there was the disenchantment with religion produced by the growing conviction among many believers that neither the sterile externalities of rationalist Christianity nor the effusive introspection of pietism provided an adequate response to the dynamics of the revolutionary age. This sense provoked a new interest in the history of Christianity and the role of history in religion. Third, the lively debate aroused by the adherents of a purely rational "natural law" and the proponents of a modern codified law raised serious questions about the entire legal system that had been based for centuries on the *usus modernus pandectarum*—that is, Roman law as modified over time by German customary law. Finally, the collapse of accepted ideologies produced by the Revolution and the "dislocation of certain traditional economic relationships and long-established social customs"[39] called into question the social beliefs that had sustained the pre-revolutionary age.

During the Enlightenment, wrote the legal historian Friedrich Carl von Savigny in 1814, "all sense and feeling for the grandeur and uniqueness of other ages, and for the natural development of peoples and constitutions—that is, everything that makes history salutary and fruitful—was lost." But the three revolutions revitalized the rehabilitation of history, which had hitherto been only tentative, and made the broader German public aware of its urgency. "If we compare the present with past conditions, we should rejoice. The sense of history has been awakened on every side, and beside it that bottomless arrogance has no place."[40] Expressions of this sort make it easy to agree that "the realm of history is the most important concern of the generation that opens the nineteenth century."[41] But it also appears to confirm the view that the new sense of history, which came to fruition in the calm of the restoration succeeding the tumultuous years of the Napoleonic wars, is the product of a conservative world-view—a conservatism exemplified by such arch-enemies as Hegel and Savigny.[42]

These various changes belong to what Michel Foucault, citing mainly French and English examples, calls the discontinuity in the *episteme* of Western culture and thought that took place generally from 1775 to 1825 and whose turning point he locates, albeit without identifying any historical causes, specifically in the years 1795–1800.[43] It was soon apparent that a significant reorganization of institutionalized knowledge was required in order to do justice to the realities of the revolutionary age, a process that occurred in Germany, principally in Berlin, in the years between the battle of Jena and the defeat of Napoleon at Waterloo.

The Four Faculties

Those of us accustomed to the organization of modern universities—with their virtually unsurveyable congeries of schools, divisions, departments, institutes, centers, programs and other units—sometimes need to remind ourselves that, for several centuries, most European universities were based on the simple quaternity of theology, law, medicine, and philosophy—in that order of precedence. The order was of course not an eternal given, but emerged gradually from previously existing arrangements. Indeed throughout the ages, curriculum provides one of the most reliable indices of social values. According to W. H. Auden, "In all societies, educational facilities are limited to those activities which a particular society considers important."[44]

As H. I. Marrou showed in his magisterial study, in classical antiquity "the history of ancient education reflects the progressive transition from a 'noble warrior' culture to a 'scribe' culture."[45] The cultivation of warrior virtues that dominated a youth's training from Homeric times down to Sparta gradually made way in Old Athens for such added accomplishments as music and poetry, while the goal of education shifted to that of a fine mind in a highly trained body (*mens sana in corpore sano*) that the Greeks called *kalokagathia* ("nobleness of character"). To this foundation, classical Athens, as represented by the academies of Plato and Isocrates, added philosophy and rhetoric. In Hellenistic times the syllabus was refined into the *ekkuklios paideia* ("rounded" or "general" education), embracing what came to be known as the seven liberal arts. By the end of the Roman empire, these *artes liberales* had been further subdivided into the *trivium* of grammar, rhetoric, and dialectic (logic)—which gradually expanded to encompass history and ethics[46]—and the *quadrivium* of arithmetic, geometry, music, and astronomy. These subjects constituted the traditional basis of education in Western Europe from antiquity through the Middle Ages.

Beyond the liberal arts, antiquity was familiar with professional schools in a rudimentary form.[47] Hellenistic Greece established medical schools in Alexandria, Pergamum, and many other cities. In Rome the science of law, which was developed and perfected by scholars from the time of Cicero down to Gaius, Ulpianus, and other great jurisprudents of the second and third centuries, was taught in a number of schools attached to temples and their libraries. The first schools of theology arose around Origen and other Christian apologists of the third century. For a variety of reasons, however, these early models disappeared from the scene for several centuries following the disintegration of the Roman Empire.

The liberal arts survived in the church schools of the Middle Ages, but gradually the rudimentary knowledge that could be acquired there became inadequate for the needs of the times. The history of universities began with the establishment of specialized professional schools: for medicine at Salerno in the eleventh century; for law at Bologna early in the twelfth century; and for theology at the Sorbonne in Paris before the end of that century.[48] By the middle of the thirteenth century, when Henri d'Andeli wrote his satirical *Battle of the Seven Arts* (*La bataille des vii ars*), the classical arts had clearly lost their precedence and given way to the more lucrative study of law (both civil and canon) and medicine. (Henri's lament sounds remarkably contemporary in its tone and relevance.) But the professional schools often found it expedient to retain one or two years of general studies, or "philosophy"—especially logic and rhetoric—as preparation for their more specialized curriculum. Philosophy, according to the saying that became current at that time, was reduced to little more than the handmaiden of theology (*philosophia ancilla theologiae*).

Gradually, as new centers of learning were established in other countries, the various faculties often joined forces within a single, loosely organized institution. By the end of the fourteenth century there were almost fifty so-called "universities" spread across Europe, from Portugal to Poland, from England to Hungary, consisting typically of three "higher" faculties—theology, law, and medicine—and the lower faculty of "philosophy," which served as a catch-all for all the other foundational subjects stemming from the original seven liberal arts. In turn, these four faculties reflected the contemporary view of humankind as consisting of soul, social being, body, and mind. This model characterized universities in continental Europe from the late Middle Ages until the end of the eighteenth century—the model underlying the lament of the Reformation Faust in Goethe's drama, who complains in his opening monologue that he has studied all the faculties without attaining true wisdom:

Habe nun, ach! Philosophie,
Juristerei und Medizin,
Und leider auch Theologie
Durchaus studiert, mit heißem Bemühn.
Da steh' ich nun, ich armer Tor,
Und bin so klug als wie zuvor!

(I've now, alas, studied philosophy, law and medicine, and—sad to say—
even theology with eager striving. Here I stand now, poor fool that I am,
no wiser than before.)

This fourfold organization did not imply an even distribution of interest, and the available enrollment statistics reflect the shifting intellectual and social priorities from the Reformation to the Enlightenment and beyond. For several centuries, the contest was between theology and law, and theology was initially, at least in name, the Queen of the Sciences. (Philosophy tended to be a holding field for students with no clear career goals.) During the late seventeenth and eighteenth centuries, enrollments in law surged dramatically in the new mercantile society as the demand for trained jurists became more urgent and ambitious young bourgeois sought careers in government. The faculty of law at a German university amounted more or less to a faculty of social sciences that trained the aspiring lawyer not so much in the practice of law as in its theory and in the cameral skills required by officials in government ministries. For the century as a whole, the enrollments in law amounted to thirty-five percent of the student population in Germany, and at certain universities with a reputation in the field—e.g., Strasbourg—the proportion was well over fifty percent. Theology, in contrast, lost much of its former prestige and was reduced to a refuge for bright but needy students without family connections (e.g., Hegel, Schelling, and Hölderlin, as we shall see). It was only with the rise of the natural sciences in the nineteenth century that medicine achieved full intellectual respectability. And philosophy—which embraced all the liberal arts, including history, mathematics, and the sciences—was regarded simply as the core curriculum or general education that preceded the serious study of a professional discipline.[49] Until late in the eighteenth century, even the professors regarded "philosophy" as a transitional position that supported them until they could move into a more lucratively remunerated "higher" faculty.[50] It was only on the cusp of the nineteenth century that a lively intellectual debate took place that produced a significant realignment of priorities among the faculties. We shall come back to this debate, which is closely tied to the historicization of the faculties.

For the moment we need only to note that the shifting priorities of the nineteenth century were clearly reflected in the curriculum, although for the time being in Germany the structure of the traditional four faculties did not change.[51] The dramatic surge in the natural sciences soon effaced developments in the other disciplines, tempting many of the humanities into an often futile effort to emulate the positivistic methods of chemistry, physics, and biology. As a result, thinkers in the "human sciences" sought new justifications for their disciplines. One of the most influential was the philosopher Wilhelm Dilthey, who in the later nineteenth century began to distinguish rigorously between the *Naturwissenschaften* (natural sciences) and what he termed the *Geisteswissenschaften* (sciences of the human mind), which are based, he argued, on "understanding" (*Verstehen*) rather than the "explanation" that characterizes the natural sciences.[52] Dilthey's categorization, which transcends the traditional boundaries between the four faculties, persisted into the mid-twentieth century as evidenced by C. P. Snow's familiar distinction between "Two Cultures." In the past half century even that binary distinction has given way in the face of an interdisciplinarity that has virtually erased all earlier boundaries and generated the organizational chaos that typifies many campuses today.

Discordant Harmonies among the Faculties

A discordant harmony (*concordia discors*) had been resounding for several decades before Kant, who borrowed the term from Horace's epistles (1.12.19), published *The Conflict of the Faculties* (*Der Streit der Fakultäten*, 1798).[53] In the introduction to this gathering of three essays, he reminded his readers that the four faculties are conventionally divided into three "higher" ones—theology, law, and medicine—whose teachings serve the interest of the state and its citizens; and a "lower" faculty of philosophy, which is concerned solely with pure knowledge and truth. While the three higher faculties are governed by official texts—the Bible, the Prussian legal code, and the medical regulations of the state—philosophy is bound only by reason. It is therefore free to question the findings of theology, law, and medicine in a manner not open to what Kant rather superciliously calls "the businessmen of the three higher faculties." Accordingly, the disharmony among the faculties can and should never be brought to a final resolution, for the philosophical faculty must as a matter of principle constantly challenge the teachings of the other faculties—not only in the interest of truth and reason, but also for the good of the state and its citizens. Indeed, it may well come about, Kant concludes, that the least will become the foremost and that the so-called lower faculty will become the upper one—not in exercising power but in advising the rulers.

In the 1790s the moment was ripe for a realignment of authority within the German universities.[54] In France, the *Convention nationale* had abolished universities throughout the country and replaced them with a group of state-run *écoles spéciales* for specific fields, while scholarly and scientific inquiry was shifted into the Institut National (the former Académie Francaise). England had as yet no true university system, since Oxford and Cambridge amounted to little more than an extension of secondary school with a focus on the ancient classics, while all serious professional training took place in other precincts.

The situation at German universities during the eighteenth century was different, but scarcely better than in France and England. The pedantry of the scholars at what was regarded as a still essentially medieval *Gelehrtenuniversität* was widely ridiculed, as in Mephistopheles' satirical interview with the student in Goethe's *Faust*. The rowdiness of the students was so notorious that the new Prussian legal code, promulgated in 1794, devoted an entire section to universities and specifically to "Academic Discipline." This débacle led to calls for reform. The utilitarian needs of a new bourgeois society, it was argued, could be more usefully provided by specialized schools emphasizing practical training. Accordingly, in the course of the century a variety of such schools was established in Berlin for surgical medicine, veterinary medicine, military medicine, architecture, mining, and agriculture. In their own defense some universities added chairs in such practical subjects as economics and public administration.

By century's end many serious reformers were urging the abolishment of universities altogether, rejecting them as relics of a past monastic life and utterly unsuited for modern realities. This call was tied to the shift moving intellectual endeavors to the scientific academies that had been established during the eighteenth century: notably in Berlin (1700), Göttingen (1751), and Munich (1759). Educational reformers proposed a radical separation at the secondary level between schools for scholars and schools for normal students on the grounds that scholarly learning is useless for professionally active citizens—indeed, it may even be harmful. Others ar-

gued that the educational needs of society would be better served by institutions of a wholly different sort and that universities had become an
intolerable budgetary burden on the state. Public support weakened to
such an extent that, during the Napoleonic era, over half the universities
in Germany disappeared, either because they simply died out, were suspended by Napoleon, or incorporated into other institutions.

As a result of these threatening developments, several young scholars
at the university of Jena in the last decade of the century—brilliant and
ambitious men who believed in the legitimacy of the university as an institution—issued a series of statements that amounted to a wholly new
Romantic theory of the university.[55] The first in the series was the inaugural lecture that Friedrich Schiller, the thirty-year-old playwright who
had been called to Jena as a professor of history in the faculty of philosophy, delivered in 1789. Entitled "What is Universal History and Why
Study It?" ("Was heißt und zu welchem Ende studiert man Universal-
geschichte?")[56] it remarkably anticipates Kant's argument. Schiller begins
by emphasizing the responsibility of the teacher, whose noble mission it is
to expose his students to truth rather than to convey practical information. Schiller makes a distinction between the narrowly focused, professionally oriented student who is studying only in order to make a living
(the "Brotgelehrte") and "the philosophical mind" ("der philosophische
Kopf"), who has loftier goals. He has nothing but contempt for the "Brotgelehrte" whose single-minded concentration on his professional training
causes him to ignore the rest of the world of learning. He argues that people with such a narrow focus actually suppress reform and hold up progress because progress requires fresh efforts and even the invalidation of
earlier training. The bread-scholar cannot tolerate the non-purposiveness
("Zwecklosigkeit") that is the prerequisite for objective judgment and
feels bereft of all context, "because he has neglected to relate his activity
to the great whole of the world."[57]

The philosophical mind works in a totally different manner, seeking
to unify where the bread-scholar differentiates.

> At an early point he convinced himself that in the realm of reason, as in
> the world of the senses, everything is related, and his vigorous longing
> for harmony cannot content itself with fragments. All his strivings are
> directed toward the completion of his knowledge; his noble impatience
> cannot rest until all his concepts have organized themselves into a har-
> monious whole, until he is standing in the middle of his art, his science,
> and from this point surveying its realm with a satisfied gaze.[58]

Schiller ends this introductory lecture by reminding his listeners that they must decide for themselves. He intends to address his lectures only to the second type, the philosophical mind, because the bread-student debases scholarship too much from its lofty purpose and makes too great a sacrifice for too trivial a profit. Schiller's academic career was brief, but his exhortation was soon echoed and elaborated by the compelling moral presence who ascended the lectern in 1794 and developed an entire philosophical system based on what Schiller, in passing, called the "midpoint" ("Mittelpunkt") from which the philosophical mind surveys and unifies its field of knowledge.

Fichte's widely acclaimed *Lectures on the Vocation of the Scholar* (*Einige Vorlesungen über die Bestimmung des Gelehrten,* 1794) began almost five years to the day after Schiller's inaugural lecture and in the same hall.[59] Philosopher that he is, Fichte begins by defining the vocation of mankind in general and then goes on to characterize man's role in society. But the scholar is not simply a member of society; he is also a member of a particular class within that society. This brings Fichte, in his fourth lecture, to his announced topic, the vocation of the scholar. While the goal of society is the satisfaction of human needs, most men are by definition incapable of assessing those needs, because they are limited to the standpoint of their own social class or profession. Among the various human impulses, however, is also an urge to *know;* and it is the cultivation of this talent that has called forth a special profession for its satisfaction: the scholar.

Fichte differentiates three kinds of knowledge: philosophical knowledge, based on purely rational criteria, studies the abilities and needs of mankind; philosophical-historical knowledge, based in part on experience, seeks to understand by what means those needs can be satisfied; historical knowledge ascertains what stage mankind has reached in its progress. It is the true vocation of the scholarly profession, Fichte sums up, to monitor the progress of the human race and to advance its progress as humanity moves toward perfection.

It is clear why Schiller was enthusiastic about the lectures, for Fichte was addressing precisely the same problems that Schiller had raised in his own inaugural lecture. Fichte's understanding of the scholar and his role as opposed to the more specialized professions is closely analogous to Schiller's distinction between the "Brotgelehrte" and the "philosophical mind." In both cases we sense a clear anticipation of the academic transformation that Kant was to formulate a few years later in *The Conflict of the Faculties*: the transformation that removed philosophy—that is, the liberal arts and sciences—from its subservient position as nothing more than a prerequisite for theology, law, and medicine, and set it over and above the three professional faculties.

When Fichte's successor, Schelling, took to the podium in 1802 to deliver his *Lectures on the Method of Academic Study* (*Vorlesungen über die Methode des akademischen Studiums,* 1803), he began with the fundamental question regarding the absolute concept of science or philosophical knowledge.[60] Schelling was troubled by the fact that talented young men at the beginning of their academic careers are confronted with a curriculum that looks either like an undifferentiated chaos or, at best, a broad ocean on which they are afloat without compass or guiding star. He proposes that universities should provide a course of general education concerning the purpose and nature of academic study. Such an introduction is doubly important, he believes, because in science (*Wissenschaft*), as in art, the particular is valued only in its relation to the whole. Even a first-rate jurist or physician can lose sight of that larger whole in his effort to master his particular field of specialization. Only philosophy, Schelling maintains, is capable of permeating the whole human being, liberating the mind from the limitations of a unilateral training and elevating it into the realm of the absolute.

Accordingly, recognition of the "sciences" (that is, all academic fields of learning) as an organic whole must precede any special training in a given field. The individual must understand how his particular discipline is related to the harmonious structure of the whole and must recognize "the living unity of all sciences." This recognition is especially urgent, Schelling claims, in the present age when all the sciences and arts appear to be advancing rapidly toward unity. Such a view, he repeats, can be expected only from the science of all science ("Wissenschaft aller Wissenschaft"), namely philosophy, whose purpose it is to strive for the totality of all cognition. Schelling not only places philosophy at the center of the university; in his survey of the sciences of pure reason—mathematics and philosophy (lectures 4–6)—he even maintains that philosophy, being the basis for all other faculties, should not constitute a separate faculty at all, but should inform and govern the other three.

It is clear that the three series of Jena lectures on the nature of the university share certain basic convictions. From the "midpoint" from which Schiller proposes to view all knowledge, by way of Fichte's "Gelehrter," who surveys all knowledge, to Schelling's idealizing conception of *Wis-*

senschaft—all three view knowledge as a totality and unified whole, in radical contrast to the cumulative erudition that had characterized university education down through the Enlightenment. Their lofty view of the university as institution leads all three to distinguish rigorously between the rightful citizens of the world of knowledge and those who do not belong in such serene surroundings: the "philosophical mind" as opposed to the mere bread-winners; the "Gelehrte" whom Fichte set above the specialist; and—in the final abstraction—that pure knowledge or science that Schelling opposed to the temporal activity of the three professional faculties. Like Kant, Fichte and Schelling placed philosophy at the center of the university curriculum in the hope of providing the unified view of knowledge that would bring together the previously disparate fields of the arts and sciences, as well as the professions of law, medicine, and theology. And both Schiller and Fichte—Schiller as a historian and Fichte through his threefold articulation of knowledge—elevated history to a level hitherto unknown. Clearly, then, by the beginning of the nineteenth century the traditional ordering of the four faculties was being challenged along with the very nature of their disciplines.

History as a Discipline

The subject of history belonged to the faculty of philosophy wherein it had long constituted an aspect of the study of Greek and Roman antiquity.[61] Because history as such was not highly regarded, for centuries it did not exist as an autonomous subject at any university in Germany.[62] The Protestant universities newly founded in the sixteenth century—Wittenberg, Marburg, Königsberg, Jena, and Helmstedt—as well as the older "reformed" institutions at Tübingen, Leipzig, Basel, Frankfurt an der Oder, Greifswald, Rostock, and Heidelberg had no chairs for history. In the thinking of such leading humanists as Melanchthon (1497–1560), history was simply a storehouse of edifying examples that could be culled for moral instruction and rhetorical effect: as Melanchthon put it in his *omnium humanorum officiorum exempla* ("examples of all human duties"), *Praise of Eloquence (Encomium eloquentiae)*. Until the late eighteenth century, educators were fond of quoting the Ciceronian adage, *historia magistra vitae* ("history is the preceptress of life").[63] There was no effort to justify history independent of ethics and rhetoric, and its professors, regarding themselves essentially as pedagogues rather than scholars, were content with a methodological eclecticism and lacked the experience or desire to deal critically with documents and testimonies from the past.[64]

It was only after the middle of the seventeenth century, first at Helmstedt and then gradually at other Protestant universities, that history obtained disciplinary acknowledgement in the narrow form of church history at the introductory level of the faculty of philosophy where it was taught as a service course for future theologians. Church history was not finally accepted in the Catholic universities until the eighteenth century. But by the middle of that century the subject had often been shifted from the faculty of philosophy into the faculty of theology where it was granted full status (at appreciably better salaries!).

A somewhat different process occurred with jurisprudence. Although history at the propaedeutic level had been taught as general education for future law students since the middle of the seventeenth century, it was not subsequently taken over into the faculties of law. (Even today only a few universities in Germany locate their chairs for the history of law within the faculty of law.)[65] Accordingly, as faculties of philosophy gradually relinquished the field of church history to the faculties of theology and history became "de-theologized,"[66] they willingly and increasingly took on the responsibility of teaching a more secularized history to the future lawyers and cameralists of the state. The chairs for this new field of European political and institutional history that was required for the pre-law curriculum remained distinct from the chairs for the older and often purely ornamental "world history" that had previously split off from rhetoric.

It was at the University of Göttingen, newly established in 1737 to train administrators for the Hanoverian government, that the discipline of history in a recognizably modern form began to emerge in the second half of the eighteenth century.[67] Unlike most other universities, Göttingen granted the theological faculty no power of censorship over the other faculties, and the Göttingen Academy of Sciences, founded in 1751, provided a research center that attracted some of the finest scholars in the historical-philological and mathematical-scientific areas—both representing fields that had hitherto occupied a lowly rank in the traditional hierarchy of faculties and disciplines. Göttingen retained its chair for "universal history" alongside the newer chair for modern institutional history. Although history had still not progressed beyond the stage of a propaedeutic subject and the professional faculties were far from being historicized, the recognition of the law faculties for the need of professionally authenticated legal materials represented a significant first step in the emergence of history as an independent academic discipline, which went far beyond the older view of history as nothing more than a source for moral edification. As yet, however, Johann Jakob Eschenburg in his standard work on aesthetics (*Theorie der schönen Wissenschaften,* 1783) could still treat "The Writing of History" under the heading "Rhetorik." And the University of Jena in 1789 could still appoint someone like Friedrich Schiller to a chair in history—a celebrated dramatist, to be sure, whose historical accounts of the rebellion of the Netherlands against Spanish rule and of the Thirty Years' War were popular but ultimately "the fruit of meagre learning and an untrained judgment."[68]

A major change took place as an indirect result of the French Revolution and the Napoleonic conquests. Napoleon abolished half (twenty-two) of the existing universities in German states, and the others, if they wanted to survive, had to cast off the medieval trappings and practices that still characterized them. The surviving institutions, and the new ones that were gradually created, organized themselves and their faculties according to more modern criteria. One of these criteria, stimulated by the new sense of history, was the recognition of history as a full-fledged independent academic discipline within the faculty of philosophy and the corresponding shift from the "Dilettantenhistorie" of outsiders like Voltaire, Hume, and Gibbon to a professionalized "Seminarhistorie."[69] The institution where this took place in exemplary form was the University of Berlin.[70]

The University of Berlin

The reasoning behind establishing Berlin as the seat of the new history and its permeation of the other disciplines is almost syllogistic in its rigor. Germany, according to the belief of many young Germans of the revolutionary age, was destined to be the new intellectual center of Europe. Prussia had proved itself to be the center of Germany. Berlin as its capital was the center of Prussia, and the university as its mind was the center of Berlin. The reorganization of the faculties had moved philosophy to the center of the university. And history, as Schiller, Fichte, Hegel and others were in the process of demonstrating, was the new center of philosophy. *Q.E.D.*

It was anything but self-evident in the year 1810 that a new university should be established—and of all places in rationalistic Berlin whose Enlightenment circles had constituted a focal point of opposition to the university as an institution.[71] But the catastrophe at Jena and its consequences changed this thinking. Ever since Friedrich Wilhelm III ascended the throne in 1797, progressive thinkers at court as well as among educational reformers had continued to discuss the idea of founding an institution that would unify and reinvigorate the various cultural and intellectual arrangements of the Prussian capital: primarily the Academy of Sciences, which had deteriorated into what some members called a "dead and mystical body" (*corpus mysticum et mortuum*);[72] the thriving medical Collegium and other professional schools; and the public lectures regularly delivered by such highly regarded scholars as the philosopher Fichte, the theologian Schleiermacher, and the classical philologist Friedrich August Wolf. In August 1807, a delegation of professors from the university of Halle, which had been shut down by Napoleon, was led by its rector to visit the king in exile at the Prussian court in remote Memel. When they appealed to the king to relocate the university of Halle to Berlin, the king was receptive and, according to the legend, expressed his interest in words that soon were circulating as a new catchword: that the state must replace through spiritual-intellectual powers ("geistige Kräfte") what it had lost in the way of physical power.

A month later and over the opposition of several members of his court, a royal cabinet order authorized privy councillor Karl Friedrich Beyme to begin planning a "general instructional institution" ("allgemeine Lehranstalt") in Berlin. Beyme got in touch with several professors, including Fichte, Wolf, and the distinguished physician Reil, and commissioned proposals for the conception of the new institution.[73] But the proposal that most decisively shaped public opinion was one that had not been commissioned: Schleiermacher's *Occasional Thoughts on Universities in the German Sense* (*Gelegentliche Gedanken über Universitäten im deutschen Sinn,* 1808). Since his unsolicited project was not submitted to Beyme in the form of a private communication, as were the others, but rather disseminated as a published document that was widely read and debated, it had by far the most extensive public influence.

In his early chapters Schleiermacher treats such issues as the relationship between science and the state; the differences among the three main types of educational institution—school, university, and academy; and the nature of universities in general, including the argument for the separation of scientifically talented students from others.[74] The fourth chapter, "On the Faculties," develops the view familiar since the Jena lectures that the faculty of philosophy should constitute the center of the university. It seems obvious to Schleiermacher that the essence of any university, as it would be envisioned by the scientific-scholarly community, is represented by the philosophical faculty. The growing sense, especially in Germany, that all knowledge is held together by an inner coherence has led to the conviction that this unity of knowledge should be incorporated institutionally. The faculty of philosophy alone embraces the entire organization of the sciences, including transcendental philosophy, the natural sciences, and history. The other faculties, in contrast, derive their unity not from cognition but from "an external occupation" and appropriate for this purpose elements of knowledge from various disciplines. "The true spirit of the university" requires that absolute freedom prevail within every faculty without any prescribed sequence of lectures. In addition, the law faculty urgently needs to be reconstituted. Mere familiarity with a volume of positive law has little scientific character. "Political science, national economics, and the philosophical and historical knowledge of legislation must emerge more strongly." Schleiermacher goes on to discuss issues of academic freedom and the award of academic honors. But the key note has already been sounded: the faculty of philosophy should occupy the center of any rationally conceived university, and history should constitute a significant part of every citizen's education.

It was first and foremost through this treatise by the popular and influential Berlin theologian that the Romantic idea of the university penetrated public consciousness in Prussia. The conception of the university as an institution in which all four faculties are unified and governed intellectually from their common center in philosophy now began to display its practical effectiveness. The power of persuasion with which Schleiermacher presented this idea of an "encyclopedic" access to knowledge contributed to dispelling Enlightenment skepticism toward the traditional university and created the groundwork for the foundation of the University of Berlin.

Early in 1809, Alexander Graf von Dohna was named minister of the interior in the reorganized government of Prussia, and he appointed the forty-two-year-old Wilhelm von Humboldt, currently Prussian envoy to the Vatican, to be director of the newly created Section for Religion and Public Education. Humboldt, who regarded the five years spent in Rome as the happiest of his life, initially had little inclination to forsake his sinecure in the Vatican City for the sake of tedious administrative activity in Berlin, and for weeks he resisted the appointment. By the end of February 1809, however, he saw himself obligated—*noblesse oblige*—to accept. Besides numerous other responsibilities, he was charged with the establishment of the new university. The task with which Humboldt saw himself confronted was anything but simple. As it turned out, he had only sixteen months—from February 1809 until June 1810—to meet the difficult challenge. The difficulties were enhanced by the fact that during most of this period the king and his court were in Königsberg. Humboldt, whose wife and family had remained in Rome, spent long months—from the middle of April until the beginning of December 1809—in the provisional Prussian residency, which was far from Berlin and the developments taking place there.

Despite these obstacles, Humboldt succeed in completing the task that Beyme had not accomplished. His success was due primarily to three factors: Beyme's not inconsiderable preparatory work, the shift of public opinion as a result of Schleiermacher's treatise, and Humboldt's own extraordinary administrative talents and philosophically grounded conception of educational policy.

Humboldt had studied law in Frankfurt an der Oder and then in Göttingen, where he had participated in Christian Gottlob Heyne's famous seminar for classical philology. But these experiences of barely three semesters determined his conception of the university at most in a negative way. Frankfurt an der Oder hosted not only one of the least distinguished but also one of the most reactionary universities in Germany, and the new institution in Göttingen was one-sidedly dedicated to the training of future lawyers and government administrators. Neither place, with the notable exception of Heyne's philological seminar, represented the kind of university cultivating humanistic scholarship characterized by teaching and research with which Humboldt's name is associated. But during the four years from 1794 to 1797, which he spent mostly in Jena, Humboldt came into close contact with Goethe, Schiller, Fichte, and other leading minds of that period during which the Jena ideal of the university was being shaped. These ideas, and not his experiences in Frankfurt and Göttingen, determined fundamentally his conception of the institution. Thus prepared, he welcomed Schleiermacher's conceptual treatise of 1808.

First of all he had to adduce arguments that the new institution should be a university and that this university should be established in Berlin. In the formal proposal for the founding of the University of Berlin (*Antrag auf Errichtung der Universität Berlin*) that he submitted to the king in May 1809, barely two months after he had assumed his new office, he made his own position clear. Specifically opposed to the pleas for special-ized professional schools, he echoed in many points Schleiermacher's thoughts, on which he later based his draft of the statutes of the univer-sity. It would be misbegotten, he argued, to establish any institution of higher education that was not a university, for theory and practice could not be separated in instruction.[75] In a subsequent document he recurred to the definition of the university as "an organic whole"[76] and insisted that the institution must be dignified with "the old and venerable name *uni-versity*." It is characteristic, he explained in his essay on "the inner and outer organization of the higher scientific institutions in Berlin" (1810) that, unlike secondary schools, which communicate established knowl-edge, the university understands the sciences to be a realm of hitherto unsolved problems. In its organization the university must reflect the prin-ciple that science is an end in itself and that, as something not yet known, it always remains an object of research.

Humboldt's conception of the university, set forth in several short and fragmentary writings, was not so much an original project but rather the institutionalization of the Jena vision and Schleiermacher's plan. After he had persuaded the king to accept his proposals, he was faced with the equally daunting task of negotiating with the professors who had to be appointed. To his credit, he succeeded in winning the most outstanding faculty in Germany for his university: Wolf in philology, Savigny in law, Schleiermacher in theology, Fichte in philosophy, Hufeland and Reil in medicine, Niebuhr in history —the list of names now renowned in intel-lectual history could easily be extended. Through a cabinet order at the end of September 1810, the king approved the proposed list, which was immediately published in the newspapers.

The founding and opening of the university was a public event cele-brated gloriously in the Berlin press with articles and poems. Rarely in the history of universities does one find a constellation of academic stars in the same place and at the same time as luminous as the group of scholars who came together in 1810–11 in Berlin to found the new institution and the period that has been called Germany's "second renaissance."[77] Many were brilliant young men—like the thirty-one-year-old legal historian Friedrich Carl von Savigny, the twenty-six-year-old classical philologist August Boeckh or the thirty-four-year-old historian Barthold Georg Niebuhr—who were at the beginnings of long, sparkling careers. Some-what older and well-known coryphaei like the philologist Friedrich August Wolf, the philosopher Johann Gottlieb Fichte, the physicians Johann

Christian Reil and Christoph Wilhelm Hufeland, and the theologian Friedrich Schleiermacher had just reached the peak of their creative productivity. From the beginning, therefore, their lectures often amounted to public events in which not only the 256 registered students participated but also the intellectually interested society of the capital. From the course catalogue, which was issued at the end of September by the Section for Religion and Public Education and published in various newspapers, we know with considerable accuracy which lectures were held in this epoch-making first semester. As one might expect, so-called "encyclopedias"— that is, overviews of an entire discipline—played a large role. In addition to Schleiermacher's "Encyclopedia of the Theological Sciences" the student could also audit medical, mathematical, and philological encyclopedias, as well as introductions to the present state of jurisprudence, the study of philosophy, the general theory of nature, and the history of older German literature. Because the professors were often gifted speakers who developed their lectures spontaneously on the basis of minimal notes, the precise wording can only rarely be reconstructed. But with the help of notes, student copies, and later publications as well as the reports of attendees we can in many cases imagine the proceedings in all their liveliness.[78]

Niebuhr's Lectures on Roman History

Despite the fame of Fichte, Schleiermacher, and Savigny the greatest sensation of this first semester was a man still unknown in academic circles: the historian Niebuhr with the lectures on Roman history that he delivered from 10 to 11 o'clock every Wednesday and Saturday morning. It is symptomatic that these lectures were so enormously appealing because they represented an altogether new kind of history. And history as a modern scholarly discipline emerged and developed to no small degree from debates concerning the problems of Roman history.[79]

On 14 November 1810, Savigny reported that Niebuhr already had ninety listeners: "not only students, and many venerate him absolutely, just as others venerate Schleiermacher."[80] Niebuhr's wife estimated the number as much higher—some two hundred, of whom about fifty were students while the others came from all classes: "a couple of princes, people from the court, officers, a large number of officials, and even quite a few local scholars," including Savigny and Schleiermacher.[81] The high attendance was all the more surprising since Niebuhr was not a man from the guild of historians but an "autodidact," as he styled himself, a "man of affairs" ("Geschäftsmann") who had long regarded a professorship as "a tedious profession."[82]

Barthold Georg Niebuhr (1776–1831), born in Copenhagen as the son of the celebrated explorer of the Middle East, Carsten Niebuhr, grew up in the rural isolation of the town of Meldorf in Schleswig-Holstein, where at an early age he became acquainted with Greek mythology through translations of Homer. He soon mastered the classical languages so proficiently in private tutorials that at age fifteen he was capable of corresponding with the Göttingen philologist Heyne about Pindar.[83] In order to acquaint the shy prodigy with the real world, his father sent him in 1793 to a business school in Hamburg and a year later to the university in Kiel, where besides his law studies he attended the lectures of the renowned Kantian philosopher Karl Leonhard Reinhold. After four semesters, the gifted young man was invited to enter the service of the influential Danish minister of finance, Ernst Heinrich von Schimmelmann, as a private secretary. (It was Schimmelmann who, in 1791, had arranged a three-year grant that liberated Schiller from what he regarded as his onerous professorial responsibilities in Jena.) In 1797 be became Secretary at the Copenhagen Library, and a year later he was sent for two years to England— mainly London and Edinburgh—to be seasoned by foreign experience. In the summer of 1800 he entered the Danish civil service as an assessor in the East Indian Bureau of the Office of Economy and Commerce, where with the generous support of Count Schimmelmann he began a brilliant career, which led him by 1804 to the directorate of the Copenhagen National Bank. During these years of administrative success the "man of affairs" could devote only his leisure hours to his beloved studies—notably to a long treatise on the Roman agrarian laws, to which he had been led by his observation of misapprehensions regarding the Roman laws of property that were put into effect at the time of the French Revolution.[84] At the same time he was depressed by the fact that the desperate financial situation of Denmark left him little space for productive work.

In 1806, when Baron Karl von Stein, the bold and imaginative initiator of the great Prussian reforms, was looking around for an experienced financial expert, he spotted the young Danish star. Niebuhr, deeply impressed by the Prussian reform movement and disappointed by the lack of opportunity for his initiatives in the Danish government, entered the Prussian civil service as a member of the directorate for maritime trade. He arrived just in time to rescue his office treasury after the Prussian defeat at Jena and to flee to Königsberg with the other members of the government. After only a few months he was delegated for almost two further years to Holland, where he conducted complex loan negotiations that were meant to save the Prussian government financially. Upon his return named privy councillor and director of the Section for State Debts, he successfully undertook measures to consolidate the Prussian currency. But as a protegé of Stein he soon became involved in Stein's power struggle with Hardenberg, whom Niebuhr despised as "ignorant au suprème degré pour les finances et pour l'administration." On 16 June 1810, a few days after Hardenberg's appointment as chancellor, he submitted his resignation and obtained the desired position as Court Historiographer. By this time, the thirty-four-year-old Niebuhr had not only experienced history as an active participant; he had accumulated almost paradigmatically the archetypal experiences of his generation. As an impressionable teenager with a politically knowledgeable father, he attentively followed the course of the French Revolution and its sequel from afar; as a student at Kiel, he was indoctrinated into the works of Kant, the inaugurator of the epistemological revolution; and as a young man in his twenties, he observed the Industrial Revolution at its source in England.

At first Niebuhr was delighted with his new-found freedom, but within a few months the discharged "man of affairs" felt that he had not yet found the proper employment of his leisure. Meanwhile Humboldt, having completed arrangements for the university, had resigned and departed for Vienna as Prussian envoy, and a provisional director had been appointed to the Section for Religion and Public Education. At the end of August, Director Nicolovius invited Niebuhr, who had recently been elected to the Academy of Sciences, to hold lectures at the newly founded university. (Niebuhr, who had never completed his studies, did not receive his doctorate of philosophy until February 1811—the first honorary degree awarded by the new university.) After a little consideration, Niebuhr reported that he planned to deal with "Roman history from the oldest periods of Italy down to the time when the last traces of Old Roman dispositions disappeared in the institutions of the Middle Ages"[85]—down to the point, in other words, at which Gibbon had begun his depiction in *The Decline and Fall of the Roman Empire*. He wondered whether he would attract any students, knowing that many among the small number of enrolled students would presumably take courses required by their fields of specialization. (In that first semester only fifty-seven students had registered in the faculty of philosophy.) The preparation of his lectures, in the absence of any available handbook, he found extremely laborious. He knew the material thoroughly as well as the most recent studies of Roman history, but found it necessary to rescue the older Roman history "out of chaos"—a topos that recurs frequently in his letters.

Unlike Fichte, Schleiermacher, and Savigny, Niebuhr was no experienced virtuoso of the lecture hall. Not accustomed to public speaking and still regarding himself as an autodidact, Niebuhr felt compelled to write down every word in advance. In addition, with his croaking voice and his largish head, with his yellowish complexion and his slight bodily frame, he made far from the imposing impression of the dynamic Fichte or the elegant Savigny. All in all, he conceived his lectures (and the resulting book) as a work that would be a learned treatise rather than a skillfully written presentation.[86] He was relieved when the opening of the university had to be postponed for two weeks because he wanted to polish his introductory lecture, which still did not satisfy him.

Despite all his concerns, Niebuhr's lectures were, according to Savigny, the most fashionable offering ("Modekolleg") of this first semester and "the most learned" that he had ever heard at a university.[87] In historiography it is reckoned among the great achievements of this historicizing "man of affairs" that he demythicized early Roman history and, through meticulous analysis and with an empathy conditioned by years of practical experience, exposed the real foundations underlying the legends and sagas, which hitherto had obscured those early centuries.[88] Leaving aside the speculations of his predecessors, including such admired writers as Machiavelli and Montesquieu, he addressed himself directly to the sources, in which it was still possible to make out the constitution, the administration, the customs and education, the knowledge of warfare, the agrarian and population questions, as well as the literature of the early Romans. As he put it in one of the first lectures, he did not want to recapitulate earlier opinions and results but to set forth the findings of his own investigations—*sine ira et studio* ("without anger or partiality")—and with a comparative view (looking toward the Arabs, the Far East, the early Germanic tribes)—in order "to discover the built-over and hidden foundations of the old Roman people and their state" (3). For this purpose he had two kinds of sources at his disposal: documents concerning the recognizable forms of the state, its laws, and its institutions; and the ancient legends that were preserved in songs and in the earliest annals. "The Roman concepts that underlie the institution of the state and its administration . . . are no less different from ours than the Romans' living space, cloth-

ing, and food" (9). He was fascinated by all these aspects in an encyclopedic vision that embraced the entirety of Roman cultural history.

Various of Niebuhr's conclusions have been rejected or corrected by
later scholarship—apart from specific details notably the theory (inspired
by Wolf's controversial *Prolegomena ad Homerum*) that the historical reports of Ennius and Livy could be traced back to earlier Roman folksongs
and heroic ballads. However, Niebuhr's great achievement must be attributed according to Wilamowitz not simply to his critical acumen but
equally to his experience as a businessman and statesman, who understood
the realities of political and administrative life and who through intuition
and "combinations" was able to feel his way into the "probabilities" of the
earliest Romans.[89] This admiration has been echoed by subsequent generations of classical scholars.[90] As G. P. Gooch summarized, Niebuhr was
"the first commanding figure in modern historiography, the scholar who
raised history from a subordinate place to the dignity of an independent
science."[91]

Quite apart from the intrinsic interest of the subject and the sensational novelty of his use of sources, what appealed most immediately to
the audience in the autumn of 1810 was Niebuhr's presentation of the Romans as a model that the German people should emulate and his effort to
depict the Romans vividly from a modern point of view. "I have written
Roman history with the feeling of a contemporary, and past history
should be written in no other way," he confessed to Goethe shortly after
the publication of his work.[92] "The political principles are here, . . .
which, had I lived as a Roman citizen, would have been in every age my
principles for action. I hope that I shall never give praise if my own heart
is not warm, or praise anything that I wouldn't have approved and supported as a contemporary with all my strength." For this reason he wor-
ried that many readers might be annoyed by his book as being too
"democratic and republican." Niebuhr, in short, took history out of the
scholar's study and made it relevant to Berlin and Prussia in 1810. In his
depiction of the early Romans, his audience could detect without difficulty allusions to contemporary circumstances: the degenerated ethical
condition of the Prussians after the debacle of 1806, the resistance of the
aristocracy to the reform movement and new legal code of 1794, the domination of the French, even his own quarrels with Hardenberg.

> The austere frugality of the old republicans, their insensitivity to posses-
> sion and the enjoyment of wealth, the rigorous lawfulness of the people,
> their unyielding general loyalty during the lovely centuries in which the

constitution, since the claims of the aristocracy were limited, existed in its full perfection; the pure instinct that never permitted them to seek foreign intervention in their internal quarrels; the omnipotence of the laws and customs, and the seriousness with which anything about them was changed that was no longer suitable, the wisdom of the constitution and the laws, the ideal of manliness in the citizens and the state: all these characteristics surely arouse in us a veneration that we can feel in the contemplation of no other people. (12)

Niebuhr was not blind to the vices of the Romans, such as their lust for power, their contempt for the laws and rights of non-Romans, their indifference toward the suffering of others, their obsessive thrift and their class system (13). But this insight gave him all the more reason to peer into the history of the ancient Romans as into a distant mirror of circumstances in the Prussia of his own day. It was with a look across the Rhine but also with an eye to the reform movement in Prussia and the quarrel between the Junkers and the bourgeois that he wrote about the Romans of the fifth century B.C.E.

Humanity and good will in the government could easily have prevented an uprising and soothed the agitated spirits; but the senate remained hard and scorned emotions. All the plebeians had to sense that they were regarded as rabble, and this rabble destroyed all aristocrats who—if they had laid down rules as loving fathers, if as wise fathers they had conceded to their growing children those rights that can be denied only to those who are still dependent—could have enjoyed their old age in love and veneration. (405)

In the dispute of the popular Consul Manius Valerius with the reactionary powers of the senate, he perceived a prefiguration of the fate of Baron von Stein, who had been dismissed at Napoleon's insistence:

The time had come when only the sacrifice of the feelings of a single man was required in order to complete what was being inexorably prepared. The people sensed it as well and accompanied him, as gratefully as if he had accomplished his work, from the forum to his house.

Niebuhr makes full and conscious use of what Novalis had called the "magic wand of analogy."[93] Even as he began with the preparation of his lectures, he was having critical thoughts with implications for the philosophy of history. Thinking in mythological terms about the distress of his own day, when fortunes lay in the hands of the most miserable human beings, he wrote:

One can then only wish for a catastrophe in which this fortune would disappear and in which a true Iron Age would appear. In the ancient world this age came quite late, and slowly, and from without. Now, to be sure, the epochs of sickness follow inconceivably fast and we may yet experience it.[94]

Though disinclined to speculations on the philosophy of history, he was pleased to undertake the lectures, he continued, because they provided him with ample material for ruminations of this sort. To another friend he confided: "The unhappy time of Prussia's humiliation has a part in the production of my history. . . . I went back to a great, but long since vanished nation, in order to strengthen my spirit and the spirit of my audience. We were in the position of Tacitus."[95]

During this first semester, Niebuhr got no further in his lectures than the early Republic, and the second installment only reached the year 338 B.C.E. While he never arrived at later centuries and while his *Roman History* remained a magnificent fragment, it profoundly influenced the future of historiography, both Roman and general. The first edition of the two volumes, based directly on the lectures, possesses a freshness of language and an immediacy of spirit lacking in subsequent editions—not least because the author later removed many allusions to contemporary circumstances, which had made his lectures into such an important public occasion.

That the most highly regarded course of lectures in that first semester at the University of Berlin, four years after the defeat of Prussia at the battle of Jena, happened to be on a historical topic, and on a topic whose relevance to the present became evident to all, is symptomatic of the new sense of history that had been awakened by the circumstances discussed above. His listeners were aware that the study of history had entered a new era, that his lectures were in fact "the birth certificate of modern historiography."[96] The significance of Barthold Georg Niebuhr both in the history of classical scholarship and of history generally has been fully appreciated and well documented.[97] Less frequently noted is the profound historicization of other fields and faculties, a process that in several cases took place conspicuously and simultaneously that first semester in the lecture halls of the University of Berlin and in the works of scholars like Hegel, who were soon called to that new institution.

Two

PHILOSOPHY

T HOSE two half-siblings, Clio and Athena, have long existed in an uneasy kinship, sometimes tolerating each other in a wary truce and sometimes quarreling bitterly in warm sisterhood. Whether out of genetic disparity arising from the fact that Clio was born from a natural union of Zeus and Mnemosyne, while Athena had to be extracted from that same father's head; or, whether out of different tastes in couture arising from the fact that the demure Clio favored laurel wreaths while Athena the radiance of being in helmet and armor; or, whether out of divergent leisure pursuits in which we find Clio with book and Athena with spear; or finally, whether for the simple reason that their mascots the swan and the owl were natural enemies, it is true that the muse of history and the goddess of wisdom have more often than not been at odds rather than in harmony.[1] When this sororal tension erupted in heated family quarrels in the later eighteenth century, their mediator was a young German philosopher named Georg Wilhelm Friedrich Hegel.[2]

Kant and the Post-Kantians

The fact that history had been rehabilitated did not immediately legitimate it in the eyes of academic philosophers. After all, the philosophy of history had been practiced principally by such outsiders as Voltaire, Iselin, and Herder. And while Immanuel Kant did not wholly ignore history, it was hardly central to his thought or his works.[3] (For this reason Walter Benjamin discarded his early notion of writing a dissertation on Kant's philosophy of history because, he sadly concluded, there was no topic there.)[4] As Kant confessed in his lengthy and essentially uncomprehending review of the *Ideas toward a Philosophy of the History of Mankind* by his former student Herder, "the reviewer . . . is not at all experienced in learned linguistic research and in the knowledge and evaluation of ancient documents and accordingly does not know how to make philosophical use of the facts related and verified there."[5] In the course of his long academic career, he never taught the history of philosophy apart from occasional and brief references in his introductory lectures on "The Encyclopedia of All Philosophy." In the proposal prepared for his lectures in the winter semester of 1765–1766, Kant suggests that "all the sciences that can actually be learned belong to one of two categories: historical and mathematical."[6] But his definition of "historical" is narrow, including little more than "physical-moral-political geography." (At that time, as a *Dozent* at the University of Königsberg, Kant was teaching science and mathematics, mainly astronomy and physical geography.) A firm grasp of the natural relationship of all the lands and seas, he continues, provides "the real basis of all history, without which it can barely be distinguished from fairy tales."[7] History as commonly taught does not constitute in Kant's eyes a respectable academic discipline.

Accordingly, in *The Critique of Pure Reason* (*Kritik der reinen Vernunft*, 1781), a work of some 880 pages in the earliest editions, the historical aspect is relegated to a four-page concluding section on "The History of Pure Reason." "This heading stands here," the author confesses, "only to designate a place that is left over in the system and must be filled out at some time in the future."[8] He goes on to specify three earlier approaches to the subject and, without analysis, to cite representatives of those approaches: by object—sensual (Epicurus) or intellectual (Plato); by origin—empirical (Aristotle and Locke) or noological (Plato and Leibniz); and by method—naturalistic (Democritus) or scientific (Wolff and Hume).During the 1780s, Kant indulged in a few short pieces that belong generally to the philosophy of history. The nine clauses of his "proposal for a general history with cosmopolitan intent" ("Idee zu einer allgemeinen Geschichte in weltbürgerlicher Absicht," 1784) amount to a grand project to expose "the history of the human race on the whole as the carrying out of a hidden plan of nature to bring about an inner and, to this end, also external-complete constitution as the sole condition in which the state can fully develop all its predispositions in humanity."[9] Even Kant realizes that his teleological notion of world history, which is based *a priori* on a guiding principle of reason, seemingly wishes "to repress the treatment of any history that is merely empirical."[10] Indeed, it was his achievement to liberate history from the mechanical chronologies of astronomy and the laws of hereditary succession and to insist that history have its own temporality.[11] Yet perhaps Kant's most famous adventure in historical speculation—his essay on "The Conjectural Beginning of Human History" ("Mutmaßlicher Anfang der Menschengeschichte," 1786)[12]—is far from being an anthropological study; rather, it is a philosophical reading of the creation story as narrated in Genesis 2–6, from which Kant concludes that the so-called fall from Paradise was nothing but humankind's move from the instinctual crudeness of animality into humanity with its reason. This transition, which amounted to a significant step forward for humankind, appeared to individual human beings as a fall because now, for the first time, they were confronted in their new freedom with the responsibility for the moral consequences of their actions.

Kant's immediate successors were hardly more kindly disposed toward a historical approach to philosophy.[13] It is perhaps unfair to state flatly that "Fichte was not a man who thought historically."[14] In his early public *Lectures on the Vocation of the Scholar* (*Einige Vorlesungen über die Bestimmung des Gelehrten,* 1794), he identifies three kinds of knowledge: "philosophical" knowledge based wholly on principles of pure reason; "philosophical-historical" knowledge based on experience; and "historical" knowledge based on the events of the past in order to determine the position of mankind in the present.[15] All three kinds of knowledge are necessary for a whole society. But Fichte's purely philosophical writings belong entirely to the first category, which he distinguishes rigorously from his more popular speeches. Among his less academic writings for a general public, his *Characteristics of the Present Age* (*Grundzüge des gegenwärtigen Zeitalters,* 1806) amounts to a philosophy of history that he presents as a succession of five epochs in the development of human freedom. And several of his popular and influential *Speeches to the German Nation* (*Reden an die deutsche Nation,* 1808) are historical in their approach, for example, the sixth on "German Basic Traits in History." Yet it is safe to say that Fichte's purely philosophical works are totally ahistorical, or at most concerned exclusively with "transcendental history."[16]

His central epistemology, the famous *Foundation of the Entire Theory of Science* (*Grundlage der gesamten Wissenschaftslehre*, 1794), contains the statement that "the theory of science ought to be a pragmatic history of the human spirit."[17] But the work as a whole, while progressive, is hardly historical. Subjective and deductive in method, it derives all knowledge from the self and the dialectical relationship between "I" and "Not-I," making no reference whatsoever to nature or history. In sum, history plays no greater role in Fichte's philosophy than it did in Kant's.

The situation is equally unpromising when we turn to Hegel's university friend Schelling. History is central to Schelling's conception of philosophy; but for Schelling "history" has a very particular meaning. Human history amounts to little more than the tail end of the *Naturgeschichte* that concerns him most. Human history begins with the fall, or man's loss of the mythic harmony with nature, and constitutes a religious process that culminates in revelation, as Schelling depicted it in his early student essay "On Myths, Historical Sagas, and Philosophemes of the Most Ancient World" ("Über Mythen, historische Sagen und Philosopheme der ältesten Welt"). In the eighth of his *Lectures on the Method of Academic Study* (*Vorlesungen über die Methode des akademischen Studiums*, 1803), he says that theology is "the highest synthesis of philosophical and historical knowledge."[18] While the process of history as the transition from a state of pure nature or imagination by way of rationality and judgment to the state of pure reason can therefore be properly said to inform his philosophy, that "history" is quite remote from the new sense of history that began to permeate the European consciousness around the time of the three revolutions of which we have spoken.[19]

A trained student of mathematics, the natural sciences, and medicine, Schelling became increasingly committed to the philosophy of nature and the relationship of spirit and nature, which remain parallel and distinct from each other. His *Ideas toward a Philosophy of Nature* (*Ideen zu einer Philosophie der Natur*, 1797) ends with the perception that "nature aspires to be visible spirit and spirit to be invisible nature." His treatise *On the World-Soul: A Hypothesis of the Higher Physics to Explain the General Organism* (*Von der Weltseele, eine Hypothese der höheren Physik zur Erklärung des allgemeinen Organismus*, 1798) devotes its two hundred pages to a consideration of "the darkest of all things . . . , matter." Toward the end of his *System of Transcendental Idealism* (*System des transzendentalen Idealismus*, 1800), Schelling devotes several pages to history, which he restricts to "the history of such beings which have an ideal before themselves that can never be attained by the individual but solely by the race."[20] Since such history is constrained by reason and freedom, it follows that neither a series of ungoverned incidents nor an absolutely law-conforming series deserves the name of history, for "theory and history are total opposites." Only on the basis of such an understanding, he continues, could any philosophy of history be based, for "the sole true object of history can be only the gradual origination of a constitution for citizens of the world."[21] In the second of his *Lectures on the Method of Academic Study*, Schelling acknowledges that the contemporary world has become increasingly historical, using the techniques of science to gain insight into the intentions of the world spirit in history. But it is one thing to make the past into the object of scientific scrutiny; it is quite another to put knowledge of the past in place of true science. Leaving it to others to write anything as mundane as history or even the philosophy of history, Schelling turns in his later career to the more mystical issues of religion, mythology, and revelation.[22] Again, then, we find little interest in human history as such and certainly no intrusion of the historical dimension into philosophical speculation.

In sum, post-Kantian philosophy for most of its first two decades restricted its interest to a "transcendental history."[23] It remained for Hegel to introduce the dimension of history into philosophy itself.

Hegel and History

Unlike his friend Schelling, who published his earliest theoretical works while still a teenager, Hegel came late to the realization that he could best fulfill his ambitions as a philosopher. His first purely philosophical work did not appear until he was thirty-one years old; the earlier (unpublished) efforts had dealt almost exclusively with issues of religion (a "Life of Jesus" and a study of "Positivity in the Christian Religion") and politics (notably the drafts for "The German Constitution"). He continued throughout his life to be grimly suspicious of the all too cozy relationship between the two powers. "Orthodoxy cannot be shaken as long as its profession, with its worldly advantages, is woven into the fabric of the state."[24]

Born in Stuttgart in 1770, the *annus mirabilis* that also witnessed the births of Beethoven, Hölderlin, Wordsworth, and several other leading figures of European Romanticism, Hegel was the son of a financial administrator in the duchy of Württemberg.[25] His love of learning and veneration of education were instilled by his parents while he was still young. When he was sent off to Latin School at age five, his mother had already taught him the rudiments of the language; and his father, a trained lawyer, later paid for private lessons in geometry, French, and other subjects. Encouraged by his teachers, Hegel read widely, making frequent use of the ducal library near his home. After his mother's death, his father enrolled him in the local *Gymnasium Illustre,* where he received a firm grounding not only in the classics but also in such Enlightenment subjects as the natural sciences and mathematics and from which he graduated in 1788 as valedictorian of his class. (It is noteworthy that he was not sent to one of the famous but educationally more conservative Württemberg seminaries, where his friends Hölderlin and Schelling were prepared for the university.)

Along with his early love of literature—his obsession with *Antigone* began in Stuttgart, but also with such contemporary writers as Rousseau and Lessing—Hegel was fascinated by history. The diary that he began keeping on 26 June 1785 opens with a recapitulation of the sermon he heard that morning concerning the Augsburg Confession (a statement submitted in 1530 to the Diet of Augsburg summarizing the religious beliefs of the Protestant princes and subsequently acknowledged as the doctrinal basis of Lutheran Protestantism in Germany). "Even if I had retained nothing else," noted the serious fourteen-year-old, who was known to his classmates as "the Old Man," "my historical knowledge would have been enhanced."[26] The next day, his entry begins with an appreciation of the multi-volume *Textbook of World History* by Johann Matthias Schröckh (*Lehrbuch der allgemeinen Weltgeschichte,* 3d ed., 1777). "No other world history has pleased me more than Schröckh's. He avoids the annoyance of the many names in a *specialized* history, relates all the main events, but intelligently leaves out the many kings, wars (in which often a only a few hundred men were scrapping) and so forth, and—best of all—combines the edifying with history." A few days later (1 July) he set down his ideas on "pragmatic history," which he defines as history "in which one relates not simply *Facta,* but also the character of a famous man, an entire nation, its ethics, customs, religion etc. and develops the various transformations and deviations of these aspects from [those of] other peoples; tracks the effect of chance and the rise of great empires; shows what consequences for the constitution and character of the nation are held by various happenings and changes in government etc."[27]

That same month (29 July) he began to keep his journal in Latin. "For the purpose of practicing style and acquiring facility it does not seem inappropriate to write down in Latin some history that has caught my attention" (*Exercendi stili et roboris acquirendi causa non alienum videtur, notam quandam historiam latino idiomate conscribere*); it is an exercise that begins with a brief outline of Roman history according to Livy and that continues off and on for the next nine months. During that same period Hegel began his lifelong practice of making "excerpts"—that is to say, abstracts or summaries in German or Latin—of his reading. This practice, foreshadowing his later "encyclopedia of the philosophical sciences," in which he sought to survey the entire realm of human knowledge, includes many passages demonstrating his interest in history: Greek and Roman, but also "Oriental" (i.e. Hebrew, Egyptian, and Persian) along with passages from the popular history of philosophy (*Grundriß der Geschichte der Weltweisheit,* 1786) by Christoph Meiners.[28] In these earliest jottings of the precocious teenager, we find anticipations of ideas that later played a central role in Hegel's thought: the notion, for instance, that human "enlightenment" took a westward course from "the Orient and the South . . . ever more westward."[29] As his earliest biographer noted, his diary jottings reveal Hegel's recurrent focus on the concept of history.[30]

In the fall of 1788, Hegel entered the Protestant seminary (*Stift*) at the University of Tübingen where his classmate and close friend was the future poet Hölderlin; two years later the *Wunderkind* Schelling, only fifteen years old, joined them to complete the legendary triumvirate who took as their lifelong motto the Spinozan pantheistic symbol *hen kai pan* ("one and all"). It was no doubt partly in keeping with his beloved mother's wish that Hegel, following the first two years of general "philosophy," continued his education as a student of theology. But even though his stipend from the *Konsistorium* was conditional on his agreement to serve the Church either in its clergy or its school system, he surely had no intention even at that point of devoting his life to theology and pastoral activities. Afflicted by a stutter whenever he had to address large groups, he was notoriously ineffectual in the pulpit; in any case, his theological interests always revolved around the culture and history of religion rather than dogma.[31]

It was Hegel's ambition at this point to become a "people's pedagogue" or *Popularphilosoph* in the tradition of such French *philosophes* as Voltaire or the Scottish philosophers—what we might today call a "public intellectual," a thinker who addresses himself on urgent issues of the day to the general literate public rather than to a coterie of fellow philosophers.[32] He even tried in vain to persuade his father to permit him to transfer from theology to law. At Tübingen, he continued his readings in the history of classical antiquity, whose writers, he noted in 1788, are remarkable for two reasons: first, for the art of historical narrative, in which they have never been excelled; and second, as a basis for the history of humankind.

> Here we see the human spirit developing in very special situations and circumstances. From the series and the spirit of their extant writings we can abstract a complete history of their culture, and many other phenomena can thereby be illuminated. To cite one example: much in the culture, the practices, morals, and customs of the Israelite people, which had and continues to have such an influence on us, can thereby be explained more naturally and made more comprehensible. For the human spirit was at all times generally the same, only that its development was variously modified by the difference in circumstances.[33]

Here we observe once again an anticipation of Hegel's philosophy of cultural history and his theory of the world-spirit. But he was not simply a bookworm immersed in the past. In the wake of the French Revolution he developed a keen interest in current events. While the story that he and his friends Hölderlin and Schelling erected and danced around a "Freedom Tree" is probably apocryphal, he followed events closely and continued to the end of his life to celebrate Bastille Day. (Schelling got himself in trouble with the authorities by translating the version of the *Marseillaise* that the friends sang together.) It is also symptomatic that, despite his interest in certain contemporary philosophical issues, revolving notably around Spinoza and Rousseau, he declined to join a study group established by Hölderlin, Schelling, and other students at the seminary to read Kant.

Following his theological examinations in 1793—he had already become a master of philosophy upon completion of his first two years at Tübingen—Hegel spent the remainder of the decade in the occupation that supported countless ambitious but jobless young men, including Hölderlin and Schelling, until they were able to obtain positions in their chosen careers: as *Hofmeister,* or private tutor, to children of prosperous families. Hegel passed the years from 1793 until 1797 as tutor to a patrician family in Bern, where he felt isolated from the intellectual excitement of Germany and, as the son of a respected bourgeois family, socially slighted by employers from an aristocracy that he regarded as corrupt and defunct.[34] But he was able, in the richly stocked library of his employer, to indulge his taste for history, studying among other works Montesquieu's *Esprit des Lois,* Gibbon's *Decline and Fall of the Roman Empire,* Hume's *History of England,* Raynal's philosophical and political history of Europeans in the East and West Indies *(Histoire . . . des deux Indes),* and Schiller's *History of the Thirty Years' War.*[35] He perused the French newspapers and was scandalized by the infamies of the "Robespierrots."[36] He followed with interest—and reported to Schelling—the political maneuvering that characterized the decennial political celebrations in Bern, when the retiring members of the *conseil souverain* were replaced by new ones. "To get to know an aristocratic constitution, one must have spent here a winter like this one, leading up to Easter, when the additions take place."[37]

In 1797, through Hölderlin's mediation, Hegel acquired a tutorial position with a merchant family in Frankfurt am Main, where he spent the next three years somewhat more contentedly in the company of his friend and closer to political and philosophical developments in Germany. Here too his reading in history continued and even intensified. The fragments of historical studies from this period demonstrate his interest in such varied topics as the social life of the Oriental world, including the Jews; in mourning women, the sense of national identity, laws, and stoicism among the Greeks; in forms of revelation in the ancient world; in witchcraft in the Middle Ages; in the security of property in modern states; in political freedom and justice in Renaissance Italy; in the death penalty; in Hume's view of the historian and Schiller's history of the Thirty Years' War; and more.[38] These studies provided Hegel with an impressive command of European history from the Middle Ages to the present which was unmatched by other philosophers of the age.[39] It should be stressed, moreover, that his interest in history and politics extended to a familiarity with the basic texts of the Scottish political economists—James Steuart, Adam Ferguson, and Adam Smith. Even though the effects of the Industrial Revolution had not yet reached those parts of Germany where Hegel was at home, he was thoroughly cognizant of its economic implications. Equally as impressive as the extent and variety of Hegel's interests is, once again, the anticipation of themes familiar from the *Phenomenology of Spirit* (e.g., national identity, revelation, freedom). During this same period his political studies focused his attention especially on England (with excerpts from English newspapers on the parliamentary debates on tax laws) and on the Prussian general code of law *(Allgemeines Landrecht),* which had recently (1794) been promulgated.[40] It was in connection with these initiatives that he studied Kant's *Critique of Practical Reason* (*Kritik der praktischen Vernunft,* 1788) and his *Metaphysics of Morals* (*Metaphysik der Sitten,* 1797)—and not, it should be noted, the more theoretical works (e.g., *The Critique of Pure Reason*) that intrigued his contemporaries.

When we take into account the extensive theological projects that he undertook during this period, it is hardly surprising that Hegel, the aspiring "public intellectual," had little time left for the more purely technical philosophy with which Fichte and Schelling were concerned. His "Life of Jesus" ("Das Leben Jesu," 1795) was an attempt, in a manner consistent with the rationalizing theology of the Enlightenment, to harmonize the teachings of the Gospels with Kant's moral imperatives. "The Positivity of the Christian Religion" ("Die Positivität der christlichen Religion," 1795) amounted to an effort to demonstrate how the living teachings of Jesus had ossified into the sterile positivism of contemporary Christianity and how, in the process, Christianity had destroyed the original character of the German nation. "It depopulated Walhalla, chopped down the sacred groves, and rooted out the phantasy of the people as a shameful superstition, as a devilish poison."[41] Both of these early works confirm Lukács' view that "the basic tendency of Hegel's thought was always historical."[42] It goes without saying that Hegel's rejection of positivism—the acceptance of "what is" as the norm—is absolutely consistent with his growing appreciation of the importance of history in human affairs.

When Hegel's father died in 1799 and left him a modest inheritance, he felt that he could at last afford to embark on the university career that he coveted and that his younger friend Schelling was already enjoying with spectacular acclaim. In 1800, with Schelling's help, Hegel was called to an unremunerated teaching position at Jena, which during the 1790s boasted the most distinguished faculty of philosophers in Germany. In Jena, Hegel was encouraged by his friend to turn his efforts toward the technical academic philosophy expected of his position as *Privatdozent.* To this end, and in short order, he wrote his first purely philosophical treatise, *The Difference between Fichte's and Schelling's Systems* (*Die Differenz des Fichteschen und Schellingschen Systems,* 1801). Together with Schelling, he founded a *Kritisches Journal der Philosophie,* to which in fact Hegel contributed most of the articles. Meanwhile, in his lectures he began to formalize his own system of philosophy, which provided the organization of his future "encyclopedia" into the triad of Logic, Philosophy of Nature, and Philosophy of Spirit. Stimulated by these interests and requirements, Hegel began to turn his attention to the problem of consciousness, which had inspired many of the principal works of philosophy since Descartes. But by the time he underwent in Jena what has been termed his "phenomenological crisis,"[43] Hegel, driven by his powerful historical impulse, had come to the conclusion that any study of consciousness must be a *history* of consciousness, not an abstract analysis after the fashion of Fichte's *Wissenschaftslehre* and not primarily a *Naturphilosophie* in the manner of Schelling: a history, moreover, in which the consciousness of the individual in its development recapitulates the historical development of the world spirit. This is Hegel's incomparable and monumental contribution to the history of philosophy.

Hegel, History, and Philosophy

Hegel's *Phenomenology of Spirit* (*Phänomenologie des Geistes*) belongs neither to the history of philosophy nor to the philosophy of history, though he made major contributions to both. Rather, it marks the first time in the history of philosophy that history constituted the essential basis for philosophy itself—a "radical historicization of philosophy"[44] and "historical revolution"[45] noted with admiration by some and disparagement by others. In his long-standard *History of Philosophy* (1892), for instance, Windelband wrote that "Hegel's philosophy is essentially historical, a systematic treatment of the entire thought-matter of history."[46] And Karl Barth, in his history of Protestant theology, observed admiringly that nothing is more characteristic of Hegel's system of knowledge than that it culminates in "the knowledge of knowledge" and has no other content than "the history of philosophy, the report of its continuous self-explication: . . . Knowledge of history and history of knowledge, history of truth, history of God."[47] Rudolf Haym, in contrast, remarked contemptuously in his early book on *Hegel and His Age* (1857) that "the *Phenomenology* is psychology cast into confusion and disarray by history, and history plunged into ruin by psychology."[48]

From his years in Jena until his death in 1831, Hegel lectured ten times on the history of philosophy. It was anything but a new field in 1805–1806 when he first delivered the lectures that constituted the basis for all his subsequent presentations.[49] In the introduction to his *Lectures on the History of Philosophy* (*Vorlesungen über die Geschichte der Philosophie*—a posthumous compilation edited from students' lecture notes and Hegel's own fragments) Hegel lists and critiques eight previous works, from Thomas Stanley's *History of Philosophy* (London, 1655) to his own present. Yet it is certainly possible in a higher sense to justify the statement that Hegel is the "founder" of the field.[50] In the turmoil succeeding Kant's "Copernican Revolution" in philosophy, the topic had recently come under fresh critical scrutiny, and Hegel's formative years witnessed a pronounced "battle of methods" in the history of philosophy, to which such major scholars as Karl Leonhard Reinhold, the leading Kantian exegete, and Fichte, his successor at Jena, added their voices.[51] A further aspect of this debate was the controversy aroused by the question set in 1791 by the Berlin Academy of Sciences: "What Progress has Metaphysics made in Germany since the Time of Leibniz and Wolff." The question's very formulation implied a history and development in philosophy and elicited responses from Reinhold, Schelling, and Kant, among others.[52]

Hegel's own history of philosophy, which significantly affected the nineteenth-century understanding of history and philosophy, most noticeably among Marxists, has with some justification been called "probably the most influential aspect of his philosophy."[53] It was Hegel's view, elaborated in the introduction to his *Lectures,* that philosophy is "system in development": that is, that philosophical thought and understanding actually progresses in the course of its history.[54] He goes on to argue that the historical sequence evident in the successive systems of philosophy is similar to the logical sequence in the deduction of ideas, that is, that history reflects logic. Consequently, "the study of the history of philosophy is the study of philosophy itself" (an epigram that echoes Goethe's similar claim in the preface to his *Theory of Color* (*Zur Farbenlehre,* 1810) that "the history of science is science.")[55]

These two notions have immense consequences not only for Hegel's history of philosophy, but also for the *Phenomenology of Spirit,* which he was composing precisely during the year when he was developing those ideas in his lectures. First, the identification of logic and history underlies the organization of the *Phenomenology,* which traces the history of the world spirit at the same time as it outlines the logical sequence of thought moving from consciousness through self-consciousness to spirit. Second, the idea that philosophy progresses through time justified Hegel's conviction that his own philosophy was not merely another post-Kantian idealistic system, but that it in fact represented the culmination—and essentially the displacement—of all earlier systems. In his lectures of 1805–1806 on the history of philosophy he discussed Schelling and warmly acknowledged his contribution, but also criticized his friend's deficiency in dialectical reasoning.[56] He concluded the lectures with words clearly implying that his own *Phenomenology,* which was then nearing completion, represented the fulfillment of progress in philosophy.[57]

> A new epoch has arisen in the world. It appears that the world spirit has now succeeded in discarding from itself all foreign, objective being and in producing from within itself everything that becomes objective and in keeping it peacefully in its power. The struggle of the finite self-consciousness with the absolute self-consciousness, which seemed to the former to be outside itself, has come to an end.

Or, to borrow the relevant lines from Lutz Geldsetzer's witty history of philosophy in verse:

> Nimmst *Hegel* du bei seinem Wort,
> geht die Geschichte nicht mehr fort,
> denn alles, was zu denken war,
> macht sein System dir offenbar.[58]

> (If you take Hegel at his word, then history no longer moves forward, for everything that was to be thought is revealed to you by his system.)

Hegel also left his indelible stamp on the philosophy of history, an undertaking that has been engaged for two centuries in a running battle with a more empirically oriented history. Jacob Burckhardt, in the introduction to his *Observations on World History* (posthumously published in 1905), labeled it "a centaur, a *contradictio in adjecto;* for history, i.e. coordination, is non-philosophy and philosophy, i.e. subordination, is non-history."[59] He attacks Hegel as the main culprit who argued that reason is the force governing world history. "But we are not initiated into the purposes of eternal wisdom and do not know them. This impertinent anticipation of a world-plan leads to mistakes because it proceeds from false premises."[60]

Burckhardt's diatribe is revealing both because it identifies Hegel as the acknowledged leader in the philosophy of history, and because it implicitly defines the philosophy of history as any attempt to understand history as demonstrating, or proceeding according to, a principle, plan, or metatheory. The philosophy of history did not of course begin with Hegel. The ancient world often recognized one of two basic patterns in history.[61] Greek political thinkers from Aristotle to Polybius saw in the history of all peoples a cycle revolving from monarchy through aristocracy to democracy and then, as democracy degenerates into violence and anarchy, beginning all over again with a strong ruler. Christian apologists, in contrast, regarded human history as a three-stage progression leading from innocence through a fall into guilt and, finally, by redemption onward to a final new paradise.

These two basic patterns, persisting for centuries, were taken up again in a radically secularized form by eighteenth-century thinkers. Giambattista Vico formulated in his *New Science* (*Scienza nuova,* 1725) a three-stage "law of cycles" according to which the history of all nations invariably proceeds in a succession of cultures that are respectively divine, heroic, and human. (The cyclical impulse continued down into the twentieth century, informing the vast cycles underlying the systems of Oswald Spengler and Arnold Toynbee.) Most thinkers of the Enlightenment were attracted, in contrast, to a view of history that documented humanity's progress toward happiness and peace through reason, for example, Voltaire's *Essay on Manners* (*Essai sur les moeurs,* 1756), Condorcet's *Outline of an Historical View of the Progress of the Human Mind* (*Esquisse d'un tableau des progrès de l'esprit humain,* 1794), or Kant's "What Is Enlightenment?" ("Beantwortung der Frage: Was ist Aufklärung?" 1783) and *At the Sign of Eternal Peace* (*Zum ewigen Frieden,* 1795).

So Hegel was working within a tradition of which he was fully aware when, from 1822–1823 to 1830–1831 in Berlin, he delivered five series of lectures on the philosophy of world history (*Vorlesungen über die Philosophie der Geschichte.* Like the *Lectures on the History of Philosophy* these were also compiled posthumously on the basis of student course notes.) Because they are presented in such a vigorous, accessible language, perhaps these lectures have remained Hegel's most popular work and feature a number of pithy formulations for which he is remembered. Thus "world history moves from East to West, for Europe is quite simply the end of world history."[62] And later in the same paragraph: "The Orient knew only that *One* is free; the Greek and Roman world knew that *Some* are free; the Germanic world knows that *All* are free." (By "Germanic" Hegel means, generally, the Protestant countries of Northern Europe.) Here too he defines his famous notion of "world-historical individuals" as those in whose undertakings we see incorporated the general will or idea of an entire people or state.[63]

In his introduction (which is sometimes separately published under the title "Reason in History") he distinguishes three types of history. "Original" ("ursprüngliche") history—represented by Herodotus and Thucydides, but also by Caesar's commentaries and Frederick the Great's *Histoire de mon temps*—describes events and circumstances that the author has personally witnessed or in which he has participated. "Reflective" history has several subdivisions: "general" histories of a people, like Livy's history of Rome or Johannes von Müller's history of the Swiss; "pragmatic" history, such as Montesquieu's *Esprit des Lois,* which uses the past in order to understand the present; "critical" history, which analyzes the sources of history; and "abstract" or specialized histories of art, law, religion, and so forth. Hegel defines the third branch, "philosophical" history, as "nothing more than the thinking contemplation of history."[64]

When Hegel contemplates history "thinkingly," as he summarizes in the concluding paragraphs of his lectures, the governing principle that he ascertains is "the development of the concept of freedom."[65] More specifically, world history "represents the development of the spirit's consciousness of its freedom and the realization produced by such consciousness."[66] Like many modern philosophers, Hegel takes the Cartesian *cogito, ergo sum*—that is, the thinking consciousness—as the basic premise of his thought. Self-consciousness, in turn, is the spirit's consciousness of itself. But the spirit, alienated from itself and subjugated to the world of nature, has often lost sight of itself. The central purpose in history is to enable the individual, the people, the state, to reach absolute self-consciousness. This perception leads Hegel to his famous definition of freedom: "I am free when I am fully aware of myself" ("frei bin ich, wenn ich bei mir selbst bin").[67] Hence Hegel sees the development of freedom as the guiding principle underlying history, and in his lectures he traces the progress of the concept of freedom as it moves from the Orient (where only the monarch is free) by way of the Greco-Roman world (where only the aristocracy is free) to the Northern European present (where all are free in the democratic state). Here, finally, the spirit has reached its goal of total self-consciousness, and history has come to its end. And simultaneously philosophy itself, as he had informed his students at Jena, had come to an end in the sprawling, dazzling work that he published in 1807, *The Phenomenology of Spirit.*

Hegel's Difficulty

The *Phenomenology,* a notoriously intricate, complex, and obscure work, was called without exaggeration by a knowledgeable authority on the eve of the twentieth century "the most difficult of all the works ever written in the entire history of philosophy."[68] The difficulties begin on the title page, where the familiar title—*Phänomenologie des Geistes*—actually turns out to be the subtitle for the first part of a larger work announced as *System of Science (System der Wissenschaft)*. Yet when the unsuspecting reader gets to the actual text of that first part, it is called "Science of the Experience of Consciousness" ("Wissenschaft der Erfahrung des Bewußtseyns"). These confusions are further evident in the organization of the work, which is preceded by a "preface" longer than the first three chapters. The eight chapters, in turn, are totally dominated by two (5 and 6), which together constitute well over half of the text. These perplexities reflect not only the hasty composition of the huge work, but also the author's shifting conception of it.

Hegel had long known that he must publish a major work if his hopes for an academic career were to be realized. In 1805, at the biblical (or Dantean) midpoint of his life, he finally undertook the challenge. Without going into the details of its complicated genesis, we can observe that the work subtitled "Science of the Experience of Consciousness" (what we know today as the *Phenomenology*) was originally intended to be merely the introduction to a work devoted mainly to logic.[69] This "logic," in turn, was to constitute the first volume of a complete "System of Science" consisting of a logic, a philosophy of nature, and a philosophy of spirit. But as the "introduction"—the first half of which (chap. 1–5) was already set in print by the summer of 1806—grew to ever more massive proportions, and under intense pressure from his publisher, Hegel decided to publish it separately without the "Logic." In the week immediately preceding the battle of Jena (14 October 1806) he sent the remainder of the manuscript to his publisher in Bamberg—amidst great trepidation, as he wrote to his friend Niethammer, lest the manuscript be lost in the turmoil of the advancing French troops. The famous "preface," which was intended as an introduction to the entire "system" and not merely to the "phenomenology," was composed in January 1807, when the rest of the book was already in press. (It has been regarded by some critics as the best part of the work and even as the key to Hegel's entire philosophy[70]—a view not shared by other philosophers.)

Several of the factors that contribute to its difficulty are characteristics of the age.[71] Let us first consider the language itself. Hegel was fully capable of writing straightforward prose, as we know from his letters, the articles he composed as editor of the *Bamberger Zeitung*, and his later lectures at the University of Berlin, notably on the philosophy of history. The difficulty of the language in the *Phenomenology* is the result of a conscious decision. By 1800 Hegel had arrived at the conviction that a revolutionary philosophy commensurate with the new revolutionary age could not be expressed in the exhausted rhetoric of traditional philosophy—that a new philosophy demanded a new vehicle of expression. In his lectures to the students at Jena he criticized in particular the terminology of Schelling's *Naturphilosophie*. "This foreign terminology, which is used in a partly useless and partly perverted manner, becomes a great evil because it makes concepts, which in themselves are *motion,* into something *firm* and *fixed,* whereby the very spirit and life of the matter disappears and philosophy is reduced to an *empty formalism,* which can easily be acquired and in which it is easy to chatter; but to those who don't understand this terminology it appears to be very difficult and profound."[72] One aspect of this innovation was Hegel's attempt to eschew the Greco-Latin terminology that still characterized the writings of Kant and Fichte and to replace it with German vocables.[73] (In Fichte's *Wissenschaftslehre,* for instance, such terms as "Reflexion," "Abstraktion," "Kategorie," "Realität," "Identität," "Kausalität," and "Thesis/Antithesis/Synthesis" are fundamental to the argument.) Furthermore, he suggested that it was best in philosophical discourse to avoid terms with fixed meanings, such as "God."[74] These efforts produced an utterly original philosophical discourse whose meaning often emerges only from the context and from the argument itself. The result, as he conceded to a friend who expressed a wish for greater clarity in his exposition, was an often impenetrable style.[75] Some matters, he explains, bring an explicit clarity with them: e.g., the reports in his newspaper about the comings and goings of the local nobility. But there is other, more abstract material, he continues, that does not permit the same clarity of exposition and which is not easily accessible at first approach. It was Hegel's conviction that the reader, by working his way through his complex prose, would be compelled to recapitulate in his own mind the process of thought that brought Hegel to his conclusions, rather than simply accepting them. (One can feel nothing but admiration for that prominent French Hegelian, Jean Hyppolite, who taught himself German by reading and then translating the *Phenomenology* into French.)[76]

At the same time, it should be realized that what might be called this language of estrangement, exemplifying the consciousness of a new age, is typical of many young thinkers of the period. During their mutual time in Frankfurt, Hegel's friend Hölderlin was creating an utterly original poetic language that did not permit the reader to fall back into the easy familiarities of earlier eighteenth-century poetry but that demanded his active participation; and much of Hölderlin's finest poetry still challenges even his linguistically and theoretically most adept admirers. The notes that Hölderlin appended to his translations of Sophocles' *Oedipus Rex* and *Antigone* and in which he expounds his "calculable law" of poetry, concede nothing in the way of difficulty to Hegel's *Phenomenology*.

Such innovations were by no means limited to the friends in Frankfurt. Their contemporaries Novalis and Schleiermacher achieved for political oratory and theology much the same degree of estrangement as did Hegel for philosophy. In the speech "Christendom or Europe" ("Die Christenheit oder Europa") that Novalis declaimed to his friends in Jena in November 1799, he manages to survey the history of Christian Europe from the Middle Ages to the present without mentioning a single name apart from Martin Luther and Robespierre. The Virgin Mary is generalized to "the holy, wondrously lovely lady of Christianity"; the saints are introduced as "long deceased heavenly human beings"; the aesthetic aspects of the great cathedrals—their images, fragrance, music—are emphasized rather than their religious aspects. Furthermore, as a trained scientist, Novalis objectifies the historical processes even further by describing them in terms borrowed from the physics, chemistry, and biology of his day. Thus he speaks of the "oscillation" of temporal periods; of the "irritability" of the religious sense; or of the "atony" of the higher organs of the age.

That same year, in his chapters *On Religion* (*Über die Religion,* 1799), Friedrich Schleiermacher achieved a similar estrangement of theological rhetoric, managing to write two hundred pages without a single specific naming of Jesus, who is introduced simply "one of the greatest heroes of religion." The great religious leaders are "mediators" between the limited thought capabilities of humankind and the eternal boundaries of the world. Revelation is defined as "every primal and original view of the universe." And although the sacred scriptures have been traditionally declared a "Bible," true Christianity would not deny that title to any other work written with equal intensity. Schleiermacher is driven by precisely the same impulse that motivated Hegel. In order to do justice to a wholly new conception of religion, a generous and all-embracing religion liberated from the artificial constraints of Christian pietism and rationalism, he felt obliged to reject the traditional vocabulary of worship and to address his audience in terms that would compel them to rethink their most fundamental beliefs concerning religion. In sum, the difficulties of Hegel's language, while considerable, not only have a purpose within his own system;

they are also consistent with basic impulses motivating young thinkers in every field at the turn of the century in that revolutionary age.

A second difficulty emerges from Hegel's effort to combine logic and history: to systematize history and to historicize reason. This accounts for what could be called the triadomania evident in Hegel's thought: the imposition of triads upon every situation, beginning with the general system of his philosophy, which is divided into Logic, Nature, and Spirit. Wherever we look we find more triads: in the Art, Religion, and Philosophy that constitute the realm of Spirit; the Law, Ethics, and Morality that govern public life; the progress from Oriental through Classical to Germanic that determines his view of historical sequence; or the aspects Symbolic/Classic/Romantic that he sees as identifying all art.

This "triplicity" is related on the one hand to Hegel's dialectics: although he never uses the terms thesis/antithesis/synthesis frequently though mistakenly attributed to him, his thought inevitably proceeds dialectically, as each stage carried to its extreme generates its opposite or what Hegel calls its "negativity." On the other hand, it reflects undeniably a manner of thought whose rediscovery he attributed to Kant and that was fashionable among young thinkers of the day.[77] Karl Jaspers has pointed out how fundamental the triadic rhythm is to Schelling's conception of the "Three Powers" ("Drei Potenzen") underlying his system.[78] And Hegel's friend Hölderlin developed a complicated theory of poetic genres and "tonal modulation" ("Wechsel der Töne") based on triads.[79]

Every poem begins with a tension between its "basic tone" and its more conspicuous "artistic effect." In order to resolve this "opposition" the poet must take his poem through a series of tonal modulations that lead by way of a "catastrophe" to its "resolution." The oppositions, in turn, involve three modes of experience—naive, heroic, and ideal—which are characterized, respectively, by pure sensation, energetic passion, and power of imagination. Depending on the sequence of tones and their resolution, the poem is then lyric, tragic, or epic. It goes without saying that, among these theologically trained thinkers—Hölderlin, Schelling, and Hegel were all, after all, educated at the theological seminary in Tübingen— the triadic mode of thought amounts to a secularization of the ancient theological triad of Father, Son, and Holy Ghost or Paradise, Fall, and Redemption. With his inevitable triads, then, Hegel is again representative of his generation.

The triadic mind-set was not limited to the friends from Tübingen. One of Friedrich Schlegel's most famous utterances—frequently cited to characterize the basic impulses of German romanticism—is the fragment defining the "three greatest tendencies of the age" as Goethe's novel *Wilhelm Meister's Apprenticeship,* the French Revolution, and Fichte's epistemology (*Wissenschaftslehre*). What is not so well known is the fact that, for Schlegel, the triadic pattern precedes its contents.[80] Scattered throughout Schlegel's writings we repeatedly encounter similar triplicities: "Bible, Faith, Church—a triangle of religion"; "Perfect mysticism = ethics + logic + poesy"; or, "Fichte's philosophy is at once point, circle, and straight line." More revealing, however, is the fact that Schlegel's "Three Tendencies" fragment with its triad of poetry, politics, and philosophy occurs in several formulations prior to the final one, where it uses altogether different examples: Georg Forster rather than the French Revolution standing for politics, for instance, or Christian Garve instead of Fichte for philosophy; and, in another case, Rousseau, Kant, and Klopstock.

A third difficulty stems from Hegel's allusiveness. Many of the allusions, sometimes involving quoted phrases or catchwords, bear, as we might expect, on the works of other philosophers—notably but not exclusively the ancient Stoics and Skeptics, the modern rationalists, and such contemporaries as Kant, Jacobi, Fichte, and Schelling—which are discussed without any specific identification.[81] Others refer to history, both ancient and modern, as well as to such current events as the recent Terror in France or the vogue of physiognomy and phrenology. Moreover, far more closely attuned to the poetic energies of his age than were most other philosophers, Hegel had the habit of introducing references to familiar literary works with little or no identification, assuming that his readers would pick up the allusions. Thus we find an (inexact) quotation from Goethe's *Faust: A Fragment,* which had appeared in 1790; several important references, sometimes attributed, to Goethe's recently published translation of Diderot's *Le neveu de Rameau* (1805); passing allusions to *Hamlet* and *Macbeth* that take for granted the reader's familiarity with those texts; quotations from Schiller's poems; characterizations of such recent novels as Friedrich Schlegel's *Lucinde,* Friedrich Heinrich Jacobi's *Woldemar,* and Hölderlin's *Hyperion*; and even oblique references to Novalis's death from consumption and Hölderlin's madness. These belonged to the cultural *koine* of the times.

By far the most important literary allusion is the extended discussion of Sophocles' *Antigone,* which provides the basis for Hegel's entire section on the ethical world of pure spirit. Hegel was an outstanding Graecist, and as a schoolboy at the *Gymnasium Illustre* in Stuttgart he was reading

Homer, the Greek poets, tragedians, and historians. Already at that time
he became obsessed with *Antigone*—an obsession that lasted throughout
his entire life and prompted him later to translate passages from the choral
odes as well as the dialogues.[82] At the same time, it was widely held by European poets, philosophers, and scholars of the period, as George Steiner
has demonstrated, that *Antigone* "was not only the finest of Greek
tragedies, but a work of art nearer to perfection than any other produced
by the human spirit."[83] No one clung to that belief more fervently than
Hegel's friend Hölderlin, who—at the very time when Hegel was shaping
the ideas that subsequently informed his *Phenomenology*—was creating
his translation/adaptation of *Antigone,* a work as joltingly original in its
language as his friend's philosophical treatise, and formulating the theoretical justification appended to the translation. (It is noteworthy that
Hölderlin's translation, too abrasive to be appreciated in his own day, was
subsequently adapted for the stage by Bertolt Brecht, who framed Hölder-
lin/Sophocles with an action exposing the play's relevance to the situation
in Nazi Germany.) As we read the pages in the *Phenomenology* dealing
with the conflict between human and divine law in the ethical world, we
are privy to what might well be regarded as a conversation between Hegel
and Hölderlin on the drama of their mutual obsession—a conversation
that, precisely because it is ongoing, does not require all the usual marks
of identification and clarification.

In sum, the terminological innovation, the language of estrangement,
the triadic patterns, the philosophical and literary allusiveness, and the
other devices that contribute to the difficulty of Hegel's *Phenomenology*
can be seen as characteristics that link him to other leading figures of the
age. This identification does not of course lessen the difficulty of Hegel's
prose, which perplexed many of his friends and reviewers. But it reminds
us that at least some well-informed contemporaries were able to read his
work with a degree of immediate understanding inaccessible to us today.
As Josiah Royce observed in 1906, "philosophy and life were then in far
closer touch than, as I fear, they are today in the minds of many people."[84]

The Organization of the *Phenomenology*

The *Phenomenology of the Spirit* is overwhelming in the sheer audac-
ity of its undertaking.[85] It was Hegel's ambition, as it had been Herder's
in his *Ideas toward a Philosophy of History,* to encompass in a single volume the entire knowledge of Western civilization—not with the taxo-

nomic encyclopedism of the Enlightenment, however, but as an integrated whole. He deals, first, with the central concerns of German idealism: the epistemological relationship of subject and object, of consciousness and nature, and with ethics, aesthetics, and religion. To this he adds an overview of modern science, from physics and anatomy to physiognomy and phrenology. He refers to the leading literary works of the period and surveys the principal philosophies of past and present against a background of informed political and economic thought. And he presents all this in a historical framework that reaches from the earliest cultures through the principal periods of (mainly Western) civilization down to the French Revolution and the Terror. Hegel, the news addict who believed that "reading the newspaper each morning is a kind of realistic morning prayer,"[86] seems to have been interested in literally everything. It is by no means farfetched when Karl Barth argues that Hegel was the Protestant Thomas Aquinas.[87]

Yet as confusing and difficult as the work often appears in detail, its general plan is simple and clear. Hegel believed, as he put it in his "Preface," that his age was "a time of birth and transition to a new period" (15).[88] Accordingly, it was time for philosophy, too, to put aside philosophy in the traditional etymological sense as mere "love of knowledge" and become "real knowing"—time, that is, "to elevate philosophy to a science" (12). Hegel proposes to demonstrate "the development of science in general or of knowing" ("Dies Werden der Wissenschaft überhaupt oder des Wissens," 26) through a process that he calls "phenomenology of the spirit." ("Wissen" is often best translated as "knowing" rather than "knowledge," since Hegel is concerned with the process rather than the product.)

The term "phenomenology"—meaning the study of the varying forms in which something appears or is manifested (in contrast to its origins, its constitution, its significance, etc.)—had become fashionable among philosophers in the second half of the eighteenth century.[89] Hegel, as his title indicates, is concerned here specifically with the phenomenology of the *spirit* ("Geist"), which he proposes to accomplish by studying the "shapes of consciousness" ("Gestalten des Bewußtseins," 75) that the spirit assumes on its way from the simplest empirical awareness to absolute knowledge. "The series of shapes that consciousness passes through along the way is the thorough history of the education ["Bildung"] of consciousness itself to knowledge" (67).

When Hegel speaks of the education of the spirit, he has two aspects in mind, general and specific. On the one hand, he is talking in the broadest sense about what he thinks of as the "spirit of the world" in its history from its primitive beginnings down to the present. At the beginning of his chapter on "The Spirit" (314–15) he defines spirit variously as "ethical reality" or "absolute real being" or "consciousness in general"; later he speaks repeatedly of the "world spirit" ("Weltgeist"—incarnated in Napoleon on horseback). On the other hand, he also means the individual human spirit because, according to a belief widespread among thinkers of the day from Lessing to Schiller, "the individual must, with regard to contents, pass through the educational stages of the general spirit" (27)—that is, ontogeny recapitulates phylogeny.[90] These stages, he continues, are "shapes already discarded by the spirit, steps along a path that has been worked out and leveled down." For the individual, education or *Bildung* consists in acquiring for himself what the world spirit has already learned in the course of history. *Knowledge,* or the sum of this internalized education, is "science" or "comprehended history" (564). For this reason, Hegel ends his enormous work with a hymn to history, which he calls "knowing Becoming" ("wissendes Werden," 563)—that is, a process of evolution that has become conscious of itself.

What does Hegel understand under the knowledge that the spirit must acquire? The spirit, according to idealism since Kant, gets to know itself only by seeing itself reflected in the other. In Kant's philosophy the individual consciousness and the phenomenal world of appearances—that is, the subject and object—remain forever separate and distinct; the subject, with no hope of penetrating to the *Ding an sich,* can at most hope to classify the object according to the categories of its own mind. It was the challenge for his successors to bring them together again. Fichte accomplished this by contending that the "Non-I" is entirely the creation of the "I" by means of its productive imagination. Schelling assumed an underlying "identity" or "duplicity" uniting spirit and nature. Hegel had a different solution. According to his understanding (563–64) the spirit "externalizes" ("entäußern") itself in two ways: *nature* is the contingent form of its externalization in space as *being;* and *history* is the form of its externalization in time as *becoming.* Having thus projected itself in space and time, the spirit must complete the process by re-internalizing through memory all that it has learned. (Hegel uses the term "Er-Innerung," a linguistic play reminding the reader that the German words for "internalize" and "memory" are closely related.) When it has thus arrived at consciousness, externalized itself in nature and history, and then internalized or "remembered" these extensions in space and time (in terms of various "shapes" or "phenomena" of being), the process is complete: history has been not simply experienced along the way but translated through understanding into concepts and thereby rendered capable of being comprehended. The individual spirit has become one with the world-spirit.

It is Hegel's project to lead us through this process from a twofold perspective. He intends for us to experience the growth of consciousness directly and immediately as consciousness itself experiences it—a process that accounts for much of the (sometimes intended, or at least unavoidable) confusion of the work. At the same time, he expects us to be able to stand back and observe each stage in the development of consciousness "phenomenologically" as a new shape of emergent consciousness. How does he propose to do this?

Provided that we set aside the long "Preface," the shorter "Introduction," and the various headings that Hegel subsequently added, *The Phenomenology* is divided into eight chapters representing states of increasing consciousness:

1. Sense-Certainty
2. Perception
3. Force and Understanding
4. The Truth of Self-Certainty
5. Certainty and Truth of Reason
6. The Spirit
7. Religion
8. Absolute Knowing

The topics of these chapters can be organized—and in later works Hegel does so—into three groups that are roughly equivalent in length. One through five deal with the development of the individual consciousness; six is concerned with the consciousness in the ethical—that is, historical and social—world; seven and eight focus on the consciousness in its relationship to the transcendental world (in art, religion, and philosophy). Borrowing the terms that Hegel used in his *Encyclopedia of the Philosophical Sciences* (*Enzyklopädie der philosophischen Wissenschaften,* 1817, 1827, 1830) to characterize these three groups, we may also call them "the subjective spirit," "the objective spirit," and "the absolute spirit."[91] Each of these groups, finally, is successively exposed in its development—both its logical development in the mind of the recapitulating individual and its historical development in the general world-spirit. How is this accomplished?

Ever since Josiah Royce's *Lectures on Modern Idealism,* which still provides a useful introduction in English to Hegel, readers have been accustomed to see in the *Phenomenology* an analogy to that form of contemporary German fiction known as the Bildungsroman and represented, in Royce's presentation, by Goethe's *Wilhelm Meister's Apprenticeship,* Novalis's *Heinrich von Ofterdingen,* Tieck's *William Lovell,* and—in English—Carlyle's *Sartor Resartus.* According to Royce's perceptive insight, which has been echoed by many subsequent scholars,[92] it was Hegel's intention, influenced by the literary practices of his day, "to make his portrayal of what he calls the experience of the *Geist,* or typical mind of the race, something that could be narrated in a story, or in a connected series of stories in which typical developments are set forth"[93]—a sort of philosophical *Orlando,* one might say, replacing Virginia Woolf's individual with the more generalized world-spirit.[94] Or, seizing a different analogy, Royce speaks of "different incarnations or transmigrations" that the world-spirit undergoes, assuming along the way different *Gestalten des Bewußtseins* or forms of consciousness.

Royce's insight, which is consistent with Hegel's tendency toward literary allusion, is helpful in enabling us to visualize the movement of this remarkable philosophical work. At the same time, the analogy must not distract us from the fact that in Hegel we are dealing not, as in the Bildungsroman, with the linear progression of an individual through his own lifetime, but with the dialectical movement of the world-spirit through history—a history of the world that is presented to us in three grand, and sometimes overlapping, spirals: of the individual consciousness and reason, of the human spirit, and of the absolute spirit as manifest in art, religion, and philosophy.

If we look for an appropriate analogy, it will be better to avoid the image of the circle, which Hegel sometimes adduces, as when he refers to "the becoming of the self" as a circle ("Kreis," 20) or describes the movement of the spirit as "a circle revolving back upon itself" (559). While the circle is appropriate, as Hegel subsequently uses it in his *Encyclopedia* (§ 15), to designate the dialectical round of timeless concepts in logic— the whole of philosophy resembles "a circle of circles"—, it does not do justice to the progressive movement of the *Phenomenology,* which traces a development from simple empirical consciousness to absolute knowing. The circle, instead, suggests a process that continually repeats itself rather than reaching higher stages and even the absolute state of perfect "knowing."[95] (In fairness, it should be noted that Hegel himself often implies, illogically, that even a circle can return to itself on a higher level.) But if the cycle is not an appropriate image, neither is the line, which is the pattern implicit in Royce's Bildungsroman of the spirit. For the line suggests a simple linear and continuous progression, whereas the development in the *Phenomenology* always takes place dialectically, as the consciousness discovers that each stage of its development generates a "negation" or opposition, which necessitates a move forward to a new stage, which is in turn "negated" and "sublated" (*aufgehoben*)—taken to a new level. In sum, neither of the images traditional in the philosophy of history—cycle and line—does justice to Hegel's conception.

Borrowing an image recently familiar from human genome research, we might envisage the relationship of the three historical strands as a *triple helix*, in which three spirals circle upward around one another, for the helix exemplifies both dialectical movement and progression. Or, to take a more homely analogy, we might think of the relationship as a braid, which in geometry designates any shape consisting of three or more interwoven lines emerging from a common point. The braid has the additional advantage of contemporary appropriateness. In pre-revolutionary Germany, and especially in Frederick the Great's Prussia, the braided pigtail was a symbol—hated by many as a sign of oppression but loved by others as a token of order and discipline.[96] In Hegel's phenomenological braid, as we shall see, the three strands are separate but interrelated, progressing in each case from simple consciousness to a much higher state and often touching or overlapping in the process.

Hegel's Phenomenological Braid

The first three chapters, amounting together to only about fifty pages and shorter than any but the last of the remaining five chapters, do not belong, properly speaking, to the three historical sequences. History begins only when the individual consciousness becomes aware of other consciousnesses with which it must interact. These introductory chapters, dealing with the development in isolation of simple consciousness, constitute, as it were, the stem or point from which the three historical strands emerge. Here Hegel discusses consciousness at its most elemental level as simple empirical certainty: we become aware of something else in time and space when it obtrudes on our senses. In a second step we begin to "perceive" the object by classifying and organizing its various characteristics according to general categories. Finally, we explain the object to ourselves according to more general laws and, in the process, become aware of our own consciousness as the place where this act of "understanding" takes place. Our consciousness has become a Self, an Ego.

It is only at this point (chap. 4) that consciousness emerges from its timeless natural state and enters history: that is, a social condition where it becomes aware of other consciousnesses. Our consciousness of ourselves as distinct from the objects we perceive has produced "desire" for those objects. In the realization that there are other selves out there with which we must compete to satisfy our desires the "I" first becomes aware of itself as part of a "We." The initial reaction of this wholly egocentric consciousness in what may be regarded as a Hobbesian state of *bellum omnium contra omnes* is that of the primitive savage whose instinct it is simply to destroy every opposing consciousness. But a natural instinct toward self-preservation (that is, desire directed toward oneself) causes the weaker consciousness to submit rather than be destroyed, and thus a higher level of development, that of master and slave, is attained. Both master and slave initially achieve the recognition they desire, each from the other. The master now determines the norms by which the slave must operate. But at the same time they both become aware of the relative nature of these norms. For the master realizes that the recognition he achieves is not universal, but only compelled from the servant; and the servant realizes that he may continue to cling to his own norms even while serving the master's wishes. The master remains dependent upon the slave while the slave, paradoxically, advances beyond the master as he comes to understand that through the work of his own hands he has created the world surrounding him—a world in which he can now see himself reflected. (Hegel describes this state in a brief but vivid section that is regarded by Karl Marx and his followers, as well as by Alexandre Kojève in his influential Paris lectures, as the heart of the book—and the point beyond which many readers seem rarely to advance.)[97]

Master and slave thus come to understand that, "on the throne as in fetters" (153), each is free in his thoughts to create his own world. Hegel defines this attitude of philosophical autonomy, which he presents as characteristic of classical antiquity, as *stoicism*—an attitude that gradually gives way to *skepticism,* as the consciousness comes to regard the world it has created and the norms by which it lives as empty and meaningless. Hegel may have intended a subtle reference to the transition in recent European thought from the still essentially Christian neo-stoicism of such Dutch intellectuals as Dirck Coornhert, Hugo Grotius, and Justus Lipsius to the Lucretian skepticism of the great French rationalist critics: Diderot, Voltaire, and Condorcet.[98] Turning away from this sham world of reality and through an act of internalization, the consciousness attains the new awareness that the relationship of master and slave, which it had hitherto projected into the outside world, actually represents a conflict within the individual consciousness itself. This sundered or "diremptted" ("entzweit") self exemplifies what Hegel terms the "Unhappy Consciousness"—a condition that he describes in a section representing more or less the world of medieval Christianity. Unable any longer to project its "master" onto a fellow mortal, the consciousness projects it into the beyond—that is, onto "God." But as the consciousness realizes that this new faith is not its own product but "revealed" by another agent, faith collapses and consciousness again seeks its justification within itself.

Having thus moved from primitive savagery by way of classical antiquity to the medieval world, Hegel arrives at the age of reason that characterizes modern times (chap. 5). When the consciousness finally retrieves its autonomy from the beyond, it becomes aware of its own power of reason, which Hegel defines as "the certainty of consciousness of being all reality" (176). "Observing Reason" first applies itself to the natural world, both inorganic and organic, where reason functions quite satisfactorily. But as soon as reason attempts to determine similar physical laws for its own self-consciousness, it degenerates into such pseudosciences as physiognomy and phrenology. (Hegel devotes what strikes the modern reader as an inordinately long section to these two forgotten "sciences," which were enormously popular and influential toward the end of the eighteenth century.)

At this point Hegel paints a series of intellectual portraits depicting modes in which reason seeks to actualize itself through its own means. These portraits, while general, are so vivid that commentators have often been tempted to identify specific examples from Hegel's favorite literary works. First we encounter the hedonistic self-consciousness that seeks to satisfy its desires through pleasure. And Hegel's quotations here suggest Goethe's Faust, and Faustian man, as the model. Then we meet the self-consciousness governed by "the law of his own heart" and the madness of self-centeredness. Hegel probably had in mind such heroes of the German Sturm und Drang as Goethe's Werther, who repeatedly appeals to his own heart for guidance. Rousseau has also been suggested.[99] Finally, Hegel presents us with the virtuous consciousness that engages in a "battle against the way of the world as against something opposed to good" (278)—a description that immediately summons up the image of Don Quixote, a figure central to the Romantic imagination.

By this point the individual self-consciousness has come to an awareness of itself as the real. Believing that "action is the development of the spirit as consciousness" (287), it initially tries to satisfy itself by total devotion to one activity or another. When this turns out to be illusory, reason seeks to establish laws of behavior for itself; but these turn out to be not universal laws but merely commandments, and "lawgiving reason is reduced to nothing more than an examining reason" (306)—that is to say, the reason informing Kant's critiques. This sobering conclusion brings Hegel to the end of the first strand of his historical braid in his own present.

Reason, having concluded that it alone cannot provide universal laws for the moral behavior of the individual self-consciousness, now generalizes itself into spirit, which is defined simply as "the ethical life of a people" and "the individual who is a world" (315). The spirit must now go through the same process as did reason: that is, pass through a series of shapes in order to arrive at consciousness of itself. But in distinction to the shapes assumed by reason in the earlier sections, "these are real spirit, actual realities, and instead of shapes of consciousness, shapes of a world" (315).

This long sixth chapter is introduced by the famous discussion of Sophocles' *Antigone,* which Hegel puts forward as an example through which to examine the breakdown of the classical ideal of ethical harmony. It turns out, namely, that the original harmony has become illusory since Greek civilization by this time pays obeisance to two sets of law stemming from entirely different sources—human and divine—and representing entirely different constituencies: male and female, nation and family. Antigone represents the family, which is governed by divine law; and Creon the state, whose laws are human. When these two sets of values come into conflict, as they do in Sophocles' play, the results are inevitably tragic for both parties. "Only an absolute lack of activity can remain innocent" (334), Hegel concludes, quoting Sophocles to show that our very suffering proves that we have sinned.

Roman civilization sought to avoid this dilemma by replacing ethical order with legal status: the authority of the emperor was the single source of all law, and therefore the conflict between human and divine law could not arise. But because this law was simply imposed from above and because the individual consciousness was reduced to little more than a legal *persona* (analogous to the stoicism of the preceding discussion), the indi-

vidual was emptied of all significance and found validation only in his possessions.

Thus alienated from itself, the spirit next seeks meaning in *Bildung* (by
which Hegel means far more than education: the term implies cultivation
of the entire personality), through which it can construct a world of its
own to afford content and satisfaction. But inevitably "the world of this
spirit disintegrates into a double one": the world of reality from which it
is alienated, and the other that it has erected in the ether of pure consciousness (350). In a bold move, Hegel skips over the entire Middle Ages
(to which in any case he has already devoted a lengthy section in his earlier discussion of the Unhappy Consciousness) and lands in the Baroque
court of Louis XIV, whose courtiers exemplify the trivialization of *Bildung* into servile gratitude for kingly favors. Heroism of service has degenerated into subservient flattery and elegance of expression into
superficial wit. Hegel refers specifically to Diderot's dialogue *Le neveu de
Rameau,* which Goethe had recently translated, as an example of individual depravity and social corruption.

In this world "torn apart" between the power of the state and the noble consciousness (Hegel repeatedly uses the term *Zerrissenheit* [368–71]
to characterize this condition, a term fashionable among the alienated
young intellectuals of early Romanticism), the individual consciousness
now moves in one of two directions that Hegel regarded as fundamental
aspects of human life: either toward a faith based on pure feeling or toward Enlightenment based on pure reason.[100] These two options, bitterly
opposed to each other (e.g., the Enlightenment war on superstition), must
ultimately also fail, because their belief is based on no higher authority.
The insight of faith (Hegel is thinking here of pietism) comes from subjective emotion and that of the Enlightenment from rootless rationality.
The French Revolution is the inevitable result of the absolute freedom and
autonomy declared by the Enlightenment. But unrestrained by any universal laws of reason or religion, the Revolution rapidly succumbs to the
Terror, for which death by the guillotine has "no more meaning than the
chopping through of a head of cabbage" (419).

Driven to this radical extreme by absolute freedom, the alienated spirit
now turns back with a new assurance to a morality that Hegel, true to his
sense of the movement of history, relocates from France to Germany and
the Kantian positing of duty as its absolute essence. Yet even this morality involves dialectical negations, for "the real moral consciousness is an
active one; therein consists the reality of its morality" (435). But the call

for action produces "deceit" or "duplicity" (434), for as soon as "pure" action is focused on an actual specific goal, it easily confuses duty with its own desires. (Hegel is alluding here, among other things, to the problem of *Pflicht* and *Neigung* that obsessed Schiller and other contemporary thinkers. Indeed, the entire section is structured around a critique of Kant's postulates.) Or else the "beautiful soul," wishing at all costs to retain its unsullied purity, refrains from the responsibility of action and melts away in sheer ethereality or mere irony. Here Hegel has in mind such contemporary phenomena as the figure of the "beautiful soul" that Goethe depicted in *Wilhelm Meister's Apprenticeship*[101] or the romantic irony practiced by such contemporaries as Friedrich Schlegel.[102]

Having exhausted reason and exposed every shape of merely human and social spirit as inadequate, Hegel now turns in the third strand of his phenomenological braid to humankind's search for a higher, transcendent, divine, or absolute meaning that he calls "religion." Religion, as culture's thoughts on meaning in the world, differs from the more theoretical preceding strand: instead of concepts, it works with representations. Starting again at the beginning with the most primitive consciousness, Hegel locates its search for the divine in the cosmic forces of natural religions: as light (in Persian Zoroastrianism), as plant and animal (in the animistic religions of India), and finally as abstract images (of the sort found in Egyptian hieroglyphs—another topic currently attractive to Hegel's Romantic contemporaries). But once the idea emerges of representation of the divine in works created by the human hand, religion in the form of art appears in Greece.

Initially the divine was portrayed in the symbolic forms of primitive sculpture, but gradually the notion of divinity was represented through language in progressively more human forms: in oracles and hymns, cultic practices, epic, and tragedy (corresponding to the level of ethical order discussed earlier in connection with *Antigone*). At length, however, this representational approach to divinity was utterly humanized and secularized in Attic comedy. In a world thus emptied of divine or transcendent meaning, the appropriate response was the Roman stoicism that Hegel analyzed in an earlier strand. "In the legal condition the ethical world and its religion have submerged in the comic consciousness, and the unhappy consciousness is the awareness of this entire loss" (523).

At this point the void and barren world is prepared for the revelation of the divine in human form (Jesus Christ) and the ensuing birth of Christianity. (In the *Phenomenology* Judaism is not discussed and barely mentioned.) Paradoxically, his death is required in order that he may be elevated into a concept. "The dead divine man or human God is *in himself* the universal self-consciousness; he must become this [i.e., he must die] for this self-consciousness" (543). His death is what Hegel calls "the abstract negativity, the immediate result of the movement that ends only in the natural universality" (545).

Religion, however, with its purely representational capacity, is no longer capable of apprehending the divine, once it has entered universality as a pure concept. In order to attain this ultimate level of "absolute knowing" we need philosophy, which constitutes the third stage in the progression of the spirit: art/religion/philosophy. "This last shape of the spirit, spirit that at the same time gives the form of the self to its complete and true content, and thereby actualizes its concept just as in this actualization it remains within its concept, is absolute knowing; it is the spirit that comprehends itself in the shape of spirit or *comprehending knowing*" (556). "Science" ("Wissenschaft") in this sense cannot appear in time and reality until the spirit has attained this highest level of consciousness regarding itself. "In knowing, the spirit has concluded the movement of its shapings" (561). As we reach the last pages of the *Phenomenology,* we have accompanied Hegel, or the spirit, on a threefold journey through time and space, through nature and history, and have reached absolute knowing— "absolute" because it recapitulates in its understanding everything that has gone before.

Hegel thought that his "phenomenology" or "science of the experience of consciousness" was merely the introduction to the greater "system of science" that he proclaimed on his title page—a preliminary exercise that, once mastered, could be internalized and forgotten. But the system remained unfulfilled apart from the detailed outlines and increasingly incisive critiques of contemporary society that Hegel provided in the three editions of his *Encyclopedia of the Philosophical Sciences* (1817, 1827, 1830). The *Phenomenology* stands alone as one of the most remarkable works in the history of philosophy—remarkable not least for the fact that Hegel, with his three-ply braid, introduced history for the first time into the actual process of knowing and the act of philosophizing. Philosophy thus historicized continued its triumphant course through the nineteenth century, notably in the thought of Karl Marx and his followers, and persisted down to the end of the twentieth century in such neo-Hegelian works as Francis Fukuyama's *End of History and the Last Man* (1992).

Three

THEOLOGY

Protestant Theology at Mid-Century

I N his autobiography, *Poetry and Truth* (*Dichtung und Wahrheit*), Goethe describes the religious instruction of his childhood in the 1750s. The official Protestantism taught in Frankfurt am Main, he recalls, was little more than "a kind of dry moralizing" that satisfied neither heart nor soul.[1] It was hardly surprising that many groups had broken with the official church: Separatists, Pietists, Moravians—all the so-called Quiet Ones in the Land ("die Stillen im Lande"). This disenchantment led, he remarks elsewhere, to a striking decline in church attendance, a decline that Goethe attributes to the lack of "plenitude" (*Fülle*) and doctrinal consistency in Protestantism along with the absence of sacraments—confirmation, the Eucharist, last unction, and others.[2] It was in no small measure its sacramental character that made Catholicism attractive to so many converts in the succeeding generation of Romantics: the political theorist Adam Müller, the critic Friedrich Schlegel, the painter Philipp Veit, the dramatist Zacharias Werner, the art historian Carl Friedrich von Rumohr, among others.

As is so often the case, Goethe has identified with succinct precision a problem analyzed and elaborated at length by subsequent historians.[3] Here he is referring to the period known in the history of Protestant theology as "neologism," the second stage in the development of Enlighten-

ment theology and lasting from roughly 1740 to 1790.[4] Martin Luther had
proclaimed a new Protestant orthodoxy informed by the substantive principle of grace through faith and by the formal principle of the authority
of Scripture.[5] But in the century after Luther, orthodoxy became ossified
into a rigid system of thought and an ecclesiastical hierarchy against
which pietism rebelled. In the name of the individual, pietists relied on private study of the Bible and on loose association among equals in informal
conventicles. It was this tension between ecclesiastical formalism and qui-
etism that caught the young Goethe's attention in the middle of the eighteenth century.

It is a paradox noted by Karl Barth that the age that humanized religion and, wresting it from the control of the clergy, handed it over to the
citizenry—that that same age was also and simultaneously responsible for
a scientific approach (*Verwissenschaftlichung*) to theology that further
alienated the normal church-goer.[6] The first stage of Enlightenment theology in Germany is usually identified with Christian Wolff, the philosopher chiefly credited with the initial accommodation of reason and the
teachings of revelation. Wolff and his contemporaries did not challenge
revelation, but they believed that certain fundamental doctrines—the
recognition of God as creator, the doctrine of moral freedom, and the immortality of the soul—could also be justified on the grounds of reason.
While other issues—e.g., the mystery of the Trinity—were apparently *su-
per*rational, they were not therefore irrational or counterrational.[7] The
second "neological" stage began to attack those doctrines that appeared
irrational—original sin, the Devil and the torments of Hell, predestina-
tion, the divine inspiration of the Holy Scriptures, the notion of the Trinity, virgin birth, resurrection and ascension, and the miracles of the New
Testament—and to explain them rationally or discount them as myth.[8]
While the Wolffians had left revelation intact, the neologians undermined
the very grounds of revelation.

In order to accomplish this mission, the neologists turned to a drastic
revision of both theological dogma and ecclesiastical institutions, exposing the personal idiosyncrasies and historical circumstances that had determined various doctrines and practices of the past that they regarded as
irrational. One of the leading neologists, Friedrich Wilhelm Jerusalem,
singled out Saint Augustine as his particular whipping boy, speaking of
"the nonsense of black-galled Augustine" who taught that human beings
living outside the Christian church as well as unbaptized children should
be damned.[9] The historian Johann Matthias Schröckh (whom the young

Hegel admired) regarded Augustine as "not much more than a beginner" in theology, lacking the linguistic ability to interpret the Bible, onto which he simply imposed his own views.[10] The Göttingen church historian Johann Lorenz von Mosheim dismissed the early church fathers Irenaeus and Tertullian as "brainless windbags and insufferable sophists"—to which other theologians added, in Tertullian's case, the charge of pederasty.[11] As far as Saint Francis was concerned, said the Göttingen historian Ludwig Timotheus Spittler, "one does him the greatest honor by assuming that he was weak in the head."[12] Obviously, and despite their laudable achievements in unearthing and editing older texts, the cause of historical objectivity was hardly advanced by these adventures in historical investigation. Generally speaking, the entire past, especially the centuries between Greco-Roman antiquity and the late seventeenth century (not to mention the whole non-Western world), was regarded as benighted. "How blessed our times appear," Jerusalem exclaimed in 1756, "when we compare the light in which religion now stands and the freedom with which it is now professed with those gloomy ages where ignorance, superstition and compelled conscience darkened its divine shape."[13]

The third stage of Enlightenment theology, representing the relentless application of reason to all the tenets of revelation, including those bracketed by the neologists, is best exemplified by two non-theologians. This is not the paradox it seems, because religion was the central issue of the day with which it behooved every Enlightenment thinker—and notably its finest minds—to come to grips. To the intellectual appeal was added a further practical concern for all professional writers: state censorship was almost wholly in the hands of the official clergy.[14] It was impossible for any critical intellectual truly engaged with his society to avoid theological controversy. Friedrich Nicolai, the chief spokesman of the Berlin Enlightenment, defined as his principal goal "the combating of ecclesiastical and hierarchical despotism, bigotry, and superstition."[15] Lessing boasted that he was "a fan [*Liebhaber*] of theology and not a theologian."[16] And in the opening sentence of his essay "Answering the Question: What Is Enlightenment?" ("Beantwortung der Frage: Was ist Aufklärung?" 1783) Kant defined Enlightenment as "the emergence of man from his self-imposed dependency"—specifying, a few pages later, "especially in matters of religion."[17]

The critic and dramatist Gotthold Ephraim Lessing (1729–1781), son of a Lutheran pastor, wrote various essays on religious topics in which he

delighted in needling the orthodox theologians. In his "Vindication of In-
eptus Religiosus" ("Rettung des Inepti Religiosi," 1754), for instance, he
asserted: "We are greatly indebted to our forefathers everywhere; only in
religion do we owe them nothing." Or: "I advise you to read the Bible without any assistance."[18] However, the real battle was aroused by his epoch-
making publication of the so-called "Fragments of an Anonymous" edited
from a four-thousand-page manuscript by Hermann Samuel Reimarus
(1794–1768), a professor of Oriental languages in Hamburg. Lessing had
become acquainted with the work during his years as a dramaturge in
Hamburg, where it was circulating in manuscript. After Reimarus's death
he obtained the manuscript from the family and proceeded to publish
seven extracts in a series he edited as librarian of the Ducal Library in
Wolfenbüttel—anonymously in order to protect the family from charges
of blasphemy: in 1774 a relatively innocuous one on "The Toleration of
Deists"; in 1777 five more dealing with such sensitive issues as revelation
and miracle; and in 1778, finally, an installment on "The Aims of Jesus
and His Disciples." In his readings of the two Testaments, Reimarus exposes the inconsistencies and implausibilities of the story recounting the
passing of the Israelites through the Red Sea and denies the historicity of
Exodus. Analyzing the accounts of the resurrection, he summarized the
discrepancies among the four gospelists and concluded that resurrection
can be reconciled with neither reason nor history. Similarly, in the last fragment he distinguished rigorously between the teachings of Jesus, who
lived wholly within the Jewish religion, and the later writings of the apostles, who interpreted—or invented—his utterances to suit their own purposes. The apostles borrowed miracle-stories from the Old Testament and
other sources in order to prove Jesus' claim to messiahship, and they con-
cocted the notion of the resurrection in order to get around the awk-
wardness of the messiah's death. Thus along with the resurrection,
Reimarus denied the entire typological theory according to which orthodoxy from earliest Christianity down to the eighteenth century had traditionally read the Old Testament as a prefiguration of the New Testament.
In *The Quest of the Historical Jesus,* Albert Schweitzer justly celebrates
Reimarus as the first writer to attempt "a historical conception of the life
of Jesus" and his work as "perhaps the most splendid achievement in the
whole course of the historical investigation of the life of Jesus."[19] Lessing
went even further than Reimarus. In the commentary ("Gegensätze des
Herausgebers") that he appended to the 1777 volume, Lessing calls all the
orthodox and even the neologist wolves out of the theological forest, chal-

lenging literalism of interpretation and the sacredness of the Bible itself along with any notion of revelation.[20] "From such things [the truths of natural religion] nothing at all can be concluded about the divinity of the books of the Old Testament."[21] "The Bible clearly contains more than is essential to religion, and it is a mere hypothesis that it must be equally infallible in this superfluous material," he continues. "There was religion even before there was a Bible. Christianity existed before the evangelists and the apostles had written."[22]

Lessing's publication unleashed a furious controversy with orthodox defenders of the faith—notably the formidable Hamburg pastor Johann Melchior Goeze—that lasted until 1778, when Lessing was forbidden by the duke of Brunswick to issue further writings on religion without the approval of the official church censor.[23] But Lessing continued to think about theological matters. If, as he had learned from Reimarus, revelation does not reveal truth, then where can truth be found? "Revelation gives mankind nothing that human reason, left to itself, would not arrive at on its own," is the conclusion that Lessing reached at the beginning (§4) of *The Education of the Human Race* (*Die Erziehung des Menschenge-schlechts*, 1780); "but it gave and gives him the most important of these things—only earlier."[24] The essay assumes a three-stage development in which mankind moves from the Kingdom of the Father (Judaism) by way of the Kingdom of the Son (Christianity) to the Kingdom of the Holy Spirit (the future Age of Reason). In sum, while revelation may have been a consolation for mankind at the second stage of its education, in the age of reason it has outlived its usefulness.

While Lessing even more than Reimarus represents a radical rationalism in its application to the history and institutions of Christianity, Immanuel Kant exemplifies that same rationalism applied to Christian dogma. Kant never wrote the "Critique of Religion" that many of his followers anticipated and hoped for. (When the young Fichte published his *Essay toward a Critique of Revelation* [*Versuch einer Critik aller Offenbarung*, 1792], it was initially attributed by many perceptive reviewers to Kant.) However, he addressed theological issues in several treatises, and notably in *Religion within the Confines of Pure Reason* (*Die Religion innerhalb der Grenzen der bloßen Vernunft*, 1793).[25] The difference in emphasis vis-à-vis Lessing and Reimarus is immediately apparent, because Kant is interested here almost exclusively in the theological question of good and evil and not at all in religious history or biblical criticism. Contrary to the traditional Christian and classical Greco-Roman belief in the original goodness of man in Paradise or the Golden Age, Kant argues that man is born with an inclination toward evil that coexists with the principle of good in his nature. History is essentially the account of the battle between good and evil for domination of man, a battle that reached its initial resolution when good conquered (in the person of Jesus Christ) and the Kingdom of God was proclaimed. But the positive church as it actually exists in reality is always inferior to the ideal Kingdom of God, by whose standards it must be is measured. In this imperfect world the struggle between good and evil must therefore continue within each individual, who thereby asserts his morality and human dignity. Kant's "theology" appalled his enlightened colleagues, because it was based on an assumption of inherent evil that seemed to be a reprise of the original sin that the Enlightenment thought it had banished through the power of reason.

There can be no proper history of religion, Kant continues, for religion is based on pure moral belief and its progress can be judged only by each individual for himself. The only aspect susceptible to a historical treatment is official dogma, and that history would constitute "nothing but the account of the constant struggle between ecclesiastical and [private] moral religious faith."[26] Such a history can have unity only if it is limited to that segment of the human race that has attained some understanding of the difference between the faith of reason and the faith of history. "The history of various peoples whose faith is not interconnected otherwise vouchsafes no ecclesiastical unity." It is this binary approach, as Kant explained a few years later in The *Conflict of the Faculties,* that justifies the role of philosophy vis-à-vis theology. "The biblical theologian is actually the scribe for ecclesiastical faith, which is based on statutes, i.e., on laws that emanate from the will of another, whereas the rational theologian is the scholar of reason for religious faith, i.e., the faith that is based on inner laws which can be developed from each individual's own reason."[27]

We see, then, that history plays a non-negligible but clearly defined and delimited role in the Enlightenment theology of the eighteenth century. It is restricted almost wholly to the critical function of disenchantment and secularization, exposing the inconsistencies, improbabilities, and impossibilities of the biblical texts and relativizing the teachings of the church fathers in the light of their perceived handicaps of ignorance, superstition, and even immorality. This critical attitude does not necessarily imply, even in the radical rationalism of Lessing and Kant, any lack of belief. But belief is firmly placed into a realm quite separate from rational proof or explanation—into a more or less timeless realm with no history.

Herder and Pre-Romantic Theology

Even as Lessing was publishing the Wolffenbüttel Fragments and Kant was meticulously defining the limits of religion, a young thinker of the next generation was engaged in an approach to religion that expanded the realm of religion well beyond the "limits" imposed by Kant and that conspicuously and consciously involved a historical dimension. Johann Gottfried Herder (1744–1803), the son of a pietist family and himself a dedicated theologian, disagreed with Lessing and Kant on almost all essentials, even though he had been an eager student of Kant's and was a friend of Lessing's. In radical contradistinction to their underlying Enlightenment belief in the essential sameness of human character, Herder believed that peoples differ according to their historical circumstances. He was opposed to the rationalists' total reliance on the autonomy of reason and to their dismissal of revelation. He rejected Kant's notion of an inherent "radical evil" and, while grateful to Lessing for putting forth doubts that needed to be answered, felt personally aggrieved by many of the "barbed points" of the fragmentist.[28] Unlike Lessing, who claimed that he was no theologian and merely a fan of theology, Herder proudly asserted: "I am myself a theologian, and the cause of religion is as close to my heart as to anyone's."[29]

Herder was persuaded that the true history of humankind could be written only by a theologian ("priest of God") because the theologian is best equipped to recognize the divine order underlying human history and, indeed, the entire universe. Appropriately, in *Yet Another Philosophy of History* (1774) he observed that religion belongs to the earliest (Oriental) stage of human society as the element of all our actions. "It was thus natural that the most ancient philosophy and form of rule in every land had to assume originally the form of theology."[30] In Egypt it became the "vehicle of education"; the Greek enlightenment removed "the sacred veil" and shifted religion to the theater and marketplace; the Romans, while contributing nothing new, tolerated the practice of all religions in their provinces.[31] Gradually the religion of the ancient world, which had come from the Orient by way of Egypt to Greece and Italy, became "a powerless thing that had lost its fragrance" ("ein *verduftetes Kraftloses Ding*")[32] and created the vacuum from which Christianity could emerge—

a Christianity that, after centuries of growth and change, has itself been corrupted by "everything that gnaws at the finer bonds of our time: philosophy, free-thinking, luxuriance."[33]

In the fifteen "provincial letters" *To Preachers* (*An Prediger. Fünfzehn Provinzialblätter,* 1774) that he composed along with *Yet Another Philosophy,* Herder reiterated the principal notions, sometimes with the identical wording. History of religion is "the great vehicle of education" for children, who learn through stories rather than dogma; religion itself is "fact! history!"; the origins of the priestly class should not be sought "where they wear red shoes or red hats and silk clothes" but among the simple people.[34] Herder maintains that the entire Bible is "casual" ("Kasual")—that is, specific to the time, occasion, and circumstances for which it was written. Accordingly, the symbolic books should also be read "casually" (that is, "case by case" or "contingently"): "just as the teacher of nature explains each animal, tree, plant, everything in its place; just as the history teacher explains each event, every incident in its place; just as the Bible exegete explains each miracle, each step in God's housekeeping in its time and in its place."[35]

This last statement anticipates the method underlying Herder's *Letters concerning the Study of Theology* (*Briefe, das Studium der Theologie betreffend,* 1780–1781).[36] Herder stresses the importance of the ancient biblical languages for the theologian, but not in the mystical sense of orthodoxy. "That the Hebrew language was spoken by human beings, by a nation, is proven; but that it also was spoken by gods, by angels and Elohim still remains to be proved; therefore I stand by the first statement."[37] Just as languages must be regarded historically, so too the stories of the Bible from Adam and Eve and the Flood to the flight of the Israelites out of Egypt and through the wilderness: Herder insists on their fundamental truth of meaning without insisting on their absolute historical validity. They are tales appropriate to the childhood level of humanity for which they were composed, a world to which the modern reader must surrender and that he must seek to enter by means of empathy ("Einfühlung").[38] Through the power of their poetry they lend themselves ideally to the purposes of instruction in school and from the pulpit. When Herder moves from the Old to the New Testament, however, he insists that "the basis of all Christianity is historical incident," which must be accepted by faith.[39] He urges the student of theology to avoid theory and abstractions and, instead, to study the history of dogma, since, through history, "every dogma becomes genetically bright and clear and even the driest terminology is enlivened."[40] True science, he concludes, has like water a twofold source: from heaven and from earth. The former is theology; the latter the human sciences. "The sea of theology can be traveled securely only in the ship of the church, with the magnet of revelation; the stars of philosophy are not adequate here."[41]

This same sense informs Herder's magisterial *Ideas toward a Philosophy of History of Humankind (Ideen zur Philosophie der Geschichte des Menschheit,* 1784–91). At the end of book 9, after he has discussed the nature of humankind anthropologically but before moving on to the earliest written evidences of humanity in the Orient, Herder devotes a chapter to "Religion as the Oldest and Most Sacred Tradition of the Earth."[42] He begins with the assertion that reason, humanity, and religion are the three "graces" that distinguish human from animal life. Of these, religion is the oldest, for traces of religion, he continues, can be found even among the poorest, crudest peoples at the edge of the earth—a religion passed along by tradition. Because religious tradition made use of symbols, the language of religion is always the oldest and most obscure language. The priests were originally the wise men of the nation, but as civilization progressed and the original meaning of the religious language and its symbols was forgotten, superficial appearance replaced truth and wisdom, the priests became deceivers, and the rulers appropriated religion for their own purposes of power. Herder concludes his chapter by summarizing the accomplishments of religion: it first brought culture and science, which were originally nothing but a kind of religious tradition. Moreover, religion was the necessary element from which both reason and humanity emerged to elevate humankind above simple animal instinct. Books 17–20 amount to a more detailed recapitulation of the history of Christianity among the various peoples of Europe, but Herder's vast fragmentary project ends before he arrives at the role of religion in his own century.

Most Herder scholars agree that his theology is guided by three principles: the conviction that God's purpose with mankind will end with the triumph of Christianity; the belief that the Bible contains the evidence for this plan; and, above all in our context, "the primacy of the historical over all speculative elements of thought."[43] Herder sought to reconcile Enlightenment skepticism with revelation and applied to theology his central historical insight that every age and every culture must be judged by its own standards and in its own integrity. On the whole, however, his contribution to Protestant theology appears minor in comparison with his epoch-making role in creating a modern philosophy of history, which he refused to reduce simply to a progression from superstition to reason, as did the Universal Historians.[44] The "provincial letters" were a conspicuous failure, and the *Letters on the Study of Theology,* while warmly received upon publication, were quickly forgotten and had little lasting influence.[45] Through these various achievements, Herder compensated for the extremes of radical rationalism and became the principal forerunner of Romantic religious thought and of the man generally acknowledged as the initiator of modern Protestant theology.

Schleiermacher: The Great Synthesizer

If Schleiermacher did in fact achieve what Tillich labeled "the great synthesis"[46] in Protestant theology, it was because he had personally and directly experienced the various forces—pietism, rationalist skepticism, and Romantic idealism—that at the end of the eighteenth century required a new amalgamation. Friedrich Daniel Ernst Schleiermacher (1768–1834) came from a line of religiously problematic clergymen.[47] His grandfather, Daniel Schleyermacher—Schleiermacher later changed the spelling of his family name—was a Reformed pastor in Elberfeld. He became involved with an ecstatic religious sect led by a self-proclaimed prophet, was himself charged with sorcery and witchcraft, and had to flee to Holland, where he gave up preaching. Schleiermacher's father, Gottlieb Adolph Schleyermacher, shocked as a young theologian into rationalist skepticism by his father's experiences, became a chaplain in Frederick the Great's army during the Seven Years' War. For practical reasons he suppressed his Enlightened views when preaching to those who still held an orthodox faith in revelation. Stationed after the war in Breslau, he married Katharina-Maria Stubenrauch, the daughter and granddaughter of court chaplains at the cathedral in Berlin. Friedrich Schleiermacher was born in Breslau on 21 November 1768 and got his early schooling there and later at Pless (in today's southwestern Poland) where his father was transferred during the War of Bavarian Succession (1778–79).

Schleiermacher's father, as the sole Reformed chaplain in Silesia, was required to travel throughout the province to fulfill his duties. In the course of these trips he encountered the Moravian community at Gnadenfrei (south of Breslau) where Prussian troops were stationed—a fateful encounter that produced in him a profound religious awakening. Although his military status did not permit him to convert formally, he became in every other sense a devout Moravian along with his wife and children. For

reasons of religious conviction, the parents decided to entrust the education of their children to the Moravian Brethren, whose school at Niesky
(near Görlitz and Herrnhut in the southeastern corner of present-day Germany) Schleiermacher entered in June of 1783. Because of the school's
rules, he never again saw his parents after his fifteenth year. His mother
died six months later, and although his father lived for eleven years more,
they communicated only by letter.

Schleiermacher adjusted happily to the pietism of the Moravians, and
in the excellent school at Niesky he received a firm grounding in humanistic studies: Latin, Greek, and mathematics, but also botany and English.
He flourished so well academically that in 1785 he was sent, along with
other graduates, to the Moravian seminary at Barby (near the university
town of Halle), which amounted to a pietist college with a general curriculum for future teachers and preachers of the Brethren. It was here that
Schleiermacher's religious doubts first began to emerge—doubts that
could not be quelled by his intellectually limited and narrowly orthodox
teachers. Although reading in modern philosophy and rationalist theology was forbidden, inevitably these texts and ideas crept in from nearby
Halle, along with prohibited works of contemporary literature (notably
Goethe's). Schleiermacher was persuaded by the Enlightenment view that
a rational world offers no justification for eternal damnation, and that insight led him to reason that the absence of damnation precluded the need
for Jesus' self-sacrifice. He communicated his growing doubts to his increasingly troubled father, who finally consented to allow Schleiermacher
in 1787 to withdraw from the Moravian seminary in order to continue his
studies at the university in Halle, one of the largest German universities
that had almost 1200 students, of whom two-thirds were theologians.

In Halle, Schleiermacher lived with his uncle Stubenrauch, who taught
church history at the university. In his studies, and under the guidance of
excellent professors, he devoted himself to modern philosophy, especially
Kant; to the history of philosophy, where he became acquainted with
Plato and Aristotle; to his beloved classics, which he continued under the
tutelage of the brilliant young philologist Friedrich August Wolf; and, at
his father's urging, to further studies in English and French. These two
happy years, enhanced by several lasting friendships, ended in 1789 when
his uncle Stubenrauch accepted a pastorate at Drossen, a small town
across the river from Frankfurt an der Oder. At the urging of his father
and uncle, Schleiermacher accompanied him there in order to prepare
himself for the theological board examinations.

Schleiermacher's letters from the year at Drossen reveal a tormented mind. "God knows what evil genius it was," he wrote to a university friend only a week after the French Revolution, "that led me so suddenly into the kitchen of philosophy, where now so much poison and gall is consumed for the fine, piquant sauces."[48] But theology offered no consolations, as he confessed to the same friend six months later. "If I study anything, it's the theological jumble with which I must reacquaint myself, because— God willing—I intend to present myself in Berlin for the examinations."[49] To his father he wrote that he was observing the "contests of the philosophical and theological athletes" without taking the side of either.[50] In May 1790, he passed the first examination with "very good" and even "excellent" marks and was rewarded by the Reformed Directorate with a position as tutor to the sons of Count Dohna at his estate in Schlobitten (in East Prussia between Danzig and Königsberg).

Following the year of aimlessness and depression in Drossen—the emotional low-point of Schleiermacher's life—his letters from Schlobitten reflect an altogether happy and enriching experience. In the person of the countess he encountered for the first time the charm and intelligence of a highly cultivated woman, the first in a series of such women who played a significant role in Schleiermacher's life. He enjoyed his teaching duties: French with the younger children and geometry, history, and geography with the older son. He had ample time to read in the count's well-stocked library. And in the village he delivered his first sermons, which often amounted to moral treatises informed by the ethics of Kant and Plato. In May 1793, Schleiermacher left Schlobitten by mutual consent with his employers. Despite friendly personal relations that continued for years, the differences between the young tutor's liberal views and the conservatism of the host family in politics, religion, and education had produced stresses.

After vacationing for the summer with his uncle in Drossen, Schleiermacher went to Berlin in the fall of 1793 and taught in Friedrich Gedike's well-known pedagogical seminar while he prepared for the second (and final) theological examination, which he passed in April 1794. Following his ordination, he accepted a position as adjunct to an elderly preacher in Landsberg an der Warthe (in western Poland). Since the young assistant preacher's sermons were a resounding success with the congregation, it was generally assumed that he would receive the position following his senior's retirement in 1796. But Schleiermacher, despite his twenty-seven years, was considered too young by the Reformed Directorate in Berlin.

When a second pastorate was also denied him for reasons of his youth, he accepted a modestly paid position as preacher in the Charité Hospital in Berlin and, in September 1796, moved to the capital, where he first had a wretched apartment on the third floor of the dilapidated hospital building (a former plague house in a desolate suburb of the city). At the Charité, where as the Reformed pastor he shared responsibilities with a Lutheran colleague, Schleiermacher not only ministered to the inhabitants of the home for the elderly on the first floor and the hospital patients on the second floor (roughly 3500 people annually), but also watched over the simple people from the neighboring outlying districts of the capital city. In addition to his sermons at the Charité, he had to hold services in the nearby home for military invalids, make visits to the sick, and carry out various pastoral duties.

Despite his demanding responsibilities, Schleiermacher found time both for his studies and for the social activities in which he took increasing pleasure. Thanks to contacts through his mother's family, he established close connections with prominent families of the Reformed church in Berlin—above all, the politically influential Consistorial Councilor Friedrich Samuel Gottlieb Sack and the aging provost, Johann Joachim Spalding. But the extraordinarily sociable young man, who was attracted not only by intellect but also by a friendly atmosphere, quickly made himself a popular figure in various reading societies and tea-clubs. Already in 1794 he had been introduced by Alexander von Dohna to the prominent Berlin physician Marcus Herz. Now he renewed that acquaintance, drawn in part by the philosophical colloquia and scientific talks that brought persons from all classes into the house of the Jewish intellectual. Above all, he became bound by a deep and—all rumors to the contrary—wholly non-erotic friendship with Herz's wife Henriette. He later characterized the relationship as "a rather intimate and hearty friendship, in which however there is not the least talk of man and woman."[51] Despite her beauty, she never affected him in a manner that could have disturbed his peace of mind. With his characteristic insight he recognized in her "a passionless being" who was acclaimed in large gatherings for her beauty but who preferred to give expression to her innermost feelings in an intimate circle of friends.

Henriette Herz, who was seventeen years younger than her husband, lived with him in a childless but harmonious marriage. She was not only a celebrated beauty with "a colossal queenly figure"[52] but also an accomplished woman who in her youth had already mastered some eight languages, to which she later added Turkish and Sanskrit. "Schleier," as his friends called him, made the long trek almost daily after work from the Charité to the Herz residence in a fashionable section on the other side of Berlin. Because at night he had to find his way back again on the unlighted and unpaved streets, his friends in their concern for his safety presented him with a small lantern that he could attach to the button hole of his coat. The friendship between the Reformed pastor and the Jewish beauty was so unusual that in 1798 Schleiermacher's superior, Consistorial Councilor Sack, disquieted by rumors, seriously thought of transferring the young preacher to the provinces, a proposal that Schleiermacher energetically opposed.

Through Henriette's mediation, Schleiermacher in August 1797 met the young literary critic and historian Friedrich Schlegel, who had just arrived in Berlin. Despite their later estrangement, this relationship developed for the next two years into one of the most intense and productive friendships of the Romantic era. Soon after their first meeting, Schlegel reported to his brother that he had found "a preacher *Schleyermacher*, who studies Fichte's writings and reads the journals with an interest that goes beyond curiosity and personality."[53] A month later he wrote to Novalis that "there is also one philosopher in Berlin" who contributes greatly to his satisfaction. "He has sense and depth, and above all a critical spirit."[54]

Schleiermacher is hardly more restrained in his praise. At the end of October he described the impression that the brilliant intellectual has made on him:

> He is a young man of 25, of such extensive learning that one cannot comprehend how it is possible in such youth to know so much; of an original spirit that here, where there is no shortage of spirit and talent, exceeds everything by far; and in his manners of a naturalness, openness, and childlike youthfulness, whose combination with all the above is perhaps by far the most wonderful part of it.[55]

After citing Schlegel's wit and lack of inhibition, the theologian goes on to say that he has hitherto never been without learned companionship and that he has had conversation partners for every discipline. But until now he has always lacked someone with whom he could share his philosophical ideas, someone capable of comprehending philosophical abstractions. "He now fills this great gap most splendidly." In short, with this friendship "a new period" began for Schleiermacher. The two friends complemented each other: to the extent that Schlegel conceded to the other a higher moral understanding, Schleiermacher found that Schlegel was "so superior in spirit that I can speak of it only with reverence."[56]

The two young men met each other in August and saw each other often at the Herz soirées and in other salons. By the end of October, as he reported to his sister, Schleiermacher was spending every morning at Schlegel's apartment, and they begin to talk about sharing living quarters. At the beginning of December, Schlegel told his brother that he would be moving into Schleiermacher's house at New Year's—to save both money and time. Renovations at the Charité had earlier forced Schleiermacher to take rooms outside the Oranienburg Gate, and there Schlegel moved in with his new friend. Their letters provide a lively picture of their life together, which lasted for almost a year and a half. Schlegel reports, for instance, that it is not hard to stay at home when it's snowing, because he has someone with him who sometimes stays home on his sofa conversing and sometimes goes into the city and brings back tidbits of news and gossip.[57] For his part Schleiermacher speaks in his New Year's letter to his sister of the "splendid change" in his existence brought about by Schlegel's move. He needs only to open the door in order to talk with a sensible person, and he can immediately share with someone else the good humor that he brings home in the evening. Schlegel usually rises an hour earlier than Schleiermacher, who wakes up toward eight-thirty when he hears the rattle of the coffee cups, whereupon the morning conversation from room to room immediately begins. Their friends jokingly called this cozy life a marriage, in which Schleiermacher played the female role. So these different but equally gifted young men lived peacefully side by side, with Schleiermacher making his excursions each evening to visit his friend Henriette Herz and Schlegel going each day to visit Dorothea Veit (the daughter of the famed Jewish philosopher Moses Mendelssohn), who in December 1798 had left her husband in order to share her life with her new lover. It was this shared life that produced two of the most important works of early German Romanticism: Schlegel's novel *Lucinde* (1799), which amounts to a poetic account of his love affair with Dorothea, and Schleiermacher's speeches *On Religion* (*Über die Religion,* 1799).

History in *On Religion*

By the time Schleiermacher wrote his great work—called by Rudolf Otto "a true manifesto of Romanticism" and one of the most famous books that history has preserved[58]—he had experienced the major spiritual impulses of the age. He had grown up and been educated in the pietist tradition; rebelling against that tradition, he had immersed himself in the rational arguments against revelation and in Enlightenment theology; and he had shared friendship and rooms with Schlegel, the most brilliant theoretical mind of early German Romanticism, the critic credited with the creation of modern literary history. He was prepared, as could be few others, to accomplish the great synthesis that would unite friends of religion in a wholly new conception.

What role does history play in this development? Apart from passing references in his correspondence to the history of ancient Greece, to Gibbon's *Decline and Fall of the Roman Empire,* and to other isolated events and books, we find no such account of Schleiermacher's interest in history as we did for Hegel.[59] (Unfortunately, most of Schleiermacher's early letters to his father, which might have contained such references—including perhaps references to Herder—have been lost.) History of course constituted part of the standard curriculum at Barby;[60] he studied church history in connection with his theological studies—and lived for several years with an uncle who taught ecclesiastical history; and history was one of the fields for which he was responsible as a tutor in the Dohna household at Schlobitten. But we have in fact more to go on, for in 1793, while teaching in Berlin and participating in Gedike's pedagogical seminar, Schleiermacher wrote a paper entitled "On Instruction in History" ("Über den Geschichtsunterricht").[61] It is not necessary for our purposes to consider Schleiermacher's specific pedagogical recommendations. But the paper provides ample evidence not only of his own knowledge of history but, more importantly, of the importance that he attributes to a command of history.

"The majority of those who have enjoyed a so-called learned education," it begins, "are less familiar with the historical sciences than with any others. At the academies, instruction in history is attended almost exclusively by future statesmen, and it appears that even clever heads rarely gained at school any taste for this interesting branch of human knowledge." Indeed many schools, he continues, provide no complete course in history whatsoever. And even though there may be history classes at others, the curriculum is not arranged according to any rational plan but pieced together at the convenience of the other subjects. If students lack guidance in general principles that would enable them meaningfully to relate the isolated facts they pick up, it is even worse with regard to stimulating any active love for the study of history. Apart from a small segment of ancient history and the history of the present century, students learn little more than an unconnected potpourri of names and anecdotes. But "it would belittle this science greatly if we purported to see its usefulness only in filling the memory rather than therein, that history alone enables us to cast an accurate, large, and general gaze into the condition of the world and to obtain from every point of view that offers itself an overview of the course of humankind or one of its parts."

Pedagogues trust too little in the capacity of youth to learn systematically, offering them only a chronicle that they are supposed to memorize. "If they were told instead to learn how the present condition of men has gradually arisen, all those difficulties would disappear." To achieve this aim, one should start by depicting present conditions and by alerting the students to interesting points of comparison with the history of past times. Then they should be led back to the earliest conditions of humankind. This should not be regarded as a waste of time, for nothing is so damaging as to neglect the systematic preparation of the mind for a science. "The beginners now have, from the vast distance between the two conditions and the explanation for the transition from one into the other, a notion of the whole extent of the science. . . . History is really the science of that which is, for everything before now is revealed as the basis of the present." If the students learn how modern bourgeois society has arisen among men, they will readily see to what extent events and people of the past are important for this rise and which reports about them are suitable for history.

Schleiermacher sounds almost like Herder when he goes on to say that "one must naturally characterize for them the condition of human beings in each of these epochs, just as initially the earliest and present one were characterized, in order to comprehend each of these great parts as a whole, to interest them in its explanation, and to help them onto the trail of the most general main events." It is desirable, moreover, to avoid the one-sidedness that arises when history is treated only politically; this can be accomplished by challenging the students to relate incidents from history according to criteria that interest them personally. Finally, in order to avoid irrelevancies the student must learn that "nothing can be a main event that is not of decisive influence on the whole of history."

This appreciation of history's centrality, which could only have been enhanced by his discussions with his roommate, shows up as a dominant theme in the speeches *On Religion*. In contrast to Schlegel, who had already published a series of essays, reviews, and fragments that had made him, well before his thirtieth year, a familiar figure on the national literary scene, Schleiermacher had up to now written relatively little: a number of sermons (published in 1801), two volumes of sermons translated from the English (published in 1795 and 1798), and several unpublished essays on philosophical-ethical topics. In the heady atmosphere of the Berlin salons and at the urging of his friends, he now turned his energies to a major pronouncement on religion, a subject newly fashionable among such young Romantic thinkers and poets as Schelling and Novalis in their opposition to the Enlightenment. In August 1798 he outlined his work and by mid-winter had written the first two speeches. (The five sections were called "speeches" ("Reden") even though they were never delivered as such.) Schleiermacher had to spend the months from February 1799 to mid-May in nearby Potsdam as a replacement pastor, and in the social isolation of the garrison-town he completed the remaining three speeches by April 15. The book was published anonymously the following month.

The very fact that he could complete such a weighty book in barely eight months shows that the author had concerned himself long and intensively—in truth, since his university days in Halle—with the thoughts that went into it. Schleiermacher knew all too well that the former authority of religion had been undermined by the rationalism of thinkers like Lessing and Kant. Among many modern intellectuals, religion, such as it was, had been secularized to at most "natural religion"—that is, a religion that proclaims itself not through divine revelation but through human reason. In the face of such attacks, pietism had withdrawn into an unworldly inwardness, while Enlightenment theology sought to adapt itself by means of allegory or demythification or otherwise rationalizing readings of the Bible.

Schleiermacher was the first theologian who fully comprehended that the radically transformed world of postrevolutionary modernity required a radically new attitude toward religion. In a very precise sense we recognize in his early work the most significant theological expression of the general consciousness of crisis at the turn of the century, a consciousness that manifested itself in every field of intellectual endeavor. As a result of his own youthful doubts, the Charité pastor understood why so many intelligent men and women of his acquaintance no longer made room in their lives and thoughts for religion. Schleiermacher's Berlin friends—Friedrich Schlegel, Henriette Herz, Dorothea Veit, and other young intellectuals of various religious heritages—represented precisely "the cultivated people among its despisers" ("die Gebildeten unter ihren Verächtern") to whom he addressed his book in its subtitle.

Schleiermacher's work, as suggested by the title of the first speech, is in the classic sense of the word an *apologia*—a defense of religion against attacks by hostile groups, whether they be heathens and Jews (in the eyes of the early patristic apologists), Moslems (for Thomas Aquinas), the Catholic pope (for Johannes Hus), or rationalism (for Hugo Grotius and other apologists of the late seventeenth century). What opponents of religion did Schleiermacher have in mind? He meant those who no longer enter "the deserted temples" and "the weathered ruins of the shrine," whose tasteful dwellings have no household deities apart from "the sayings of the sages and the songs of the poets," and whose minds are so filled with thoughts of fatherland, art, and science that no feeling remains for eternal and sacred being (3).[62] Schleiermacher was not addressing himself to the simple folk of his congregations at the Charité or in the Berlin suburbs, but to the men and women he encountered in the Berlin salons that he frequented. He was turning against "excessive enthusiasm" and "insatiable sensuousness" (7-8)—that is, the Moravian piety of his youth as well as the enlightened theology of Halle and other universities. Moreover, the form of presentation that he selected—the "speech" or "talk" ("Rede")—was not the scholarly treatise of traditional apologetics, but a more social variation of the scholarly lecture, which was gaining popularity among intellectuals of his generation.[63]

Schleiermacher clearly defines his own role at the outset. Though a member of a churchly order, he intends to speak to his audience as a fellow human being (4). Religion was "the maternal body" that nourished him as a child (12). Filled thus with religion, to whom should he now bear witness? Not those "proud islanders," the English, whose empiricism has reduced religion to dead letters of the alphabet. And not to the French, whose "unreined arrogance" defies the eternal laws of the world (13). Only in Germany does religion find the wise moderation and quiet contemplation that are necessary if it is to find a refuge from barbarism and "the cold, earthly sense of the age" (14).

In order to attain his goal he begins by analyzing the reasons for the contempt that modern intellectuals bring to religion. Every work of the human spirit can be viewed from a double perspective: either as "a product of human nature" or as "a product of time and history" (17). If religion were acknowledged as an expression of human nature, it would not be despised. So it is more likely that it is despised because it is regarded as nothing more than the empty product of certain ages of faith. But if that were the case, then the despiser ought to be able to prove from case to case where and why the content is false. Schleiermacher proclaims no desire to traverse "the various buildings of religion"—from the fables of the savages to deism, from "the crude superstition of our common people down to the poorly stitched fragments of metaphysics and morality called rational Christianity" (18). These phenomena are nothing but transitions on the way to a true religion based on "an astonished contemplation of the infinite" (19). In all these systems, to be sure, there is some trace of spiritual substance, but it will remain hidden from those who make no effort to penetrate its contingent form. Whoever seeks religion must direct his gaze to individual hints and moods that can be found in all utterances and deeds of God-inspired people—the heavenly sparks that arise "whenever a holy soul is touched by the universe" (22). Modern attempts to transplant religion to other realms—to ethics or law—simply expose their contempt for it. Schleiermacher ends his first speech with the bold assertion that religion "necessarily arises of its own accord from the innermost being of every better soul," that it belongs to "its own province in human nature" ("Gemüt"), and that it therefore deserves "to be recognized in its innermost being" (26). The disdain of the intellectuals is exposed as contempt for the Enlightenment disfigurements of religion, but not of religion itself.

In his introductory *apologia*, Schleiermacher made the important point that religion can be viewed either from within or from without, either psychologically or historically. The second speech "On the Nature of Religion," by far the longest and most famous one, is devoted wholly to the first proposition. Schleiermacher begins by distinguishing religion from metaphysics, which seeks simply to classify the universe, and ethics, which sets up a system of rules of behavior vis-à-vis the universe. Religion, in contrast, is "neither thinking nor acting, but contemplation ["Anschauung"] and feeling ["Gefühl"]" (35). "Contemplation of the universe," he summarizes in his most famous formulation, "I beg you, make friends with this concept; it is the hinge of my entire speech, it is the most general and highest formula of religion" (38). One feels true religion in the "mysterious moment" before contemplation and feeling are parted, "when the sense and its object have as it were flowed into one another and become One" (50). At such moments man feels wholly at one with the universe. "I lie on the bosom of the infinite world; at this moment I am its soul." Schleiermacher's prose rises here to its rhapsodic peak. He calls such moments "the holy embrace," "the highest blossom of religion," "the birth hour of everything living in religion" (51). The meaning of such moments is not action: "To love the world-spirit and joyously to observe its operation, that is the goal of our religion" (54). And he cites as an example "one of the greatest heroes of religion"—he means Jesus, whose proper name is never mentioned in this entire book on religion by a Christian theologian— who in his own contemplation of nature chose such lovely images as the lilies of the field. Modern man, in contrast, knows other aspects of nature—"its chemical powers, the eternal laws." But the universe is ultimately comprehensible only humanly—that is, existentially. (Here the speaker adduces the example of Adam, for whom the meaning of the world became clear only through his love for his wife.) There follows a hymn of praise to the variety of humankind, in which each individual is a necessary part, and to the manifold degrees of human powers, which we can all sense in ourselves. Each of us is in this sense "a compendium of humankind" (67). But we no longer recognize this harmony of the universe because we are caught in the "miserable isolation" of conventional morality; we need mediators between our "limited mode of thinking and the eternal boundaries of the world." We must seek to contemplate humankind not only in its being, but also in its becoming. "History in the truest sense is the highest object of religion. . . . All true history has everywhere had first of all a religious purpose and emerged from religious ideas" (67). Schleiermacher goes on in the second half of the speech to discuss the ideas of immortality and divinity; but with the principle that history is the object of religion he has reached the logical conclusion of the speech.

The third speech "On the Cultivation of Religion" amounts to a critique of the Enlightenment, which has obscured the harmony of the universe by its incessant analysis and classification, and of pietism and mysticism, which find no access to the universe outside because they look only inward. Nevertheless, he argues, "our age is no less favorable to religion than any other" (108), and he concludes with his vision of the rebirth of religion: in a science that reveals the shrine; in a new morality; in a philosophy that elevates humankind to the understanding of its interaction with the world; and in a physics that leads the viewer directly into the center of nature (115).

The fourth speech "On the Social Aspect of Religion or on Church and Priesthood" argues that everyone who has been illumined by religion feels a need to communicate with others who have experienced the same thing—for instance, through hymns and choral music. In this sense, everyone is a priest and the whole religious world is an indivisible whole, for only "the religion of society taken together is the entire religion" (126). In our present-day reality, however, truly pious individuals turn away from the church because it clings so desperately to lifeless concepts. Schleiermacher offers no solution—only his vision of the ideal, where the family is "the truest image of the universe" (153). This produces a final critique, fifty years before Karl Marx, of the deplorable social conditions under which people live and which constitute the greatest hindrance to religion. True religion will be possible only when each individual is free and has "the peace and leisure to contemplate the world within himself" (154).

If the great second speech analyzed religion from within and psychologically, presenting it as the feeling of awe that fills the individual in his contemplation of the universe, the fifth (and final) one "On Religions" looks at religion from without and historically. Schleiermacher begins by defending the diversity of religions, for "man is finite and religion is infinite" (160). By justifying the "positive" religions of the world, he takes a standpoint directly opposed to that of many rationalist critics, who rejected positive religions in favor of a universal "natural religion." Hegel, for instance, who during these very same years was writing his long study, "The Positivity of the Christian Religion" (published only after his death), rejects any positivity in religion or law that is based on authority rather than independent thought.[64] For Hegel, Jesus was proclaiming a virtually Kantian ethics of freedom; it was the church that corrupted his teachings into the "transitory contingency" that became the authority of a positive religion, which must be rejected if mankind is to get back to any authentic Christianity.

Schleiermacher, in contrast, disparaging natural religion as "meagre and thin" (183), invites us to ignore the empty practices and abstract concepts of the various religions and, instead, to consider their source and original components. "You will find that all the dead cinders were once glowing outpourings of the inner fire" (165). History becomes essential, for "every positive religion appears most youthful and fresh, and therefore can be most surely recognized, during its development and its blossoming" (169). It is not easy, to be sure, to expose what is typical and individual about each religion if one eliminates the details. Yet in all can be found a certain development of the innate religious aptitude, and here instinct is a better guide than rationality. Religion requires a basic view of the universe; otherwise it is nothing. It may be little more than a "dark premonition" that attracts the individual to a religion. "His religion is determined by the earliest definite religious view that penetrates his feelings with such power that through a single impulse his organ for the universe is brought to life and from now on is always active" (176). In contrast to this vigorous experience, the so-called "natural" religions emerge from no vivid sense of the world and have no history and no center (183).

If the skeptics are serious about their interest in religion, then they cannot get around "the despised positive religions" (185). That does not necessarily mean that we can simply abstract from them the element common to all specific religions in order to reach the truth. "Religious men are wholly historical" (188), and Schleiermacher's Christology is entirely based on his belief in the historicity of Christ's life and mission.[65] But this fact is also a source of great misunderstandings. That moment when those religious leaders became overwhelmed by contemplation of the universe, it turned into the crux of their religion; it is a moment that ossified in the hands of their successors all too readily into a lifeless ritual. Generally speaking, in every religion there have always been, on the one hand, rigid systematizers, who delimit religion with propositions, and, on the other, "shallow indifferentists," who decry everything unique as dead literalism (190).

As examples of positive religions, Schleiermacher scrutinizes Judaism, which he designates as a "dead" religion because it has long since been reduced to its political and moral elements, and then finally considers Christianity. The underlying idea of Judaism is "general and immediate retribution": everything is regarded as the direct intervention of the deity (191). The original view of Christianity, in contrast, is "that of general striving of everything finite toward the unity of the whole" (193). Nowhere, the Charité preacher believes, is religion so wholly idealized as in Christianity. He has no intention of glossing over its deformations, for everything sacred becomes unavoidably corruptible as soon as it becomes human. He sketches the role of Jesus as a mediator, even if Jesus never claimed to be the sole object to whom the idea of mediator should be applied. (Schleiermacher points out that "one numerous party of Christians" [the Catholic church] has celebrated as mediators those who have led a godly life [the saints].) Similarly the holy writings have been declared a "Bible," although true Christianity would not prevent any book written with equal power from being integrated into the Bible (203). The underlying idea of every positive religion is eternal, but the religion and its cultivation are transitory. Christianity, "sublime above all others and more historical and humble in its splendor," has expressly acknowledged this transitoriness (205), teaching that the time will come when no further me-

diators are needed and its positive institutions will become irrelevant.
Hence nothing is more irreligious and un-Christian than "to seek unifor-
mity in religion" (206). Schleiermacher closes the fifth speech and thus the
entire work with the observation that he and his contemporaries are living in an age that "is obviously the boundary between two different orders
of things" (207). When the mighty crisis has passed—he is of course referring to the French Revolution and its consequences— it might again
bring forth a moment that could stand for future generations as the center-point for the contemplation of the universe. "Out of the void there always emerges a new creation."

Schleiermacher's *On Religion* received a mixed reception among his
contemporaries. Friedrich Schlegel was one of the earliest admirers, and
other young intellectuals read the work with equal enthusiasm. But outside the small circle of Romantics, the "speeches" had no broader impact,
and the professional churchmen, in particular, found them too nebulous
to be intelligible. Indeed, Consistory Councilor Sack, the official church
censor, suspected that his young friend and ward had been infected insid-
iously by the revolutionary ideas of his roommate. No doubt Schleiermacher's psychological understanding of all "religion" contributed to this
lack of comprehension among the orthodox. And his justification of all
positive religions, including Christianity, as historical phenomena would
have been unacceptable to the rationalists and the advocates of natural religion, "who do not even want the religion of humankind to have its own
history" (182). But the work survived to become recognized by later generations as the keystone of modern Protestant theology.

History in Systematic Theology: *Brief Outline*

Schleiermacher's *On Religion* marked the culmination of the first major (Romantic) period of his development, which was intuitive and creative
and revolved around the general idea of religion *per se*.[66] The next period
was governed, in contrast, by his growing impulse to bring into a theological system the ideas that in the "speeches" and other early publications
often did not go beyond vague notions and to apply them specifically to
Christianity. Despite the turmoil of his life during these years, his literary
productivity was prodigious.

In 1801—Schlegel and Dorothea Veit had left Berlin because of the
scandal surrounding their liaison—Schleiermacher became involved in a
passionate but Platonic affair with Eleonore Grunow, the unhappily mar-

ried wife of a Berlin clergyman. Hoping for her divorce so that they could marry but unwilling to pressure her unduly by his presence, Schleiermacher requested a transfer and, in 1802, was reassigned to the Pomeranian town of Stolpe near the Baltic coast, where he ministered to a cluster of small Reformed congregations. Frustrated by the meaningless busywork of his position and miserable in his isolation from friends and the intellectual life of Berlin, Schleiermacher even sought forgetfulness in gambling at cards. Yet the two years in exile were intellectually fruitful. Since he had no decent library at his disposal, he had to rely on the few texts available to him and the resources of his own mind. This produced, on the one hand, the first two volumes of his great translation of Plato's dialogues (1804–05) and, on the other, his most exhaustive purely speculative philosophical work: a critique of ethical systems from Plato and Aristotle down to Kant and Fichte (*Grundlinien einer Kritik der bisherigen Sittenlehre,* 1804).

In 1804 he was rescued from Stolpe by a call to the university of Halle where he became the sole Reformed member of an otherwise solidly Lutheran and unwelcoming theological faculty. Even his former professor of philosophy, Johann August Eberhard, with whom he had studied Kant and the history of philosophy, denounced him as an atheist. While Schleiermacher's views were unacceptable to the rationalists and pietists on the faculty, he found friends in his former teacher, the classicist Friedrich August Wolf, with whom he could discuss Plato, and Henrik Steffens, the Norwegian philosopher of nature, through whose influence nature was introduced into Schleiermacher's thinking, which had previously been almost exclusively limited to human culture. Meanwhile, for his lectures he was compelled for the first time to organize his sometimes disparate thoughts on religion into a theological system.

The happiness of his life in Halle is reflected in one of his enduringly popular works and the only purely literary prose that he ever wrote: *Christmas Eve: A Dialogue (Die Weihnachtsfeier: Ein Gespräch,* 1805)— a work that exemplifies the thought developed in the fourth of the *Speeches* on the social aspect of religion and the impulse of religious people to share their thoughts with one another. This fiction, the portrayal of a Christmas Eve celebration by a group of ten men and women of different ages and dispositions, also amounts to a poetizing of his thoughts on history. The theme is sounded close to the beginning, when the young daughter of the house invites the assembled guests to her room to admire a panorama of tiny carved figures that she has set up for the occasion and that represent significant moments in the history of Christianity: the baptism of Jesus, the crucifixion, the destruction of the temple, the battles of Crusaders and Saracens over the holy sepulcher, the pope in a procession at St. Peter's, the martyrdom of Hus, Luther's burning of the papal bull, the conversion of the Saxons, Christian missionaries to remote parts of the world, a churchyard of the Moravian Brethren, and the famous orphanage of Halle (32).[67] This enterprise leads the rationalist among the adults, the lawyer Leonhardt, to worry that her childish piety might lead her eventually to don "the revolting little cap and graceless gown of a Herrnhuter sister" (37).

It is only in the last section of the work—after the celebration has been described, after the women have related various personal stories involving Christmas Eve, and after interruptions by other friends passing by—that the actual Platonic dialogue on the meaning of Christmas takes place. The voices represent different points of view that, taken together, constitute a synthesis of Schleiermacher's own experience and development from pietism by way of skepticism to idealism. Leonhardt, the rational skeptic, advances views that remind us of Schleiermacher's thoughts on the teaching of history (70–75). In his analysis of Christmas, he focuses on the importance of the festival as ritual, which, he argues, preserves the meaning of the Redeemer's birth much better than the biblical accounts. Ritual, he continues, constitutes the principal access to religion for uneducated people. As an example, he moves easily to antiquity, where memories of the past unnoted by historians and poets are often preserved in ritual. (In his essay of 1793 Schleiermacher had suggested that teachers of history should make connections between present and past and between different cultures.) This leads him to the suggestion—to borrow a term from modern theories of folklore—that myth is the narrative accompanying a ritual: that Christian doctrine and its institutions represent a subsequent attempt to justify and rationalize the earlier rituals. This brings him to the typical rationalist critique of positive religion. "It remains doubtful whether it was at all in accordance with Christ's will that such an exclusive and tightly organized church should be formed, without which Christianity as we know it—and consequently our festival as well—would be inconceivable." He regards the resurrection and ascension with suspicion, "for [Christ's] life belongs to this planet, and what can be divorced from the same cannot have stood in any vital connection with it." He ends with the paradoxical conclusion that the Christmas celebration, based as it is on ancient rituals, should be praised "since what might be experienced and historically valid regarding the personal existence of Christ has become so precarious because of the diversity of views and doctrines" (74).

The next speaker, the pious Ernst, rejects this ritual interpretation of Christmas: in his eyes the festival is simply intended to incite joy. Presents are distributed not to stimulate joy but "only because there is already great cause for rejoicing" (77). And we regard Christ as the Redeemer because we, who live in a cleavage between time and eternity, recognize in him "that original, natural state of vitality and joy in which there are no opposites of appearance and being, time and eternity" (79). Finally Eduard, going beyond Leonhardt's rationalism and Ernst's emotional piety, offers an idealizing theological interpretation based on the mystical evangelist, John, who celebrates Christ as the Word become flesh, whose human nature enables us to see "humanity as a living community" (83). This community by which man-in-himself is restored—here we are close to Schleiermacher's own defense of positive religions in the fifth of the *Speeches*—is the church. "Everyone, therefore, in whom this genuine self-consciousness of humanity arises enters within the bounds of the church. That is why no one can truly and vitally possess the fruits of science who is not himself within the church, and why such an outsider can only externally deny the church but not deep within himself." For this reason "the festival breaks forth like a heavenly light out of the darkness" (84). At this point a late visitor interrupts the solemn colloquy, reminding the group that Christmas is after all not an occasion for speech-making but for communal celebration.

Schleiermacher's happiness in Halle was short-lived. On 14 October 1806, Napoleon defeated Prussia at the battle of Jena and, two days later, entered Halle. (Unlike Hegel, who had euphorically acclaimed "the world-spirit on horseback" in Jena, Schleiermacher, the ardent nationalist, refused to watch the victor's triumphant entry into Halle.) The French closed down the university, and, although Schleiermacher continued through the winter months to deliver sermons in the university church, he soon realized that the outlook was hopeless. In the summer of 1807 he returned to Berlin, where he delivered public lectures on religious topics and, at the same time, engaged in various political activities of opposition, which took him on secret missions to the court-in-exile in Königsberg and to other parts of Prussia. During this same period he also managed to produce two major scholarly works: a critical exegesis of I Timothy, which is still regarded as a classic of biblical hermeneutics, and a philological-philosophical study of Heraclitus (1808).

In 1809 his life took an appreciable turn for the better. He became the pastor at Trinity Church in Berlin and, having broken off his connection to Eleonore Grunow, married the widow of a friend, Henriette von Willich. While Schleiermacher's sermons soon attracted a colorfully motley audience—"Moravians, Jews, baptized and unbaptized, young philosophers and philologists, elegant ladies," he reported; "the image of Saint Anthony invariably suggests itself"[68]—their residence in central Berlin rapidly became one of the social and intellectual centers of the capital. Schleiermacher had already involved himself significantly in the discussions about a university in Berlin with his *Occasional Thoughts on Universities* (1808). So it was hardly surprising that he was summoned by the Section of Religion and Public Education to join the commission to establish the university. In July 1809, he was among the first scholars appointed to the faculty of the new institution and, a year later, was named the first dean of the faculty of theology. He was also elected a member of the Berlin Academy of Sciences, to which he devoted considerable energies.

In addition to his work at the Academy, his weekly sermons and pastoral activities, his frequent meetings with the university commission, and his decanal responsibilities, Schleiermacher regularly lectured for fifteen hours every week (beginning at 7 A.M.). Among the lectures that he delivered during the first semester was his "encyclopedia," which was simultaneously published under the title *Brief Outline of Theological Study for the Use in Introductory Lectures* (*Kurze Darstellung des theologischen Studiums zum Behuf einleitender Vorlesungen*, 1811). Schleiermacher had already presented an "Encyclopedia and Methodology" three times before—in 1804/05 and in the summer semester 1805 in Halle and then again in the winter of 1808 as a series of public lectures in Berlin—in each case speaking ad lib from notes.

It was not an uncommon academic practice for professors to base their lectures on someone else's textbook, and various "encyclopedias" of theology had been available since Mursinna's *Primae lineae encyclopaediae theologicae* of 1764—works that extended from the empirical listing of otherwise disparate materials and disciplines to what has been called the "fanatical apriorism of idealistic systematization," which sought to organize faith and Christianity speculatively with no regard for history.[69] But Schleiermacher, uncomfortable (as he tells us in the preface to the first edition) when following anyone else's outline, developed his own curriculum, which he intended to publish for the benefit of his students. For a variety of reasons (as suggested by his schedule above) he did not get around to it until the semester was well underway. The individual short paragraphs of the two editions (1811, 1830) represent no more than the starting point for the free rhetorical development of his ideas as he spoke.

This document, which opened "a new epoch for the self-understanding of Protestant theology"[70] and which "presents the whole of theological effort in a cohesive manner never before achieved," only slowly gained recognition in the course of the nineteenth century.[71] For decades it was largely ignored in favor of Schleiermacher's two other major works, *On Religion* and his magisterial *Christian Faith* (*Der christliche Glaube,* 1821–22). Its radically new historical approach and its synthesizing conception of theology as a unified discipline were disseminated gradually by Schleiermacher's students, and not by contemporary reviews or publicity. Indeed, Schleiermacher's historicization of theology aroused the indignation of many theologians of his day, who accused him of relativizing the absolute values of Christianity.[72]

Today the *Brief Outline* has achieved recognition among theologians as a classic work that created a critical method based on history. Even Schleiermacher's great twentieth-century nemesis, Karl Barth, acknowledged that it was the achievement of nineteenth-century theology, thanks to Schleiermacher, to recognize that Christianity is distinct from other faiths to the extent that it is determined historically through its relationship to the historical person of Jesus Christ.[73] The same cannot be said, however, for the historians. Even though the work contains what amounts to a detailed theory and methodology of historical research, it goes unmentioned in most standards works on historiography.[74]

In the first of 338 paragraphs, Schleiermacher defines theology as "a positive science, the parts of which join into a cohesive whole only through their common relation to a particular mode of faith, that is, a particular way of being conscious of God."[75] (In the first edition he writes "religion" rather than "mode of faith.") In his general introduction (§§1–31) Schleiermacher notes that he will use the term consistently to designate Christian theology (since he will be dealing here—unlike *On Religion,* where the topic was religion in general—specifically with Christianity). Theological interest can focus either on knowledge concerning Christianity or on activity concerning church governance: the former attracts the theologian, the latter the clergyman. No one can master all the theological disciplines in their scope and variety, but it is essential for the theologian to have an overview of the entire field, the manner in which the various parts of theology are related, and the auxiliary disciplines. That, he summarizes, is the intent of the encyclopedic outline.

Schleiermacher divides theology into a "trilogy" of philosophical, historical, and practical theology. "Philosophical" theology uses the philosophy of religion to define the essential nature of Christianity and the divisions of the Christian community. It is the goal of "practical" theology to train the leadership of the church. But "historical" theology provides the actual "corpus" or center of theological study, for the church cannot be guided without an understanding of its nature as a historical institution, and the essence of Christianity cannot be grasped without an understanding of its historical relation to the timeless idea. "Ethics" (by which Schleiermacher means the human sciences in distinction to the natural sciences) is "the science of the principles of history," which is the necessary basis for all study of theology. Following this introduction the work proceeds according to the "trilogy" of aspects. (Despite this over-all triadic organization, Schleiermacher tends to think in terms of binary opposites rather than dialectical progressions.)

Part 1 (§§32–68) immediately puts "Philosophical Theology" on a historical basis by acknowledging that the distinctive nature of Christianity can be grasped neither in a purely scientific nor in a purely empirical manner: it can only be determined "critically" by comparing what is historically given in Christianity and the oppositions by which religious communities differ from one another. This is achieved either by apologetics, whereby Christianity looks outward and stakes its claim to a distinct historical existence by the manner of its origination, or by polemics, whereby it looks inward and, in recognition of its nature as a historical organism, analyzes its inner afflictions. Apologetics explores the nature of Christianity through the historically developed phenomena of canon and sacrament; and polemics considers its weakening through such illnesses as indifferentism and separatism. Philosophical theology, he summarizes, "presupposes the material of historical theology as already known; its own prior task, however, is to lay a foundation for the properly historical perspective on Christianity."

Schleiermacher takes it for granted that "Historical Theology" should be an integral part of the modern study of history, and his introduction to this long part 2 (§§69–256) amounts to a general statement on the theory and method of historical study. Any historical phenomenon can be regarded either as a sudden new start or as a gradual development (§71)— that is, as revolution or evolution. A series characterized by quiet progression constitutes a historical period; a series in which sudden beginning predominates represents a historical epoch (§73). Since every historical whole can be considered not just as a unity but also as a composite, it can be considered synchronically—that is, the period as a whole—or diachronically, following any one of various parallel lines of development (§§74–75). Accordingly Christianity can be treated as a single period in the development of religion; or as an independent whole divided by epochs (§79).

Since historical theology concentrates entirely on Christianity, only the second method is appropriate. For church leadership the present moment is the single most relevant one; but since the present can be understood only as the outcome of the past, knowledge of the entire earlier sequence is necessary (§§81–82). And since it is the goal of theology to represent its nature as purely as possible, a knowledge of primal Christianity (*Urchristentum*) is an indispensable part (§84). Accordingly, historical theology falls naturally into three parts: knowledge of primal Christianity, knowledge of the development of Christianity, and knowledge of its condition at the present moment (§85).

To this end, theological history makes use of the various tools at the disposal of all historical study. For the understanding of the ancient documents upon which Christianity is based, a knowledge of exegetical theology is indispensable (§88). The further development of Christianity can be studied either as a whole or broken down into two parts: the history of its teachings (dogma) and the history of the community (church history) (§90). The representation of the present condition of the church is the realm of what Schleiermacher calls *Statistik,* by which he and his contemporaries meant more or less what we would now call sociology of religion (§95). Dogma, in contrast, is "the systematic presentation of doctrine that has currency at any given time" (§97). Historical criticism, he concludes his introduction, "is the all-pervasive and indispensable organ for the work of historical theology, as it is for the entire field of historical studies" (§102).

Schleiermacher's recommendations for the exegesis of canonical writings (§§103–48) are applicable to any field of history. For an understanding of the documents, first, it is essential to know the original language(s). Second, their interpretation requires a mastery of hermeneutics: every text must be understood in the context of the notions from which it emerged and of all the circumstances governing the lives of the authors as well as their audiences. In addition, it is important to be familiar with the cultural and political circumstances of the period. No study of the canon without adequate philological preparation can rise above simple edification or go beyond pseudodogmatic confusion.

Church history (§§149–94) is "knowledge concerning the total development of Christianity since its establishment as a historical phenomenon." If it is to transcend mere chronicle, history must concern itself with primary and secondary sources. The student arrives at the inner reality of a situation only by combining a mass of relevant details. The two principal functions in the development of Christianity are the growth of doctrine (dogma) and the shaping of a communal life (church history), which in turn can be traced through the closely interrelated developments of worship (*Kultus*) and morality (*Sitte:* that is, the meaning that Christian principles impart to the various areas of daily life). When the church is unhealthy, one group may want to go beyond the primal-Christian utterances in their determination of doctrine while others introduce philosophical principles into Christian doctrine without any appeal to the historical canon. (Schleiermacher is clearly referring to the contemporary extremes of pietism and rationalism.) In order to understand these phenomena it is necessary to make use of all the auxiliary tools produced by the specialists (whom Schleiermacher calls "the virtuosos"). Generally, from the infinite scope of theological history every theologian needs to master at least as much as he requires for his own independent participation in church leadership, including an acquaintance with local circumstances and present conditions. The section on the current state of Christianity (§§195–250) deals with dogmatics and "statistics," in both of which a historical perspective is necessary for any proper assessment of the present. Dogma and "statistics" vary, of course, from period to period in church history. In his concluding remarks (§§251–56), finally, Schleiermacher makes the point that in the Christian church, while the influence of the individual on the group is declining, it is more important than elsewhere to attach our understanding of specific epochs to the lives of influential individuals. In the words of the first edition: "The elements of any historical-theological presentation are far more biographical than historical." While philosophical theology requires nothing more than a chronicle knowledge of history, the scientific treatment of historical sequence in historical theology presupposes the results of philosophical theology: the former (in the words of the first edition) assumes a point of view above Christianity, and the latter a point of view within it. Although philosophical and historical theology inevitably follow different paths of development, they can attain fulfillment only by complementing each other. Those theologians who at present pursue philosophical alongside historical theology are accused— sometimes wrongly and sometimes rightly—of reading history according to predetermined hypotheses. Conversely, the analogous reproach is made that others, lacking the philosophical perspective, are transforming historical theology into a mindless empiricism.

Schleiermacher's final section on "practical theology" (§§257–338), which deals with church service (liturgical and sermonic; pastoral and communal) and church governance (authoritative and independent; teaching and writing), can be disregarded in the present context, since history plays little or no role there.

Schleiermacher's *Brief Outline* represents the systematizing culmination of his thoughts on religion and theology. In it Schleiermacher succeeded in presenting a view of theology that could accommodate and explain the two extremes noted by Goethe in his autobiography: the pietism and rationalism of his youth, which he viewed as unhealthy excrescences due to the predominance of either primal Christian views or philosophical systematization. In addition he was able to relate his practical experience as a clergyman, both in preaching and in pastoral work, and his experience of church politics to his scholarly understanding of the history of dogma and the church as an institution and to incorporate as well his first-hand acquaintance with the philosophical idealism of his Romantic contemporaries. Above all, he demonstrated that any meaningful theology must be based on a historical understanding of religion generally and Christianity specifically, and he presented a clearly outlined methodology of historical research as applied to the field of theology— an approach that came to dominate theological thinking of the entire nineteenth century.

It is no accident that in that same first semester at the University of Berlin, Schleiermacher was also delivering his lectures on hermeneutics. Although he never published a work on the subject that in intellectual history is linked inextricably with his name, his ideas—based essentially on a few aphorisms from the years 1805 and 1809, a short (44-page) handwritten manuscript, and lecture notes of his students from the later years of his career—constitute the basis for modern hermeneutics.[76] But the fundamental principle of his hermeneutics—"All understanding of the specific is qualified by an understanding of the whole"[77]—is evident already at this point and determines, as we have seen, his approach to historical sources.

Schleiermacher's utterly original conception of theology did not immediately reshape the discipline outside Berlin. But his publication sig-
naled the imminent end of theologies that sought their inspiration solely
inwardly (pietism) or externally (rationalism) and provided, instead, the
basis for a modern theology that synthesized the separate disciplines con-
stituting the field and historicized the idea of Christianity and the institution of the Christian church. His *Brief Outline,* in sum, accomplished for
theology what Hegel's *Phenomenology* had achieved for philosophy and
constituted the theological response to the revolutionary spirit of the age.

Four

LAW

German Law in the 1790s

LOOKING back some fifty years later, the great legal scholar Friedrich Karl von Savigny considered it "undeniable that, at the time when the composition of the Prussian Territorial Code was undertaken, German juristic writing for the most part was trivial and clumsy and had lost the capability for any beneficial influence on practice." Savigny was referring to the last two decades of the eighteenth century, when three different forms of law were vying for authority in the courts and in the popular mind—local customary law, Roman law, and natural law. It was reasonable, he continued, that "the awareness of this defective legal situation led at the time to the attempt to relieve the predicament by means of an indigenous law book and thus to transform wholly the basis of practical law."[1] How had Germany reached this impasse?

During the Middle Ages most of Europe was governed by one of two principal systems of law. In the north, stretching from Iceland across England and northern France to Germany, men and women lived according to a set of customary laws going back at least as far as the tribes described by Tacitus in his *Germania* and gathered in such early collections as the sixth-century *Lex Burgundionum* in southeastern France, the *Lex Salica* of the Franks, and the Langobardic law of northern Italy.[2] For almost a thousand years these laws and procedures grew and changed more or less radically in scores of different political entities across Europe, with the result that much of northern Europe was ruled by a patchwork of often overlapping systems of law. Yet they shared their origin in a common Germanic law, an origin still evident in the great wave of thirteenth-century gatherings: Philippe de Beaumanoir's *Coutumes de Beauvaisis,* Eike von Repgow's *Sachsenspiegel,* Henry de Bracton's *De legibus et consuetudinibus Angliae,* and the Icelandic *Grágás.*

In the south, in contrast, and extending from Constantinople across Italy to the Mediterranean coasts of France and Spain, towns and principalities were still ruled by a form of ancient Roman law as formalized by Emperor Justinian's juridical commissions in the sixth century: the famous *Corpus Iuris Civilis.*[3] In the political disarray following the decline of the Roman empire, to be sure, that law lost many of its broader powers. But in the towns of northern Italy, and elsewhere, it maintained a continuous existence as the authority in matters of private or civil law. In the year 1000, this law was still being studied and discussed by the learned nobility at centers in Pavia and Ravenna. The methodical study of Roman law began in the eleventh century as European society evolved, economically and socially, to a post-feudal stage at which it again required the subtleties of a sophisticated legal system. By the middle of the twelfth century, the School of Bologna had achieved renown for its law faculty, whose professors rediscovered the texts of the *Corpus Iuris Civilis* and, in the next two centuries, encrusted them with commentaries and glosses that often obscured the material's classical sources, while appropriating statutes for modern use in total ignorance of the social needs to which they had originally responded. The students who flocked to Bologna from every country in Europe in order to be certified in the increasingly profitable profession of law were trained not in Justinian's original "Roman Law" but in the corrupted form of the so-called *mos italicus.*

In the fifteenth century, the vast lands of the Holy Roman Empire were still governed by a fragmented system of overlapping and often conflicting sets of laws. Citizens were subject to the municipal laws of their hometowns, to territorial rule as represented by such compilations as the *Sachsenspiegel,* and to a rather weak imperial *ius commune.* The situation was complicated by the fact that, under the Germanic conception of "personal" law, each individual was governed and judged by the law of his own tribe or community, even if that law was inconsistent with the local law of the territory where he happened to be at the time. The whole complex system, based essentially on ancient Germanic principles and procedures that had been infiltrated by various Roman ideas, was regulated by often minimally trained judges presiding over tribunals of elected lay judges (*Schöffen*).[4] The system was most highly fragmented in the southwest; in the north the *Sachsenspiegel* played the unifying role that was fulfilled in northern France by over sixty collections of *coutumes*.

By the end of the fifteenth century, many citizens of the Holy Roman Empire were profoundly convinced of the need for change.[5] In many towns and cities the traditional local law, in a series of "reformations," had already been adapted to the demands of modern commerce and business. The merchants were distressed by the legal uncertainties that made business between cities and principalities needlessly complicated and dangerous—where, according to a current saying, a merchant traveling from place to place had to change laws more frequently than coins. The princes for their part were dismayed at the medieval practice of feud, which still constituted the normal and fully legal means of resolving territorial or even personal disputes. Toward the end of the century they began clamoring for reform in return for their support of the emperor in his war against the Hungarians. Specifically, the estates demanded a Perpetual Public Peace forbidding feud justice and a reorganization of the emperor's judicial system, making it a permanently established court with judges not subject to the whim of the ruler. These goals, which were consistent with imperial desires—to impose a unified code of written law on the patchwork of largely unwritten "customary" law, to centralize political authority, and to emphasize the continuity of the Holy Roman Empire with the ancient Roman empire—were achieved in 1495, with the agreement of Emperor Maximilian, and led to the official "Reception" of Roman law in northern Europe.[6]

The newly established Imperial Supreme Court (*Reichskammergericht*) now began to apply *ius commune* systematically to all cases not covered by the local customary law and territorial statutes. This contrasted starkly with the rough imperial justice originally instituted to hear cases involving parties directly responsible to the empire and administered haphazardly by the emperor as he journeyed from place to place (in a so-called *placitum generale*).Initially only half of the new assessors had to be *doctores* while half were chosen from the knights' estate; but soon it was expected that even the knights should have or be represented by men with at least some legal training—a trend that appealed mightily to the growing fraternity of lawyers freshly trained in the *mos italicus,* either in Italy or in the recently established German universities.

Because the affairs of the empire were increasingly dominated by trained jurists, and even in the territorial courts the learned *doctores* gradually displaced the lay justices (*Schöffen*), around the year 1500 Roman law was prominently replacing the older system of customary law. But this displacement brought with it many complaints about the old and the new law alike—a disgruntlement summed up by the proverbial saying *summum ius, summa iniuria* ("the highest law is the highest injustice").[7]

A combination of these various factors, plus the desire to join the growing European community of lawyers, who were linked by their common commitment to Roman law, produced in Germany by the middle of the sixteenth century the so-called *usus modernus pandectarum* ("modern application of the [Roman] pandects").[8] This system, named from a book of that title (*Specimen usus moderni pandectarum*, 1690–92) by the Brandenburg legal scholar Samuel Stryk, combined ancient Roman law, medieval canon law, and elements of the indigenous customary law. This bastardized "Roman" law did not simply replace the older Germanic customary law: it had only secondary validity and was consulted in cases when some form of customary law did not apply or when there was some other justifiable reason for its use. Ever since the Reception of the fifteenth and sixteenth centuries, then, the towns and principalities in the German territories of the Holy Roman Empire had been governed by parallel systems of the *usus modernus pandectarum* and the familiar Germanic customary law.

Around the middle of the seventeenth century, a new element was added to the mixture: natural law.[9] There is no single "law of nature"—a "law" that might most simply be understood as the ideological system on the basis of which an age seeks to justify its existing positive law. In antiquity and the Christian Middle Ages, this legitimation was sought mainly in transcendental authority. For classical Roman law, in the words of Justinian's *Institutes* (bk. 1, title 2), the authority is nature itself: *Ius naturale est, quod natura omnia animalia docuit* ("natural law is what nature teaches all living beings"). Thomas Aquinas and other Christian thinkers also perceived behind the secular laws of the thirteenth century an eternal law (*lex aeterna*), but they believed that it expressed the will of God underlying all nature. The rationalism of the seventeenth and eighteenth centuries shifted the emphasis: a man-based natural law, emancipated from all medieval moral theology, sought the justification of universal human rights not in God but solely in human reason (e.g., the "Laws of Nature" cited in the first sentence of the American Declaration of Independence). Instead of regarding human rights as the secular expression of a higher will, Hugo Grotius and his successors in Germany—Samuel Pufendorf, Christian Thomasius, Christian Wolff, and others—deduced their ideal law from reason alone. To the extent, however, that natural law gradually liberated itself from the existing positive law (whether Roman or customary), natural law became less and less a juristic and increasingly a philosophical exercise. In 1796 Fichte published a *Foundation of Natural Law (Grundlage des Naturrechts)*, and in the following year Kant brought out his *Metaphysical Rudiments of Legal Theory (Metaphysische Anfangsgründe der Rechtslehre)* as the first part of his *Metaphysics of Morals.* This led, on the one hand, to the circumstance that natural law became a widely discussed topic of intellectual discourse. On the other hand, it rapidly degenerated into a discourse in which everyone, even the juristically unsophisticated, felt qualified to participate.[10] By the last decade of the eighteenth century, this gaining popularization had largely discredited natural law, which was loosed from all the practical restraints of positive law as well as historical reality.

It was this situation of legal confusion, as Savigny recalled, that led to the wave of codifications that produced in 1794 the Prussian General Territorial Law (*Allgemeines Landrecht,* or ALR), the Napoleonic *Code Civil* (1804), and the Austrian *Allgemeines Bürgerliches Gesetzbuch* (ABGB, 1811).[11] However, despite official hopes that the new codes would resolve the dilemma, they were often regarded with suspicion and even hostility by a populace comfortable with their "good old law." In the countryside, customary law continued to prevail, as Heinrich von Kleist amusingly portrayed in his dramatic comedy *Der zerbrochne Krug* (1808). And in the universities a pandemonium of competing systems reigned.

It was generally and widely understood at the time by professors of every disposition that German legal scholarship was in a state of crisis at the turn of the century.[12] At Göttingen, Johann Gottfried Reitemeier maintained in 1785 that jurisprudence was still fragmentary and immature. "How great is the incompleteness of this science with regard to representation, organization, and presentation; how incomplete is the connection of its parts, how undisclosed the spirit of the laws, and how barbaric and repulsive the language of its art—this is proved by the repeated complaints of the initiates as well as of the laymen in legal science."[13] In 1810 Anselm von Feuerbach, a philosopher of law, complained that among the professors of Roman law "a certain pedantry, a spirit of pettiness and poor taste has become indigenous and prevalent."[14]

At the turn of the century, Heinrich von Kleist, leaving his military career behind, studied law for three semesters at the undistinguished university in his hometown, Frankfurt an der Oder, where seventy percent of the two hundred and twenty students were enrolled in the faculty of law. The faculty was dominated by natural law, as expounded by Ludwig Gottfried Madihn, on the basis of his textbook, *Principles of Natural Law for the Use of His Lectures* (*Grundsätze des Naturrechts zum Gebrauch seiner Vorlesungen*, 3d ed. 1795). Madihn's lectures precipitated in the impressionable young Kleist an intellectual crisis that prompted him to give up the study of law. "In the course on Natural Law I recently heard debated the question whether the contracts of lovers could be valid because they are made in a state of passion," he confided in 1800 in a letter to his fiancée.

> And what am I supposed to think about a discipline that racks its brains over the issue of whether there is such a thing in the world as property and which for that reason would only teach me to doubt whether I may ever justifiably call you *mine*? No, no, Wilhelmine, I don't want to study law, not the vacillating, uncertain, ambivalent laws of reason. I want to cling to the laws of my heart, and I want to practice them, no matter what all the systems of philosophy may object.[15]

Even though Kleist, in his deficient preparation as well as his literary genius, was no typical student, his reaction attests to the inadequacy of the teaching of law, which was often presented more as a popular philosophy than as a practical or historical field.

The mood was recalled in a similar way years later by others. In an oration that he delivered in 1838 to commemorate the fiftieth anniversary of the doctorate of the Roman legal historian Gustav Hugo, Savigny pointed to the degeneration of legal scholarship at the time Hugo was studying in Göttingen—a condition recognized, he stresses, by everyone concerned, quite independent of their own points of view.[16] "Even someone who understood nothing of juristic matters was able to perceive that legal science, in comparison with other areas of intellectual activity, enjoyed incomparably less esteem than previously; but precisely this fact is the most certain sign that teachers and writers must have neglected the possession entrusted to them." (Savigny goes on to emphasize the major contribution made by Hugo in rectifying those circumstances.)

Jakob Grimm, who studied law at Marburg in the first decade of the new century—more to satisfy his family's wishes than out of any love of the subject—provides in his autobiography a detailed account of his own curriculum: logic and natural law with Bering ("without getting any true benefit from either"); the institutions and pandects of Roman law with Weis; pandects and canon law with Erxleben; history of the empire, constitutional law, and feudal law with Robert; German private and criminal law with Bauer.[17] Weis's presentation was lively and learned; Erxleben's monotonous and antiquated. "But what can I say about Savigny's lectures other than that they gripped me powerfully and achieved a decisive influence on my entire life and study." In the winter semester of 1802–03, he heard Savigny on juristic methodology as well as the laws of intestate succession; and in the following semesters the history of Roman law, Justinian's Institutions, and the law of obligations. If the study of law was revitalized in the first decade of the nineteenth century, it was due in no small measure to the remarkable achievements of Savigny and the Historical School with which he was associated.

Forerunners of the Historical School

Savigny is commonly regarded as the leader of the school that has been publicized by the journal of the foundation for legal history enhanced by his name: *Zeitschrift der Savigny-Stiftung für Rechtsgeschichte* (1880 to the present). But inevitably Savigny's achievement was based on the work of accomplished forerunners. Although Savigny's charisma, his compelling presence as a professor, and his accessibly written publications enabled him to establish a "school," Gustav Hugo is usually credited with having first created a historically based legal science.[18] The field of law, as a mirror of contemporary social thought and historical circumstances, has always existed in an intimate interaction with its supporting culture.[19] It would be surprising, then, if the study of law toward the end of the eighteenth century did not reflect the new sense of history that was emerging in philosophy, theology, and other fields of intellectual endeavor.[20]

Roman law had of course been studied and professed at German universities ever since the Reception; but scholars had been concerned almost wholly with the *usus modernus pandectarum* and not with the original Roman sources. In the *laudatio* that he wrote in 1838 on the fiftieth anniversary of Hugo's doctorate, Savigny depicted the situation.

> The malady consisted therein, that people had worked up the positive
> material, for purely practical ends and without critical scrutiny or dis-

crimination of its components, into an apparent whole. While the incommensurate and incompatible was lumped together in this manner [i.e., elements of Roman, canon, and German law], it was difficult to say whether this was more for the benefit of historical truth or practical purposes. All this had not proceeded from any mistaken belief that it was right; rather, it had been allowed gradually to happen out of sheer mindlessness. This dead mass was handed down from one scholar to the next; in each hand new errors were imperceptibly added; and even the better people were unable to extricate themselves from the traditional respect for the false method.[21]

It was Hugo's accomplishment to see through the wrongness of this procedure and to address the German legal system in its present positive form, inquiring into the source of each concept and each legal statement. "It was his basic principle that in every age the positive law was a living whole, and he recognized it as the responsibility of science to reconstruct this whole from the scattered stock of individual evidence. The more completely this kind of investigation was carried out, the more each individual would obtain his rights—in history as well as the present."

Gustav Hugo (1764–1844), the son of a high official of the Baden government in Lörrach (southwestern Germany), spent almost his entire career in Göttingen.[22] Following secondary studies at Montbéliard and Karlsruhe, he enrolled there as a student of law in 1782, but found the study of law as then taught at Göttingen quite dispiriting with the exception of two professors—the constitutional scholar Johann Stephan Pütter (1725–1807), a disciple of Montesquieu, and Ludwig von Spittler (1752–1810), a historian of modern Europe. Until he won a faculty prize for a paper on intestate succession (*Commentatio de fundamento successionis ab intestato*) Roman law held little appeal for Hugo. But the paper impressed his faculty mentors, Pütter and Spittler, so greatly that they arranged for Hugo, after further study and practical experience, to return to Göttingen as their junior colleague in Roman law. After serving from 1786 to 1788 at the court of Dessau as tutor in law to the prince and as a legal consultant, he completed his doctorate in 1788 at Halle with a dissertation on ownership (*De bonorum possessionibus commentatio*) and returned to Göttingen, first as a professor *extraordinarius* and, from 1792 until his death, a full professor.

According to Hugo, in a series of textbooks that he prepared for his courses (*Lehrbuch eines civilistischen Cursus*), the student of law must distinguish clearly among three fundamental questions: (1) "What is lawful?" (a question with purely practical implications that may be answered by the layman by referring to the existing positive law); (2) "How did it become lawful?" (a question for the historian of law); and (3) "Is it reasonable that it is lawful?" (a question for the philosopher of law). Hugo devoted considerable energy to the last question with his critical attack on the influential theory of natural law as promulgated by Christian Wolff, which he called ahistorical and a "plague,"[23] insisting on a complete separation of natural law and positive law. He presented his own views of legal philosophy in his *Textbook of Natural Law as a Philosophy of Positive Law (Lehrbuch des Naturrechts als einer Philosophie des positiven Rechts,* 1798), in which following Kant he denied that laws could be deduced a priori from transcendent legal principles and argued that natural law is nothing but the philosophy of positive law. However, he is best remembered for his efforts on behalf of a responsible history of Roman civil law.

Hugo remarked in 1791, "For at least fifty years the study of civil law as a whole has made no progress; on the contrary, it has sunk."[24] He pointed by way of contrast to Gibbon's magisterial survey of Roman law in chapter 44 of *The Decline and Fall of the Roman Empire,* which he translated into German in 1789. It was Hugo's ambition to make a clear distinction between German customary law and Roman law, between the *usus modernus pandectarum* and historical Roman law, and between the later Justinian law and the earlier classical Roman law. He set out to achieve this goal in a variety of ways: with his editions of classical legal texts (Ulpian, 1788; Paulus, 1795); with the journal whose six volumes he issued periodically from 1791 to 1837 and in which he reviewed some four hundred works on legal history; and above all in his classic textbook on the history of Roman law, *Lehrbuch der Geschichte des römischen Rechts,* first published in 1790 and much reprinted in later editions. Its "combination of the free, unlimited overview with penetrating knowledge of the material," Savigny wrote in 1806 in his admiring review of the third edition, "is the most gratifying thing that can occur in a science—and one that normally occurs most rarely."[25] Formerly, he continues, the history of law had been treated separately only as a preparatory subject. "The present work is based on a higher idea, according to which the whole science of law is nothing else than the history of law."

Hugo's work is divided chronologically into four periods bounded by the Twelve Tables, Cicero, Alexander Severus, and Justinian—a division that still constitutes the basis of "external" Roman legal history and that displays a pronounced similarity to Herder's closely contemporaneous philosophy of history. The "inner" history of each period, in turn, was exposed by a systematic analysis of its sources, commentaries, and systems. "The genial work," Savigny's review concludes, "acquaints us with demands and challenges of which we had no conception. By heightening and enlarging our concept of science, it guides the free view beyond itself into an undefined distance."

Clearly, the historicizing of law did not begin with Savigny nor even with Hugo, who himself had been taught by professors like Pütter and Spittler. They in turn were inspired by Montesquieu's *Esprit des Lois,* which appreciated the influence of social and historical circumstances on constitutions, and by Herder's *Ideas.* And the pragmatic history of law, which led to the discovery of important new materials, goes back even further, to such figures as the seventeenth-century polymath Hermann Conring (1606–1681).[26] It is no accident, moreover, that Hugo was taught and in turn taught at Göttingen, the center of historical studies in other fields: e.g., the famous and influential classical seminar of Heyne. In addition to Pütter, other colleagues on the law faculty made contributions to the fledgling historical study of law, notably Johann Friedrich Reitemeier (1755–1839) and Gottlieb Hufeland (1760–1817).[27] Appropriating Montesquieu's pragmatic view of history, Reitemeier was the first to relate the development of law to political and intellectual history in his *Encyclopedics and History of Laws in Germany* (1785). "The history of the state according to the various stages of culture or the description of the condition and the changes of the nation in population und area, in prosperity and poverty, in strength and weakness, in crudeness and refinement—all this constitutes the basis on which the history of laws is erected as upon its proper base."[28] Hufeland, the cousin of the famous physician, was strongly influenced in his conception of history by his colleague Reitemeier; but in his *Textbook of the History and Encyclopedics of All Positive Laws Valid in Germany* (1796), he makes a fundamental distinction between general history and the history of law, which belongs strictly to legal science and which he defines as the history of the origins and alterations of laws.[29] Neither Reitemeier nor Hufeland succeeded in freeing legal science wholly from the influence of natural law, and neither they nor Hugo advanced beyond a descriptive and analytical pragmatic history to a genetic view of history; but their invaluable preparatory work provided the firm basis on which the Historical School of law of the following generation was able to build.[30]

Savigny: Founder of the Historical School

The Savignys were descended from a family of ancient Burgundian nobility, some of whom in the seventeenth century emigrated from their na-
tive Lorraine to Germany to avoid persecution for their Protestant faith;
they rapidly established themselves and their fortunes in their new home.
Friedrich Karl von Savigny (1779–1861) was born in Frankfurt am Main,
the son of a wealthy and highly regarded lawyer who served as privy councilor in the legal and diplomatic affairs of several princes of the Upper
Rhine.[31] In 1792, the thirteen-year-old boy found himself an orphan, pre-
deceased not only by both parents but also by his twelve siblings. Taken
into the home of his father's close friend Constantin von Neurath, an assessor at the Imperial Supreme Court (*Reichskammergericht*) in nearby
Wetzlar, Savigny was privately tutored along with Neurath's son Constantin, where he obtained the solid grounding in Latin (though not
Greek) that later led even the most learned philologists to consult his opinion on textual matters. The boys, who were both intended for legal careers, were introduced by Neurath himself to the fundamentals of
encyclopedic law according to the catechistic method of rote memoriza-
tion of questions and answers. (This was not an uncommon practice at
the time: both Goethe and Jakob Grimm, for instance, were first exposed
to law by their fathers in a similar manner.)

At Easter 1795 the two friends enrolled at the regional University of
Marburg, where Savigny in 1800 was to receive his doctorate from the faculty of law. While he duly inscribed himself for the usual law courses—
pandects (i.e., *usus modernus*), German private law, procedures of common civil law—Savigny was less attracted initially by law than by lectures
and readings in literary and philosophical subjects. Indeed, during these
years of his "philosophical apprenticeship," he was intensely engaged,
along with a close group of like-minded friends—notably the classicist
Friedrich Creuzer and his cousin, the theologian Leonhard Creuzer—with
Kant's writings on ethics and such aesthetic works as Friedrich Schlegel's
essay on philosophy, "Über die Philosophie," Friedrich Heinrich Jacobi's
popular philosophical novel *Edward Allwills Papiere,* and Goethe's *Wilhelm Meister's Apprenticeship.*[32] In addition, his letters from this period
speak of his readings in Wieland's verse romance *Oberon,* Goethe's drama
Iphigenie auf Tauris, the novels of Jean Paul, the tales of Ludwig Tieck,
and the writings of Fichte. (Herder, mentioned occasionally in an offhand
manner, became a significant influence only later, when Savigny's interests

had shifted decisively to history.)[33] This early preoccupation with German cultural affairs is revealing, because Savigny's subsequent turn to history generally, and to the history of law specifically, was motivated in no small measure by his all-embracing view of national culture, which became as all-encompassing as Herder's.

The only professor of law to whom Savigny formed a close and lasting personal attachment was Philipp Friedrich Weis (1766–1808), a philologically trained Roman historian in the French tradition of "elegant" jurisprudence: that is, the cultivation of medieval legal antiquities from a purely antiquarian standpoint and with no concern for their implications for legal practice, past or present. Weis, who quickly recognized his student's talent, his power of judgment, and his solid knowledge of Roman law, unhesitatingly called him in a report on the seventeen-year-old "the most excellent among all my students during my academic teaching career."[34] It was not from Weis's scholarly writings that Savigny learned— Weis published unusually little during his brief career, only six short pieces—but rather from his example of personal erudition, his gifted teaching, and his lovingly cultivated library, where the future historian of Roman law first encountered the principal works of medieval jurisprudence and acquired the passion for collecting old editions and manuscripts that prompted him eventually to assemble a personal library of some ten thousand volumes. (Savigny's letters to Weis amount to a detailed account of his search for books and manuscripts in libraries, archives, bookshops, and auction houses all over Europe.)[35]

Savigny's studies at Marburg were twice interrupted. He spent the winter semester 1796–97 at Göttingen, where—surprisingly—he neither met nor heard Gustav Hugo, whose works he later praised as the greatest single influence on his thinking. The most powerful impression was made, rather, by the brilliant lectures of Hugo's colleague, the historian Spittler. The following summer Savigny suffered a serious deterioration of his health, symptomized by hemorrhaging, which was believed to have been brought on by the extreme application to his studies evident already at this early age. He retreated to his inherited estate at Trages where he continued his reading.

On his return to Marburg, his interests began to turn increasingly toward law. In the winter of 1798–99, he reported to his friend Constantin von Neurath in a revealing letter that he had finally decided to dedicate himself to jurisprudence.[36] He realizes, he confesses, that he has lost a good deal of time because of the disorderly manner of his previous studies. But already the direction of his future studies is clearly evident. "Since last summer I have reviewed Roman law (which I love extraordinarily) according to Hofacker [the author of standard textbooks] and also studied individual materials. I'll soon be finished and will then cursorily go through the other juristic disciplines (which I heartily despise)." His plan, he continues, leads him to something that is necessarily connected with it—the study of natural law. "I want to say nothing about the general interest of natural law as the basis of our jurisprudence but only a few words of its particular relevance for the present time." At this point the young scholar reveals how firmly his interest in the law and its history is grounded in the social disruptions of the revolutionary era and to what an extent his conservative view of evolutionary change is already taking shape.

> Now at a time when the old forms are threatened with general destruction it is more essential than ever to seek a standpoint which, independent of everything positive and conventional, is based *within us*. Look at Paris, whence the dominance of philosophy was supposed to emerge, and behold actions of the most flagrant injustice—to convince yourself that the revolution created only the potentiality, but that reform must proceed from the inner sanctuary of the spirit—that in Paris people remained *under* the events, and that we all must strive to raise ourselves *above* them. And if (as I hope and wish) the spirit of the violent revolutions should be extinguished, then that higher standpoint will be no less necessary—no longer, to be sure, so as not to go under with the positive [law], but to bring about through free action that quieter reform which, without the great price of bloody reform, has a slower but more certain effect.

These are the reasons, he concludes, why he hopes that his friend will consider natural law "with seriousness and respect."

At this point Savigny does not appear to be sure of the specific focus of his interest in law. His words suggest a commitment to legal practice and practical reform. A few weeks later (10 Feb. 1799), he congratulates his friend on the seriousness with which he is preparing himself for his legal career as a judge—an attitude, he says, that is becoming increasingly rare. "And can it be any different when even the most exceptional caretakers of science—men like Hugo—out of idleness or egoism find it convenient to separate theory more and more from practice and thus to permit the content of the latter to become increasingly more contemptible and its effect more harmful rather than that both should coincide fully in content."[37] This attitude is fully consistent with his interest in ancient Ro-

man law, whose authors, he felt, were men equally at home in legal theory
and the reality of everyday Roman life. He himself was coming increasingly to the conviction that "one's own thorough study of the sources is
not only the surest, but also the easiest and most pleasant way to satisfaction in our field." However, despite his youthful contempt for the
purists of law, Savigny was already known among his friends at Marburg
for his ambition to become "the reformer of jurisprudence, a Kant of legal learning."[38]

In the summer of 1799 he undertook a traditional *Bildungsreise,* which
in Savigny's case turned out to be an academic peregrination through
Thuringia and Saxony. Following an initial tour of Eisenach, Weimar,
Jena, Dresden, and Freiberg, he spent the winter in Leipzig pursuing his
research. The following summer he returned to Jena, where the lively intellectual atmosphere of the university and the Romantic cénacle had appealed to him. He found particular stimulation in the person and home of
Gottfried Hufeland, a man of "universal culture," whose writings he had
not yet adequately studied and appreciated. "He has a great respect for
Roman law, stemming from a detailed familiarity with it."[39] Savigny was
especially pleased to find that Hufeland confirmed his view of Hugo and
other scholars, and was impressed by Hufeland's knowledge of current
events and political affairs. Returning to Marburg, Savigny submitted his
dissertation *De concursu delictorum formali*—the only work on criminal
law that he ever wrote—and received his doctorate from the faculty of law
on October 31, 1800.

Savigny's decision to become a professor of law shocked many of his
friends. It was unusual in the extreme for a member of the nobility to undertake a university career, which was regarded as socially inferior. (In the
early years of the University of Berlin, the king of Prussia was willing to
receive the rector for a ritual visit at court, but not deans and certainly not
ordinary professors.) In the winter semester of that same year, he began
his teaching at Marburg with lectures on the topic of his dissertation, but
quickly shifted his interests to Roman civil law, the field to which he devoted the remained of an increasingly distinguished career.

In the summer semester of 1801, Savigny offered a course of lectures
on the last ten books of the pandects (the part of Justinian's *Corpus Iuris
Civilis* known as the *Digest*) because, as he explained, the material treated
there frequently did not get covered: Roman law was normally taught systematically according to the order of books and titles in the pandects and
time ran out before the end was reached. In the course of preparing his lec-

tures, which he based directly on original sources, he focused particularly on the question of possession, and it soon became clear to him that views had changed significantly in the course of subsequent treatments of the matter in the *usus modernus pandectarum.*[40] Encouraged by Weis, he decided to write a book to rid the law of its post-classical ballast. Perhaps Savigny was also influenced in his turn to history by his friend, Friedrich Creuzer, who just at this time was writing his account of Greek historiography, *The Greek Art of History in Its Origin and Development (Die historische Kunst der Griechen in ihrer Entstehung und Fortbildung,* 1803).[41]

In the second half of 1802—his work was delayed by his preparations for a different course of lectures—he began his intensive studies for the book, which he wrote in just six weeks. The five-hundred page volume, *The Law of Possession (Das Recht des Besitzes,* 1803), was an immediate success and required several further revised editions (1806, 1818, 1822, 1837).[42] The epoch-making novelty of the work, which was immediately noted by scholars and reviewers, consisted in the fact that, rather than beginning with the *usus modernus,* it went directly to the sources to define the original Roman concept of possession (that is, occupancy of land and other properties in contrast to ownership) and to show how that concept (notably by taking into account the manner in which possessions are acquired and lost), along with the terms that define it, changed over time during several hundred years of Roman history. Only in the brief sixth section—following sections on the Roman understanding of possession, acquisition, loss, interdict, and usufruct—does Savigny deal with "Modifications of Roman Law" in the *usus modernus.* "The theory of possession has been presented in the first five sections of this work in total abstraction from everything that could have been added to Roman law in more recent times; and this method of investigation is necessary if, in the confusion of old and new, both are not to be simultaneously misunderstood."[43] It is necessary, he continues, because, among all the significant misapprehensions concerning the Roman view of possession, all were produced by the conflation of canon law or German law. But it does not suffice simply to eradicate those elements from Roman law. "If a theory of possession is justifiably to make a claim for application in civil law, then the relationship that it bears to the determination of recent law needs to be investigated and set forth."

The work of the twenty-four-year-old professor *extraordinarius* was epoch-making for its style, which in its classic simplicity and elegance—

a style carefully modeled on that of Goethe and the other German classical writers whom Savigny admired—was accessible to specialist and interested layman alike, unlike Hugo's diffuse works or the often pedantic
compilations of the pragmatic historians. More importantly, the work
clearly exemplified in rudimentary form the principles of what soon came
to be known as the Historical School, distinguishing rigorously as it did
between Roman law and the *usus modernus* and, at the same time, demonstrating the relevance of the past for our understanding of the present law.
Above all, it related law to life in a manner unknown to earlier pragmatic
or "elegant" historians of law. His teacher Weis and the work of Hugo, to
be sure, had fostered Savigny's inherent love of history; but it was his own
research that convinced him of the genetic development that he elegantly
traced over time in the laws of possession.[44]

While *The Law of Possession* presented the practice of historicism but
not its theory, the latter had already been expounded for Savigny's students in the lectures on methodology that he delivered in the winter of
1802–03—and that were attended and recorded by his most famous and
loyal student, Jakob Grimm. In his course of lectures, Savigny treated the
methods of jurisprudence, the available secondary literature and how it
should be read, and the ideal academic study of law.[45] Only the first section is relevant to our concerns. According to the first of Savigny's three
principles, "jurisprudence is a historical science" (87)—one that should
be studied historically and philologically. Secondly, "it is a philosophical
science"—that is, one that should be analyzed systematically. Finally, the
proper method of jurisprudence combines the exegetical and the systematic elements. With this statement of principles Savigny advances well beyond all contemporary study of jurisprudence, which, as we have seen,
tended to be either historical/practical (*usus modernus*) or theoretical
(natural law). Each aspect must, of course, be treated separately; but the
complete method inheres in the combination of both. Savigny offers a genetic view of legal science that differs from all preceding pragmatic history: "a *historical* treatment in the literal sense, i.e., consideration of
legislation as constantly developing in a given time" (88). The connection
of legal science with the history of the state and its people needs to be set
forth. "The *system itself* must be thought of as progressive." The proper
approach is threefold: "interpretation, history, system" (89). "Interpretation = reconstruction of the law. He who explains it must permit it to take
shape again artificially; he must put himself into the standpoint of the legislator." The exegete accomplishes this by a genetic representation of the

thought that the law expresses (logical aspect), by a representation of the medium whereby the thought is expressed (grammatical aspect), and by a representation of the historical object that the law determines by describing the moment that brought forth the law (historical aspect)—a process that Savigny illustrates with examples taken from his own work on the laws of possession. As Savigny explained in 1809 (and after his study of Herder) in a subsequent revision of his methodology, "every writer and every work is qualified by its time and by its prehistory; it is a member of a historical whole and can be fully recognized only in this whole" (154). (It should go without saying that Savigny is defining with astonishing precision a hermeneutical method similar to the one that Schleiermacher was expounding almost simultaneously for his students in Berlin.) After a review of the inadequacies of earlier scholarship, Savigny goes on to explain that the greatest challenge for the historical approach is knowledge of the sources—an approach for which Gustav Hugo provides virtually the only model (97). As for legislation as a part of general history, a model is provided by Gibbon's chapter 44, which requires more jurisprudence than almost any modern jurists have at their disposal (99). Savigny's only criticism stems from the fact that Gibbon's standpoint from the "decline of the empire" distorts his view of Roman law, whose true value arose in the most splendid period of the republic.

As early as 1802–03, then, Jakob Grimm and the other students at Marburg were exposed in their earliest form to the principles that Savigny was to elucidate and exemplify a decade later in Berlin as the leader of the Historical School—principles of historiography that have been largely ignored by historians of the field.[46]

Years of Preparation

Savigny's teaching career at Marburg did not last long. Though quiet by temperament and studious by disposition, he had a large network of lively friends. During his visit to Jena in 1799 he had met not only the legal scholar Hufeland, the physicist Ritter, and various members of the early Romantic group; most importantly, he had formed—despite Brentano's humorous references to him as a "study machine"[47]—a close attachment to the brilliant, tormented poet Clemens Brentano, who came from a prominent and prosperous family in his hometown of Frankfurt. (In his poetic novel *Die Romanzen vom Rosenkranz* Brentano subsequently created, in the person of the medieval legal scholar Jacopone, a fond and vivid portrait of Savigny's manner and appearance.) The friendship soon led to the acquaintance with other members of Brentano's family, notably his impulsive and mercurial sister Bettine and another sister, Kunigunde (Gunda)—the most dignified and restrained of the entire family—to whom Savigny in due course became engaged and whom he married in May of 1804, at the end of what turned out to be his final semester of teaching at Marburg.

Savigny was hugely successful as a teacher at Marburg where he was surrounded by an admiring circle of students and friends, including Friedrich and Leonhard Creuzer. Clemens Brentano had moved to Marburg with his new wife, the beautiful and gifted poet Sophie Mereau, in order to be close to Savigny. And during these early years two of Gunda's sisters, Bettine and Meline, were virtually members of the household. Among his most famous and devoted students were the brothers Grimm, Jakob and Wilhelm, who always recalled Savigny's friendship, hospitality, and mentorship with appreciative gratitude.[48] His teaching along with the éclat surrounding his book promptly brought calls to other universities, notably Heidelberg and Greifswald. But Savigny had other plans. Encouraged by his mentor Weis, he had long been contemplating and for several years collecting material for a book on the history of Roman law in the Middle Ages based on original sources. Now, happily married and with his professorial appointment, Savigny determined that the moment was at hand to undertake the indispensable archival researches in European libraries.

In September 1804, he set out with his wife and her sister Meline and journeyed by way of Heidelberg, Strasbourg, and Metz to Paris, where he arrived on December 4 to continue his research in the archives of the capital. The Paris sojourn began with a disaster: the trunk containing all his notes and research plans was lost or stolen from his carriage as the family entered the city. "It's nothing trivial," he reported to a friend several weeks later, "to be so completely interrupted in an undertaking calculated in years. You know the kind of collecting energy that I had; . . . it gave me a feeling of security, certainty, and progress. . . . But that loss has given me on the contrary a feeling of uncertainty and incompleteness that will perhaps cling to me for a long time. A thousand notes, found by chance or composed, were important to me because in my thoughts a flock of unresolved questions were connected to them. And all that is gone."[49]

His solution, which turned out to be a boon for them both, was to send for Jakob Grimm to come to his assistance. The faithful student arrived in early February, and the two of them were soon able to reconstruct most of the material that Savigny had lost. They worked intensively in the libraries, which were open only from 10 A.M. to 2 P.M., excerpting material from the abundant but poorly catalogued manuscripts in the Bibliothèque Nationale. At home, Gunda and Meline helped with the copying and the voluminous correspondence—a virtual cottage industry enlivened by occasional visits to the Paris sights and museums. Grimm stayed with Savigny until the fall, and the work they accomplished provided Savigny with valuable material for his project. The findings that Grimm made on his own—of medieval German literary works—set him on the course that would eventually lead him away from the study of law and into his career as a scholar of German language and literature.

The Savignys returned to Marburg in September of 1805, their family enlarged by the birth of their first child. But Savigny did not go back to teaching. After spending the winter organizing the material collected in Paris and at libraries en route, the family set out again in the summer of 1806 on a second research trip, which led by way of Nürnberg, Erlangen, and Munich to Vienna, where they spent the winter of 1806–07, gathering new material. (Savigny's letters during these years—especially to the Creuzers, the Grimms, and to his teacher Weis—provide a fascinating and detailed account of his research and book acquisitions, as well as informative technical discussions of terms and concepts from medieval Latin and Roman law.) The return trip the following summer brought them to Weimar where Savigny met and spent several days in the company of his revered Goethe. Savigny, still not ready to return to his teaching responsibilities, spent the following months circulating through Marburg, Frankfurt, and his estate at Trages and organizing the materials he had collected at the twenty-six libraries in France, Germany, and Austria that he had visited since 1804. During the winter, he conducted negotiations with Jena and Heidelberg and then, in the spring of 1808, accepted a call to the Bavarian University of Landshut because he now felt the need to settle down in a quiet academic surrounding to complete his project. His negotiations included a substantial stipend for the transportation of his vast library, which—since it was far better for his purposes than even the finest public library—he required for his own "special plan."[50]

It was now his highest priority, he announced to Jakob Grimm in August 1809, to complete his first-hand study of the sources, of which at present he had worked through only about half.[51] By April of the following year he felt that he had virtually completed his task.[52] His twofold ambition, as already defined in his "methodology," was to write a *history* and a *system* of Roman law, both based directly on the original sources. "To this end I have most of the material assembled, but the execution may still have to wait for some time because it is supposed to be also a complete and critical bibliography, and I don't want to cite anything that I haven't read myself." In the process, he continued, he hoped to treat many legal writers of "the misunderstood twelfth and thirteenth centuries, whom I intend to restore to honor."

Savigny's tenure at the Bavarian university, where he arrived in September 1808 and accomplished substantial productive work, was brief. He enjoyed several of his colleagues and during his three semesters succeeded again in attracting a following of students so devoted to him that many of them accompanied his carriage for miles through the countryside—some even followed him as far as Salzburg—when he left Landshut only a year and a half later.[53] He and his family became fond of the lovely surrounding countryside and made frequent trips to Munich, where he explored the rich manuscript holdings. But he was dismayed by the provincial nature of the small university, by the scholarly lethargy of most of the faculty, and by the inadequate preparation of the students, most of whom came from peasant and working-class families. The tranquillity was further interrupted by the antics of his brother-in-law Clemens and his second wife, who also showed up in Landshut; by the major battle of Landshut in the spring of 1809; and by the denunciations and persecutions of Protestants in Catholic Bavaria. So when his future brother-in-law Achim von Arnim—the Prussian writer who was now engaged to Bettine—wrote about the establishment of the new university in Berlin and communicated Humboldt's interest in attracting Savigny, he was delighted.

Humboldt regarded it as his priority to obtain the finest faculty, if the university was to be a success. Humboldt assured King Friedrich Wilhelm III that Savigny was the man "of whom the king may expect the deepening of legal consciousness, the proper treatment and leadership of the entire study of jurisprudence."[54] And to Savigny himself he wrote flatteringly, but honestly, that "You must be there even before the university itself." Savigny, in turn, was able to win the assurance that the basis of legal study in his new faculty would be Roman law, and not the new Prussian legal code (ALR). Savigny had at last found the place where he was to spend the remainder of his long life.

In the opening semester of the new institution in the fall of 1810, Savigny introduced himself to his new audience (according to the official catalog of courses) with lectures on "Institutions, History, and Antiquities of Roman Law" (ten hours weekly). His tenure started propitiously. While he had only forty-six students in the first semester, they responded to his personal commitment and quiet dignity as gratifyingly as those at Marburg and Landshut. "When he raised his resonant voice and, with an incomparable mastery of the material and a vivid plasticity of representation, conjured up the ancient Romans, their social conditions, and their legal concepts, finely worked out into all their consequences, one was almost reconciled with the superiority with which he initially blew away in a few concise and accurate words all the errors and foolishness with which the more recent jurists had obscured and deformed the noble features of Roman antiquity."[55] Savigny was also attracted to the culture of Berlin, optimistic about the future of the new university, and impressed by many of his new colleagues: the philosopher Fichte, the theologian Schleiermacher, and the classicist Boeckh. He was an enthusiastic auditor at Niebuhr's lectures on Roman history and soon became best of friends with the historian, whom he greatly admired and never tired of praising in his letters. In April of 1811 he was elected into the Academy of Sciences. And in 1812 he was the unanimous choice to replace Fichte as the second rector of the university when the philosopher resigned as the result of a bitter dispute with the faculty.

In the second semester of that first year, 1810–11, the faculty of law—which besides Savigny included the founding rector, the constitutional lawyer T. A. H. Schmalz (1760–1831), and the young historian of post-classical Greco-Roman law, Friedrich August Biener (1787–1861)—was joined by a colleague superbly qualified to profess the history of German law, Karl Friedrich Eichhorn. While the history of law, both the older pragmatic and the more recent genetic form, was first applied to Roman law, that initiative was rapidly accommodated to the study of German law. As the new historians sought to cleanse the *usus modernus pandectarum* of its various alien elements and to uncover the pure sources of Roman law, questions arose concerning the history of the German law that had become intermingled with Roman law even before the Reception. Within a short time, while the history of law established itself as a formal field of study, a practical distinction had to be made between "Romanists" and "Germanists"—a bifurcation that initially worked in productive reciprocity and only later in the nineteenth century deteriorated into an antagonistic separation.[56] It was the latter field that rapidly captured the interest of Jakob Grimm, who applied the methods he learned from Savigny—and Savigny's obsessive search for sources—to his later study of German legal antiquities (*Deutsche Rechtsalterthümer*, 1828). In a seminal essay "On the Poetry in the Law" ("Von der Poesie im Recht," 1816), Grimm formulated the archetypal Romantic view that law emerged out of an original cultural unity in which language embraced both law and poetry, and thus legitimized the connection between the field of law and the dozens of Romantic writers who studied law at university and then addressed legal issues in their writings.[57]

The true founder of the history of German law was Eichhorn (1781–1854), the son of the distinguished Göttingen Orientalist J. F. Eichhorn, who had studied law at his hometown university with Pütter and Hugo.[58] Following the completion of his doctorate, he made study-trips to the principal sites of law in the Holy Roman Empire—the Imperial Chamber Court at Wetzlar, the Imperial Diet at Regensburg, and the Imperial Court at Vienna—and then, returning to Göttingen in 1803 as a Privatdozent, began lecturing on trial law in the Empire. Two years later he was called to the faculty of law at Frankfurt an der Oder, where he lectured broadly on every aspect except criminal law. It was there that he published the first edition of his four-volume political and legal history of Germany (*Deutsche Staats- und Rechtsgeschichte*, 1808–23), the work that warrants his reputation as the father of German legal history.

Eichhorn justifies his undertaking, in the preface to the first edition, with the familiar appeal to history in the face of present uncertainties.

> At the present moment, when the social condition of Germany and especially its legal circumstances have suffered so many important changes, when both must perhaps still undergo many equally important changes, and everything is still in a state of becoming and still in transition from one state of affairs into another, it appears more important than ever to focus our attention on the past and to acquaint ourselves with the spirit of our former circumstances. . . . Without a detailed knowledge of what was, and the manner in which it became what it was, it will always be impossible to understand its spirit and its relation to what remains in existence.[59]

Prior to Eichhorn, there had been works on German political history; but German legal history was limited essentially to its constitutional aspect. "Since the legal circumstances of a people assume a conspicuously important place among its political institutions," he argues, "the history of law stands in such a precise connection with the history of the state that the latter cannot even be represented without appropriating much from the former" (3). Despite earlier preliminary works, he continues, it is necessary to uncover new truths and to correct erroneous views rather than simply to compile and organize the existing materials (xv). Eichhorn's work was the first, following the model of Hugo and Savigny, to go back directly to the sources for a history of German law, which he divides into four parts: the oldest history of the Germanic tribes (114 to 561 B.C.E.); the Frankish monarchy (561–888); the Holy Roman Empire of German Nation (888–1517); and the German state system (1517–1815).

It was on the basis of this striking achievement that Savigny brought him to Berlin as a colleague sharing a similar historically-oriented view of law. Eichhorn returned to Göttingen in 1817, but for much of that second decade he and Savigny represented the entire spectrum of the history of law in Germany and, as we shall see, co-founded in 1815 the first journal for the history of legal science.

The brilliant start of the University of Berlin, which had assembled Niebuhr, Schleiermacher, and Savigny along with other distinguished scholars at the peak of their careers, was brought to an abrupt halt in 1813 by the War of Liberation against Napoleon and his armies. As students deserted the lecture halls and flocked to the fronts—in the winter of 1813–14 only twenty-nine of the previous six hundred students were enrolled in the university— the professors who remained behind sought to contribute in their own way. Savigny belonged to the organizers of the local militia, to whose exercises according to his amused sister-in-law Bettine he rushed off before lectures every morning at 3 o'clock with spear in hand. (He belonged to a rifle company along with the classicists Boeckh and Wolf, the theologian Schleiermacher, the philosopher Fichte, and the physician Reil, who were twitted by popular wit with nicknames taken from Falstaff's followers.)[60] Although the company never saw action and was disbanded in the summer of 1813, Savigny's efforts were subsequently recognized through the award of the newly created military decoration, the Iron Cross. It was precisely during this period of turmoil that Savigny finally began writing his history of Roman law. "After the great examples of destruction that lie behind us," he wrote to the Grimm brothers in December 1813, "one must doubly hasten—with all the power of concentration one has acquired—to finish it and thus to guard it against ruin."[61] Following Napoleon's defeat and a typhus epidemic, which claimed the lives of several colleagues, including Fichte and Reil, things began to return to normal. By the winter semester of 1814–15, the university could again enroll some five hundred students returning from the field. Savigny was commissioned to tutor the Crown Prince in law. But in the meantime another problem had arisen.

The Codification Controversy

In 1814–15 the close coincidence of three major events marked the beginning of what came to be known as the Historical School of legal studies. The first and triggering event was the so-called codification controversy.[62] Following the defeat of Napoleon, Germany was threatened by the legal chaos at which Eichhorn had already hinted in the preface to his history of German law. There were essentially three possibilities: to retain the Code Civil, which had been imposed by the French upon the entire left bank of the Rhine and extensive territories in western Germany (the kingdom of Westphalia, the cities of Frankfurt and the Hanseatic League, and elsewhere); to create a new code for all of Germany; or to revert to the old fragmented system of Roman law as supplemented by local customary law. The debate was set off by a pamphlet, *On the Code Napoleon and Its Introduction into Germany* (*Über den Code Napoleon und dessen Einführung in Deutschland*), published early in 1814 by August Wilhelm Rehberg, a royal councilor in the kingdom of Hanover. Rehberg, rejecting those "philosophical enthusiasts who want to introduce total freedom and equality among men,"[63] argued from a position of legal conservatism that Germany should renounce the superficial unity of an all-embracing Roman legal system and return to a crazy-map of particularized legal systems.

Rehberg's proposal was immediately challenged by Anton Friedrich Justus Thibaut (1772–1840), one of the most highly respected civil jurists of the day—first in a review and then in a pamphlet *On the Need for a General Civil Law for Germany* (*Ueber die Nothwendigkeit eines allgemeinen bürgerlichen Rechts für Deutschland*, 1814). The star of the distinguished faculty of law at Heidelberg, which constituted the principal competition to the University of Berlin, Thibaut was fully aware of the risks and opportunities inherent in the historical moment. It was inevitable, he thought, that Germany would reject the artificial political unity imposed by Napoleon, but he felt that it would be a tragedy if the nation should also relinquish the benefits of a unified system of law. "I am of the opinion that our civil law . . . requires a total, immediate change and that the Germans cannot become content in their civil circumstances unless all German governments seek with unified forces to effect the promulgation of a single law code valid for all Germany and removed from the whim of the individual governments" (67).[64] Traditional German law, he argued, was so defective that, given any hundred questions, ninety had to be answered from Roman or canon law. Roman law, in turn, a product of Rome's period of most abysmal decline, was so vast and complex that not even the most learned scholars could master it in its entirety. What was needed was a new code written specifically for Germany. "A simple national code of law, executed with German vigor in the German spirit, will be accessible in all its parts to every mind, even the average one, and our lawyers and judges will finally be in a position where the law will be available to them for every case" (74). Such a code would also serve scholars and students by consolidating for the first time the legal theories of the universities and the actual practice in the courts. A common code of law, finally, would provide a legal and ethical unity for the nation transcending the inevitable political separation of states.

Thibaut's authority and charisma might well have carried the day against the rallying forces of conservatism, which were hastening at the Congress of Vienna to regain the privileges lost under Napoleon, had his opponent been anyone but Savigny. Though both were historians of Roman law and of Huguenot descent—indeed, Savigny had recommended Thibaut for the chair at Heidelberg, and ten years earlier Thibaut had been among the first reviewers to hail the achievement of Savigny's *The Law of Possession*—the two men were utterly unlike in temperament and personality. Thibaut's profoundly republican sentiments were the product of his family circumstances. Growing up in Hanover as the son of an officer, he was bourgeois in his aspirations—"Jacobin," according to his friends—and sociable by disposition. In Heidelberg he was beloved for the evenings of choral music that he conducted every week in the attic of his house. ("Jurisprudence is my business; my music room is my temple.")[65] This contrasted sharply with Savigny's elitist nobility, the seclusion he preferred, and his single-minded dedication to his studies.

Even before Thibaut's response to Rehberg, Savigny had been reasoning against codification in his lectures and drafting a statement of his own, which he now rushed into print under the title *On the Vocation of Our Age for Legislation and Legal Science* (*Vom Beruf unsrer Zeit für Gesetzgebung und Rechtswissenschaft*, 1814). Savigny objects that Germany has no need for codification and, moreover, no capacity for its challenges. All that is required is a thorough understanding of Roman law—not according to the principles of natural law, which had contributed to the deterio-

ration of legal culture in Germany, but according to the historical principles of a science of law for which Savigny adopted the neologism *Rechtswissenschaft,* which is printed prominently in large letters on the title page
of his brochure.

Savigny acknowledges the urgent need for a generally accepted system
of civil law now that the threat of oppression by the French has been
warded off and the Napoleonic code largely discarded, a code that Savigny abhors as a disease that "consumed everything around it like a can-
cer" (98).[66] He maintains, however, that rationalist jurisprudence is
mistaken in its belief that law can be produced through the prescriptions
of authority. "The historical sense has awakened everywhere" (100), and
history teaches us that law everywhere has a specific character, unique to
its people, like language and customs—that law is everywhere unified by
the feeling of the people and exists in an "organic connection" of law and
folk (103). The true seat of law, he insists, is the sacred consciousness of
the people (105), for which he later adopted the new term *Volksgeist.*
Common law always arose from custom and popular belief—through
quietly working inner forces rather than the will and caprice of individual
legislators (chap. 2). Until recently such a *ius commune*—that is, Roman
law as modified by local law—had prevailed in Germany (chap. 5). Although Savigny concedes that the system involves both delays and confusing variety, he insists that this combination is best suited for Germany.
He rejects the view that every age is equally well qualified to formulate its
own laws (chap. 6). The capacity for legislation varies as greatly from age
to age and from country to country as do the arts. His own age lacks precisely the two qualities essential for any gifted jurist: the sense of *history*
needed to comprehend the uniqueness of every age and every form of law,
and the sense of *system* needed to understand each concept in its context
and relation to the whole. (We easily recognize here the principles stated
earlier in his "methodology.") But matters may improve. "Unless all signs
deceive us, a more lively spirit has come into our science, which can in the
future once again raise it to a unique formation" (125).

Savigny devotes the middle section of his pamphlet (chap. 7) to a detailed analysis of the three most prominent modern codes—the French
Code Civil, the Prussian Territorial Law, and the Austrian Civil Code—
in order to expose what he considers the inadequacies of each. The defects
in the legal education of an entire generation are evident not just in specific shortcomings of those projects but in the character of the whole enterprise.

What is needed in the universities is a new science of law—"Rechts-wissenschaft"—that will address Roman law, German law, and the modifications of both systems (chap. 8). Students should immerse themselves in the works of the Roman jurists until they can actually think as the Romans did. (Again, Savigny is reiterating an idea underlying his early methodology.) The generation of jurists educated in this manner will then be capable of creating a living common law that will enable judges to settle new controversies on the basis of old precedent. While he compares the French code to "a political disease that has been survived" (176), he believes that too much confusion would result if both the Prussian and Austrian codes should be discarded at this time (chap. 9). Although the codes need to be retained temporarily as a practical expedient, the teaching of law in the universities should focus on Roman law presented according to Latin textbooks (as at Berlin). The goal of university juristic education is not practical training (as at Heidelberg) but the knowledge and understanding of law and its assumptions. A new code would divide Germany into three areas: Austria, Prussia, and the other lands (chap. 10). It would be preferable for all to share and study the common sources of their law ("die Urquellen unsres Rechts," 187).

While he agrees with his one-time friend Thibaut on the goal of national unity (chap. 11), he rejects the possibility of any code by committee: a book of law should be an organic whole rather than an aggregate of separate decisions. At present, Germany has no jurists capable of conceiving a truly popular code and lacks a language in which to write it. It should therefore be the most immediate goal to establish the basis for a reliable system of law, which in turn can bind the nation together in a true community (chap. 12). "I see the proper means in an organically progressing science of law, which can be common to the entire nation" (192). The problem does not reside, as the codifiers argue, in the ancient sources of Roman and common law, but in the nation itself. Recapitulating his title, and quoting no less an authority than Melanchthon for support, Savigny sums up by stating that Germany has at present no true vocation for legislation but an enormous talent for the study of law.

The codification controversy was not limited to these two most passionate spokesmen. The battle was waged in the salons, the discussion clubs, and the leading journals as jurists and public figures all over Germany joined the fray.[67] Gustav Hugo predictably weighed in on the side of Savigny and the traditionalists, along with Niebuhr and Jakob Grimm, while the fiery philosopher of law, Anselm von Feuerbach, came to the support of Thibaut. Savigny's pamphlet was also the target of a person-ally invidious attack by the Bavarian jurist Nikolaus Thaddeus Gönner, an old enemy from Landshut. But for all practical purposes the debate was won in 1814. While Savigny's pamphlet may not in itself have been the de-cisive factor, it contributed enormously to the publicity surrounding the controversy.[68] His arguments, as well as his rhetoric, appealed to the forces of restoration mustering themselves at the Congress of Vienna. In the realm of jurisprudence, Germany returned in effect to the status of the years before 1806, and this situation prevailed, for better or for worse, until the end of the nineteenth century. It was not until 1896 that a newly unified Germany finally adopted a civil code valid for the entire nation, the *Bürgerliches Gesetzbuch,* which took effect on the first day of the new century.

The Historical School

With his eloquent plea against codification Savigny contributed to the political battle for Roman law.[69] Now, with the first volume of his classic history of Roman law in the Middle Ages (*Geschichte des Römischen Rechts im Mittelalter,* 6 vols., 1815–31), he struck a powerful blow for its scholarly centrality. The author tells us (in the preface to the first edition) that he had initially intended to write a history that would have extended from Irnerius, the great twelfth-century luminary of the School of Bologna, to the present—an interest inspired by his teacher Weis at Marburg and furthered by his own appreciation for the spirit of the late medieval com-mentators whose works he had studied at Paris and elsewhere. That plan would have been appropriate if, in fact, Roman law had completely dis-appeared at the end of the western empire, only to be reawakened six cen-turies later—if, in other words, the history of law and juristic scholarship were separated by an absolute break. "But a thorough investigation of the true origins of law exposes this view to be just as dismissible in its way as the assumption of a long and total interruption of Roman law."[70]

Savigny came to understand that it was his challenge "to show how the legal circumstances of modern times, insofar as they are based on a Ro-man foundation, emerged from the circumstances of the existing Western Roman empire through straightforward development and transformation and without interruption." By the same token, it now seemed advisable not to extend the investigation down to the present, since Western legal science, from the sixteenth century on, has undergone such profound changes. These considerations led Savigny to treat the entire Middle Ages as an integral whole. The legal history of the Middle Ages, as now defined and justified, consists of two principal parts: the six centuries preceding Irnerius, during which the continuity of Roman law can be proven, but without any scholarly activity; and the four centuries after Irnerius, which were dedicated principally to scholarly assimilation and communication.

Savigny's researches to this point had brought him to the startling new conclusion that Roman law led a continuous existence through the entire Middle Ages quite independent of the existence and condition of the Roman people to which it originally related. How was this to be reconciled with the other view, which he shared with Grimm and the young Romantic nationalists to whom he was tied by friendship and marriage, that "all law is produced with an inner necessity by the people themselves" (x)? It was this dilemma that caused Savigny to relate his history of law to the history of the peoples in which Roman law continued its underground existence: notably the Burgundian, West Gothic, Frankish, East Gothic, and Lombardic kingdoms and Italy under Greek and papal rule. At this point, he pays tribute to his friend and colleague Niebuhr, whose lectures on ancient Roman history provided an exemplary model. "Nothing in all history is more engaging than the periods in which the strengths and capabilities of various nations grow together into new, living formations" (xii). An equally creative period, Savigny believes, is apparent in the Middle Ages, when modern Europe arose from the mixture of various elements, principally Roman and Germanic. But the manner of this mixture, and the reasons for it, have been little investigated—and notably with regard to the history of law.

This was the challenge that Savigny took upon himself as he began writing his long-planned work in the fall of 1813, making extensive use of hitherto unknown sources that he had discovered in the course of the past fifteen years in various libraries and archives.[71] He expresses his gratitude to Niebuhr for his help and advice, especially with regard to Roman sources. (Niebuhr was responsible for putting Savigny on the trail of the *Institutiones* of the classical Roman jurist Gaius, which he had discovered in Verona and which were now edited and published [1816] by Savigny's former student and present colleague J. F. L. Göschen: the first major pre-Justinian legal source.) He is indebted also to his friend and colleague Eichhorn for his treatment of German legal history. Finally he singles out with generous gratitude his student Jakob Grimm, whose assistance in many libraries, and notably in Paris, advanced the progress of the enterprise.

It was especially the powerful narrative of the first two volumes that captured the imagination of Savigny's contemporaries, the story of the peoples populating Western Europe during the early Middle Ages and assuring the continuity of Roman law. The essentially biographical portraits of the later volumes, focusing on legal scholars of the later Middle Ages, had less popular appeal; but they provided evidence for Savigny's insistence, ever since his early "methodology," that not only the law proceeded according to historical principles, but also the scientific study of law (*Rechtswissenschaft*). His work certified, for the time at least, his insistence that Roman law in its original form should constitute the center of the legal curriculum, providing as it did in its continuous existence the basis of the law governing modern Europe. At the same time, he made the point that law is not a subject of peripheral interest to be left to the specialists but that it should be relocated to the center of education and consciousness, since it is an integral aspect of every culture. For all these reasons, Savigny's magisterial work made a profound impression on contemporary readers and was soon translated into every major European language.

In spite of its intellectual appeal, the purely theoretical nature of Savigny's approach attracted fewer students than the more practical law professed by Thibaut and his colleagues at Heidelberg and elsewhere. As a result, by 1819 Savigny was requested officially to supplement his lectures on Roman law with a course on the Prussian Territorial Code (ALR). However, the notes taken by students in that course suggest that, notwithstanding its title, Savigny actually continued to deal with Roman private law, conceding little more than a brief presentation on differences between the Prussian code and the law of the pandects.[72]

While the codification controversy and the publication of Savigny's *History of Roman Law in the Middle Ages* provided the political impetus and scholarly foundation for the Historical School, its institutional basis was established with the journal *Zeitschrift für geschichtliche Rechtswissenschaft,* edited by Savigny, Eichhorn, and Göschen, the first volume of which appeared in 1815. In his introductory piece "On the Purpose of this Journal" ("Ueber den Zweck dieser Zeitschrift") Savigny states "the complete agreement [of the three editors] about the manner in which the science of law must be regarded and treated" (1). He explains that jurists of his day can be assigned to two classes or schools divided by a fundamental difference. One school is adequately characterized, he continues, by its name as the "historical" school. But he finds no suitable designation for the other, which manifests itself in various forms, sometimes as philosophy and sometimes as natural law; in the absence of any accepted name he chooses (rather unfairly) to call it the "unhistorical" school.[73] Regarding the relationship of past and present, of becoming and being, the latter group believes that every age produces its own world for better or for worse, but that the past is nothing more than a collection of moral-political *exempla,* one of many aids to understanding, and one that genius can easily do without. "According to the teaching of the others there is no wholly individual and separate human existence: rather, whatever can be regarded as individual is, seen from another side, a member of a higher whole. So every individual human being must necessarily be thought of as a member of a family, a people, a state; and every age of a people as the continuation and development of all past ages" (5). "History is . . . the only way to a true recognition of our own circumstances" (6). Applying this principle to "the science of law," the Historical School assumes that "the matter of the law is given by the entire past of the nation, but not arbitrarily, so that it could at random be this or that, but proceeding from the innermost essence of the nation itself and of its history" (6). It is the special responsibility of the present to penetrate and rejuvenate this matter, in contrast to the "unhistorical" school, which assumes that law is brought forth arbitrarily at every moment by persons authorized with legislative power. The editors, totally committed to the Historical School, intend to further the development and application of the views of that school, particularly at a moment when the highest possessions of the nation have been rescued and fresh hope is at hand. In particular, they aspire—and here political ambition is linked to the scholarly one—"to give a new stimulus to the historical grounding of the national law" (7). They intend to do this over the opposition of the "unhistorical" school, which focuses its hostility on the treatment of Roman legal history while ignoring German legal history. They have chosen the form of a journal, rather than more comprehensive monographs, in the hope of reaching a broader interested public. While not susceptible to any blind faith in the ability of legal science to dispel the present gloomy night of affairs, they believe nevertheless that things are now possible that were unheard of by the great scholars of the sixteenth century.

Savigny's eloquent proclamation was accompanied by Eichhorn's more restrained statement, "On the Historical Study of German Law" ("Ueber das geschichtliche Studium des Deutschen Rechts"), which begins with the sobering assertion that the study of German private law, despite its growing significance in the practice of law, remains at a low level. This he attributes to no lack of interest but to the treatment of German law in the absence of the necessary preliminary studies. German law exists principally in the form of the territorial law of individual lands. "But no single one of all the German territorial legal systems [*Particularrecht*] has a separate existence in itself, and none can have it because no German land was ever wholly separated by history and the characteristics of its people from the rest of Germany" (125–26). While all the local laws enjoy a certain uniqueness qualified by the history of the individual lands, still the legal circumstances of every German land must be imagined in their inner connection with those of the rest of Germany and all local law in connection with the common law standing above and linking them. "Since the German territorial laws stand in a commonality of origin based on various circumstances and in an inner relationship arising from it, any rule based on that commonality and not simply on an accidental correspondence of particular determinations is necessarily applicable everywhere, as long as the existence of an anomaly in the territorial law cannot be demonstrated, and thus has the nature of a common law" (130).

This principle produces the appropriate method of study. For every German legal arrangement one should seek the legal idea underlying the particular law and develop from it what should be regarded as essential (common law) and contingent (particular law). Such determinations can be made only from a historical point of view—a point of view largely lacking in earlier investigations, which had been content with the existence and compilation of particular laws and not with the history of their development and the evolution of their idiosyncrasies. In addition, there is a shortage of local histories of the various German lands, written on the basis of documentary sources, from which alone it is possible to become acquainted with the unwritten territorial laws. "I believe that one cannot adequately appreciate the benefit that can be anticipated from the sketched preliminary work for German legal science, and perhaps even more for the future legislation about matters of German law" (138). In addition to these two statements of purpose and principle the first volume of the journal contained articles by Savigny and Eichhorn, as well as Hugo and Göschen and Jakob Grimm, that put into practice the genetic method exemplified by the Historical School.

With the appearance of the *Zeitschrift für geschichtliche Rechtswissenschaft*, in sum, the sense of history made its way officially into the faculty of law at the University of Berlin and, for the next half-century, into

German law.[74] The Historical School was not without its critics. The two principals continued the battle to the end of their careers. In 1838, only two years before his death, Thibaut defended the position of the codifiers against the charge of anti-historicism leveled at them by Savigny and his followers. Thibaut's article in defense of his views was entitled "Über die sogenannte historische und nicht-historische Rechtsschule" and castigated the vanity and pedantry of the historians.[75] Savigny restated his opposition to codes in the preface to a second edition of his monograph in 1828 and again in the preface to his *System of Present-day Roman Law* (*System des heutigen Römischen Rechts,* 1840). "The historical view of legal science is wholly misunderstood and distorted if, as frequently occurs, it is understood as though it represented the highest form of legal construction emerging from the past—a form that can claim the unchanged domination over present and future. Rather, it consists essentially in the uniform acknowledgment of the value and independence of every age, and it places greatest weight only on the recognition of the living connection that ties the present to the past, without the knowledge of which we can grasp only the external appearance of the legal life of the present, not its inner essence."[76]

Other critics arose. Among the fiercest was Anselm von Feuerbach, the prominent legal philosopher and president of the Bavarian Appeals Court in Ansbach, who wrote in 1832 that "the historical jurists strike me as being like people who gnaw the bones of a mummy and count the fibers on the sarcophagus."[77] Hegel, who came to the University of Berlin in 1818, waged a war against the Historical School from the moment of his arrival.[78] In his first semester, he offered a course of lectures on "The Philosophy of Law," in which he informed the students that "It would be one of the greatest insults to a cultured nation or the juristic profession to deny to either the ability to make a code of laws."[79] A particular thorn in Savigny's side was Eduard Gans (1797–1839)—a student of Thibaut's, an enthusiastic disciple of Hegel's, and himself a considerable scholar of comparative law—who was appointed to the faculty of law in Berlin in 1828 over Savigny's violent objections. Savigny's dissatisfaction with this appointment and other developments at the university led to his resignation from the university and his appointment from 1842 to 1848 as Minister of Legislation, where by an ironic twist of fate he was charged with the revision of the Prussian Territorial Code (ALR).

History's verdict on Savigny and the Historical School has been mixed.[80] It is generally agreed that Savigny, both as the acknowledged leader of the School and as Minister of Legislation (and subsequently Minister of Law) in Prussia, delayed the inevitable progress toward a modern code of law for a unified Germany, which was finally enacted in 1900. The poet Heinrich Heine, as a student of law in Berlin, was among those infuriated by the ceremonious dignity of the "cloying troubadour of the pandects" (in his late poem, "Everybody Does It" ["Die Menge thut es"]). Karl Marx and subsequent Marxist analysts objected to what they considered Savigny's advocacy of the interests of a feudal nobility.[81] Yet despite many mistakes of detail that have been corrected and despite a significant revision of his theory concerning the continuity of Roman law, most knowledgeable historians of law would agree with the twentieth-century legal historian Hermann Kantorowicz, who after a careful consideration of the pros and cons concluded: "If I had to choose between Savigny's work and the whole flotilla of books that follow in its wake, I would not hesitate in choosing the *Geschichte des Römischen Rechts im Mittelalter*."[82] Today his name resonates not only in Germany, where the *Zeitschrift der Savigny-Stiftung für Rechtsgeschichte* still bears his name, but also abroad. In England he has been called "the greatest jurist that Europe has produced."[83] In 1989 *The American Journal of Comparative Law* published a special number on "Savigny in Modern Comparative Perspective," which investigated such topics as "The Influence of German Legal Theory on American Law: The Heritage of Savigny and His Disciples" and "Savigny and His Anglo-American Disciples." In any case, by way of Hugo, Savigny, Eichhorn, and Grimm we have traced the gradual historicization of law and its study during the period between the French Revolution and the post-Napoleonic restoration—a process precisely parallel to the one already observed in philosophy and theology.

Five

MEDICINE

The Discovery of Life

SOMETIME in or around the year 1800, Life was discovered. This is not to suggest that life (lowercase) had not been a matter of considerable interest and speculation for earlier ages, which had conceived a variety of striking images to symbolize the relationships connecting the various realms of known being. Analogies between man as microcosm and the macrocosm as a whole, for instance, were as familiar to philosophers in China, India, and Persia as they were to Plato and Aristotle, and this mode of thought remained attractive, notably to astrologers, throughout the Middle Ages and Renaissance.[1] A vision of this sort appears to Faust in the first scene of Goethe's drama, when he opens the "mysterious book" of Nostradamus and contemplates the sign of the macrocosm.

> Ha! welche Wonne fließt in diesem Blick
> Auf einmal mir durch alle meine Sinnen!
> Ich fühle junges, heil'ges Lebensglück
> Neuglühend mir durch Nerv und Adern rinnen.
>
> (430–33)

(Ah, what bliss suddenly flows through all my senses at this sight! I feel a young, holy joy of life coursing with a new glow through my nerves and veins.)

Studying the sign, he understands the unity of all being.

> Wie alles sich zum Ganzen webt,
> Eins in dem andern wirkt und lebt!
>
> (447–48)

(How all being is woven into a whole and each part works and lives in the other!)

The sense of analogy obtaining between and among the various aspects of nature—summed up in Novalis's phrase "the magic wand of analogy" ("der Zauberstab der Analogie")—emerges repeatedly, as we shall see, in the various Romantic theories of nature and medicine, which regarded the macrocosm as a vast organism and the individual organism, in turn, as a tiny microcosm.

Another notion is that of the *archeus* (from Greek *archaios,* "ancient," "primeval"), a term coined by Paracelsus (1493–1541) to designate in his alchemy the immaterial force that generates and regulates life in every individual object in the mineral, plant, and animal realms. The term was subsequently appropriated by Paracelsus's Belgian follower, J. B. van Helmont (1579–1644), as a label for the rarefied spiritual essence that could penetrate the patient and cause disease, an essence for which he coined the word "gas" from Greek *chaos.*

A third powerful image emerged in the great Chain of Being, envisaged at least since Plato as the universe itself. This conception attained its widest acceptance in the eighteenth century and found what is perhaps its most familiar expression in the lines of Alexander Pope's *Essay on Man* (1733–34).

> Above, how high, progressive life may go!
> Around, how wide! how deep extend below!
> Vast chain of Being! which from God began,
> Natures aethereal, human, angel, man,
> Beast, bird, fish, insect, what no eye can see,
> No glass can reach; from Infinite to thee,
> From thee to Nothing.
>
> (235–41)

The notion was widely current in Germany too, as we see in Herder's *Ideas toward a Philosophy of History of Mankind* (*Ideen zur Philosophie der Geschichte der Menschheit,* 1784-91) where he describes the planet earth as "a great workshop for the organization of very diverse beings": "The immeasurable chain extends from the Creator all the way down to the nucleus in a grain of sand."[2]

The notion of the unbroken Chain of Being underlies the widespread encyclopedic impulse that produced Chambers' *Cyclopaedia* (1728), Zedler's *Großes vollständiges Universal-Lexikon* (1735), and Diderot's *Encyclopédie* (1751). Its specifically scientific implications—the conviction that "nature makes no leaps" (*natura non facit saltus*)—are strikingly evident in the taxonomic passion of the Swedish botanist Carl von Linné (Linnaeus), whose *Species plantarum* (1753) listed some eight thousand varieties of plants and named them all according to his binomial method of classification. (The final edition of his *Systema naturae* [1758] identified 5,897 animals.) Antoine-Laurent Lavoisier's *Traité élémentaire de chimie* (1789), which introduced a new method of identifying and naming the chemical elements, as well as such nosologies as J. B. M. Sagar's *Systema morborum symptomaticum* (1771), which classified some 340 types of disease,[3] are equally indebted to the ideal of plenitude, continuity, and gradation that characterized notions of the Chain of Being.[4]

Yet in all these often ingeniously elaborated and essentially centrifugal systems, "life" is a force as detachable from the individual as, say, the "breath of life" that God breathed into the nostrils of newly created man (Gen. 2.7) or the humiliated "life" that in the last line of Virgil's *Aeneid* leaves the body of the defeated Turnus and "with a groan flees to the shades below": *vitaque cum gemitu fugit indignata sub umbras*. In reaction against the prevailing encyclopedic empiricism, which catalogued according to differences, a tendency toward simplification and unification began to emerge in the late eighteenth century—a monistic urge to identify a single force unifying the disparate phenomena.[5] It was this desire that underlay and popularized such notions as Anton Mesmer's "animal magnetism," Galvani's electrical "galvanism," John Brown's "excitability," the "world-soul" of *Naturphilosophie,* or Lorenz Oken's organization of the animal world according to the senses. The related desire to temporalize the timeless Chain of Being and to move from the spatio-mathematical thinking of the eighteenth century to an essentially biocentric orientation—a classic scientific "paradigm shift"—is altogether typical of Romanticism.[6]

Symbolic for the dramatic change in thinking about Life is the fact that the word "biology" was simultaneously and independently coined in 1802 by Gottfried Reinhold Treviranus and Jean-Baptiste Lamarck, in Germany and France respectively, to designate the realm of living beings, both animal and vegetable, in distinction from the inanimate mineral world.[7] In his *Biologie* (1802), Treviranus defined biology as "the science of life," while Lamarck in his *Hydrogéologie* (1802) called it the division of "terrestrial physics" that includes "all which pertains to living bodies."[8] Both men, reacting against the taxonomic obsession of the eighteenth century and responding to changing scientific views, believed that it was the responsibility of the newly defined discipline to concern itself with those functions that were coming to be recognized as characteristic of Life as opposed to inanimate matter: organization, generation, nutrition, growth, and susceptibility to illness and death. (This trend ran counter to Kant's pronounced resistance, in his *Critique of Judgment* [*Kritik der Urteilskraft*, 1790], to all attempts to regard biology as a science.)[9]

The creation of biology was preceded by several developments in scientific thought of the late eighteenth century. The natural world had long been traditionally divided into the three kingdoms of mineral, animal, and vegetable, as in Paracelsus's alchemy. Goethe's extensive scientific writings still fall clearly into the separate realms of geology, zoology, and botany—the sciences known collectively as *Naturgeschichte* (natural history). (Chemistry and physics, in contrast, were generally classed separately as *Naturlehre*, "theory of nature.") But increasingly this division was eroded as naturalists in Germany and France—Johann Blumenbach, Antoine-Laurent de Jussieu, Félix Vicq d'Azyr, among others—began to conclude that living things of the plant and animal world were characterized by the organization of their integrated systems. As these "organic" beings were fundamentally differentiated from the inorganic objects of the inanimate world, the field of physiology was redefined to designate the study of the life-force that inspires such living organisms.

In the last decade of the eighteenth century, scientists began to envision something that they called the *vis vitalis*—"vital force" or *Lebenskraft*—that characterized living beings.[10] Among the many works of the decade that addressed the topic, Christoph Wilhelm Hufeland's work on *The Art of Prolonging Human Life* (*Die Kunst, das menschliche Leben zu verlängern*, 1797; in later editions called simply *Makrobiotik*) was one of the most successful. Hufeland had already discussed *Lebenskraft* at length in an earlier work on the genesis of disease (*Ideen über Pathogenie*, 1795) in which he designates it as "a mere word-sign" that he is prepared to give up as soon as someone defines life more precisely. In the meantime, he continues to use it for "the inner cause of vitality."[11] But this book, written as the text for specialized lectures for medical students, did not reach the same broad audience as did *Makrobiotik*.

Based on his phenomenally popular lectures at the University of Jena, where he edited a *Journal of Practical Medicine and Surgery* (*Journal der practischen Arzneykunde und Wundarzneykunst*), and written for a general audience, *Makrobiotik* went through four editions within ten years, was rapidly translated into all the major European languages, and soon established itself as a classic among Western medical texts. In his second chapter, Hufeland defines "Lebenskraft" as the force that "fills and moves everything; it is probably the basic source from which all other forces of the physical and especially the organic world flow. . . . inexhaustible, infinite,—a veritable breath of divinity" (31–32).[12] It is further described as "the finest, the most penetrating, most invisible activity of nature that we have hitherto known," exceeding even light, electricity, and magnetism, to which it appears to be closely related (32). "When the life-force enters a body, it is translated from the mechanical and chemical world into a new organic or living one" (35). It is not only the force that holds the organized body together; it also resists the destructive influences of rotting, weathering, frost, and other natural forces (36). Yet the life-force is only a potentiality; life itself means action. "Every life is accordingly a continuous operation of expressions of force and organic stimuli" (49). In the preface to the third edition (1805), Hufeland, now in Berlin as personal physician to the royal family of Prussia and professor at the Collegium Medico-Chirurgicum, remarks that he might well have replaced the word "life-force" with the term "excitability" ("Erregbarkeit"), which had been made recently fashionable in Germany by the interest in Brunonianism.

Johann Christian Reil, who was later to be Hufeland's colleague at the University of Berlin, founded the *Archiv für die Physiologie* in 1795 and in its first number published a long article entitled "Von der Lebenskraft."[13] Reil argued that the animal body should not be regarded as a mysterious and super-sensual being but as a physical object subject to general laws of nature. It will be the task of future science, he continues, to determine the specific qualities of living matter ("Lebensstoff") and of the vital force as a material organization. Reil (1758–1813) did not live long enough to carry out his project. But as the chemical analysis of these "organic" beings by Justus von Liebig and others ascertained the universal presence in them of carbon, the field of organic chemistry gradually emerged in the course of the nineteenth century. Almost simultaneously the Romantic physicist Johann Wilhelm Ritter, inspired by Galvani's experiments, created a sensation among his contemporaries—and sent his Jena students and friends into the nearby marshes in eager search of frogs—with his "proof that a constant galvanism accompanies the life-process in the animal kingdom" (*Beweis, daß ein beständiger Galvanismus den Lebensproceß in dem Thierreich begleite,* 1798).[14]

Alexander von Humboldt viewed the life-force in negative terms, a conception that deserves mention because that great naturalist publicized it in virtually the only poetic work he ever composed. According to one of the Latin aphorisms that Humboldt published in 1793 as an addendum to a work on the subterranean flora of the mines at Freiberg (*Flora Fribergensis subterranea*), the *vis vitalis* is "the internal force that dissolves the chains of chemical affinity and prevents the elements of bodies from being freely conjoined"[15]—that is, the force that makes organic life possible by preventing the elements from reverting to their normal state of crude matter. In 1795, in response to a suggestion by Schiller, he put this idea into the form of a short allegorical tale, "The Life-Force or the Genius of Rhodes" ("Die Lebenskraft oder der rhodische Genius"), which was first published in Schiller's journal *Die Horen* and later included as the final section of Humboldt's own favorite and most popular work, his *Aspects of Nature (Ansichten der Natur,* 1807).[16] The story concerns a mysterious painting that allegedly hung in the market hall in ancient Syracuse portraying a group of healthy, handsome young men and women who reach out longingly toward one another while gazing with earnest eyes at a childlike genius hovering above them with a butterfly on his shoulder and a burning torch in his right hand. For a century not even the most ingenious critics were able to provide a satisfactory interpretation of the painting. At length a merchant ship arrived from Rhodes bearing along with other treasures a twin to the mystery painting: here the genius stands with extinguished torch and without his life-symbolizing butterfly among the youths and maidens, who rush past him to embrace one another with expressions of wild abandonment. The tyrant of Syracuse approached the aged poet-philosopher Epicharmus, who finally was able to provide an adequate interpretation. The genius of Rhodes, he explained, represents the life-force; in his vital presence the elements of life are kept distinct though they long to be together; but when his power is exhausted, those same elements flow back together in utter disarray. Humboldt's own genius did not reside in poetry; the allegory is clumsy, and his notion of life-force idiosyncratic. But the fact that Schiller requested the piece and published it in the leading literary-cultural journal of the day indicates how widespread was the general interest of the 1790s in the new question of Life and life-force.

These various developments in the study of living beings marked a radical shift in the conception of life—a shift that has been called the temporalization of science.[17] Earlier systematizations of nature—the Chain of Being, Linné's taxonomies, the great encyclopedias—had been conspicuously atemporal and ahistorical, presuming a timeless universal order. Toward the end of the eighteenth century, however, and as a result of the same revolutionary forces that produced the general sense of history informing the other faculties, static order in the world of nature gave way to progress as the new understanding of Life emerged involving genesis, growth, and death; synchronicity yielded to diachronicity, status to development, and mechanics to dynamics. Young naturalists sought, in particular, to find in nature correspondences to the progressive ideas of Herder.

Accordingly, students of nature turned their attention to these newly prominent aspects of life. Genetic thought had been dominated for two centuries by the theory of pre-formation—the notion that the organism exists pre-formed in the germ and that development is nothing more than the unfolding of the pre-existent form.[18] (This mode of thought is reflected iconically in Baroque paintings in which the child is represented simply as a tiny adult or in which the unborn Jesus is exposed as a perfectly shaped small person within the Virgin's womb.) As the sense of history, temporalization, and development began to take hold, however, the idea of "epigenesis," a term originally coined by William Harvey, was revived by such German naturalists as Caspar Friedrich Wolff (*Epigenesis,* 1768) and Karl Ernst von Baer, who concluded that form emerges only gradually from the activated egg. It has been suggested persuasively that embryology was "the science in which Germany stood foremost at a time when it was behind other countries in most branches of positivistic research."[19] Simultaneously, the doctrine of recapitulation, or the so-called biogenetic law, began to take shape: the view that ontogeny recapitulates phylogeny—a biological doctrine that neatly paralleled the currently fashionable idea that the individual in his *Bildung* recapitulates the education of the entire species (e.g., Lessing's *Education of the Human Race* or Schiller's letters *On Aesthetic Education*).[20] It was this conviction that motivated Goethe's quixotic quest in the gardens of Sicily for the "Urpflanze," the primal plant that he imagined as being the Platonic model for all botanical forms and that was the subject of the conversation in Jena in 1794 that ignited his friendship with Schiller. Similarly, the desire to counter the decentralizing taxonomies of Linné and other rationalists led Goethe to his experiments in comparative anatomy, which could be understood essentially as the search for unity in the seeming disparity of animal life.

An excellent summary of contemporary thinking on these issues is contained in the "observations on morphology" that Goethe jotted down in 1794 or 1795 following conversations with the young Alexander von Humboldt.[21] Morphology—a term that Goethe coined—is concerned with organic structures: that is, those with the capability of reproducing themselves. This capability, he believes, "favors the idea of evolution." But the fact that the new being cannot be developed from the old one unless the old one has come to maturity through the consumption of nutrition, in turn, favors the idea of epigenesis. Goethe then discriminates among the various approaches to the natural world. Natural history deals with the external form of living objects and the relationship among their outwardly visible parts. Anatomy, in contrast, is concerned with the inner and outer parts of the organic body with no view to the whole. Chemistry analyzes the parts of the organic body to the extent that they have ceased to be organic or that they are regarded simply as material components. Zoonomy (roughly equivalent to physiology in the modern sense of the study of functions) deals with the whole insofar as it is alive and motivated by a special physical power. Physiology, in contrast, focuses on the living whole insofar as it is alive and informed by a spiritual power: in short, it designates the theory of life as generally inspired by a life force. Morphology, finally, considers the form in its parts and as a whole, as well as its correspondence to and deviations from other organic bodies.

This is roughly the point that thinking in natural history had reached in the decade following the French Revolution. In reaction against the differentiating taxonomies of empiricism, scientists were seeking a single unifying principle to account for "Life," which had come to be recognized as a process governed by an animating and temporal force that distinguished organized bodies of the animal and vegetable worlds from the inanimate and timeless matter of the mineral and cosmological worlds. These organic bodies of zoology and botany, studied with the techniques of physiology and morphology, were soon to be united under the common heading of biology. Historicization appeared in natural history as the temporalization of a world that had previously been understood solely in spatial terms and of a life-force that was now believed to inspirit all being.[22] If science in Germany for the next decades took a direction distinctly different from the empiricism that governed science in England and France, it was due largely to the influence of one man.

Schelling: *Naturphilosoph* as Physician

Schelling's philosophical career differed strikingly from that of his university friend Hegel or, for that matter, from the careers of Kant, Fichte, and most other thinkers of the age. In the first place, his work is marked by no single *magnum opus* such as the *Critique of Pure Reason,* the *Wissenschaftslehre* ("theory of science"), or the *Phenomenology of Spirit.* Instead, his oeuvre consists of a series of disparate essays, letters, systematic projects in paragraph form, dialogs, speeches, treatises, critiques, and lectures.[23] His productive career, despite his longevity, was almost wholly restricted to his twenties; during this time, he bounced from topic to topic with a seeming will-o'-the-wisp randomness. Beginning as a follower of Fichte, Schelling achieved sudden fame—and also notoriety—as the creator of *Naturphilosophie*; then with a quick about-face, he turned to transcendental philosophy and aesthetics, only to spend the remainder of his long life as an often ridiculed philosopher of religion and myth. It is the second stage of *Naturphilosophie,* brief but epoch-making, that concerns us here.[24]

Friedrich Wilhelm Joseph Schelling (1775–1854), like his roommates Hegel and Hölderlin, was a Swabian and a beneficiary of the renowned Swabian educational system. Born at Leonberg near Stuttgart, he spent most of his childhood just over the hill from the university town of Tübingen at Bebenhausen, where his father had become a pastor and professor at the well-known preparatory school. Having mastered Latin and Greek as a child, at age ten Schelling was sent to the Latin School in Nürtingen, but returned home two years later because he had already exhausted the educational possibilities of that institution. While only fifteen, three years before the normally permissible age, the *Wunderkind* was admitted to the university and theological Stift at Tübingen, where he shared quarters with Hegel and Hölderlin, who at that time were both five years older.

Schelling's precocious publishing career began in 1793 when he was eighteen years old and still a student. That year, his essay "On Myths, Historical Sagas, and Philosophemes of the Most Ancient World" ("Über Mythen, historische Sagen und Philosopheme der ältesten Welt") appeared in a prominent theological journal. The following year—Hegel and Hölderlin had just left Tübingen—and under the direct impact of

Fichte, whom he had met the preceding summer, Schelling published a treatise on the formal possibilities of philosophy (*Über die Möglichkeit einer Form der Philosophie überhaupt,* 1794). In 1795, having concluded his own theological studies, he brought out the work that seemed firmly to establish him as Fichte's leading disciple: *On the Ego as a Principle of Philosophy, or on the Absolute in Human Knowledge* (*Vom Ich als Prinzip der Philosophie oder über das Unbedingte im menschlichen Wissen*).

Like his friends, Hegel and Hölderlin, Schelling spent several years on the traditional career track for aspiring intellectuals. But unlike Hegel, who was isolated in a Swiss household where he read history and observed local politics, Schelling as tutor to the young barons von Riedesel accompanied his wards for two years (1796–98) to the University of Leipzig, where he undertook intensive studies in mathematics, the natural sciences (especially physics and chemistry), and medicine. With the astonishing power of assimilation that characterized his eager mind, Schelling rapidly mastered the sciences of the day, including notably the phenomena of physiology, electricity, animal magnetism, and Brunonian medicine—the system named after the genial Scotsman John Brown (1735–1788) that profoundly affected medical practice in Germany in the decade following the French Revolution.[25]

According to Brown, excitability was the fundamental property of living bodies, which when properly stimulated produced excitement (more or less equivalent to Hufeland's life-force). Health resulted from an equilibrium between stimuli and excitability. Diseases were caused by an imbalance: asthenic diseases, produced by inadequate excitement, were treated by stimulation (e.g., opium and alcohol). Sthenic diseases, resulting from overstimulation, required depletion through such means as bloodletting and purging. The center for Brunonian medicine in Germany was Bamberg, where Andreas Röschlaub, translator of Brown's *Elementa Medicinae,* and A. F. Marcus, personal physician to the bishop of Bamberg, had established a rapidly famed hospital and, beginning in 1793, lectured at the university on the popular new theory.[26] Many contemporary thinkers were convinced that Brown had identified the diseases of which the French Revolution was the historical manifestation.[27]

Captivated by his new-found passion for nature, Schelling became disenchanted with Fichte's philosophy, in which nature (Fichte's non-ego) was reduced to nothing more than a projection of the ego through its "productive imagination." It became his ambition, using his recently acquired scientific and medical ideas, to provide a new foundation for the non-ego and thereby to reestablish the balance between spirit and nature that Fichte, and before him Kant, had upset.[28] As the first stage in this process—Hegel later joked that his younger friend conducted his education in public—Schelling at age twenty-two wrote his *Ideas toward a Philosophy of Nature* (*Ideen zu einer Philosophie der Natur,* 1797), which laid the groundwork for German *Naturphilosophie*. (It was his restitution of nature to its dignity that made Schelling's *Naturphilosophie* so enormously attractive to his Romantic contemporaries.) Rejecting the mechanistic separation of mind and matter, which had prevailed at least since Descartes and down to Fichte, Schelling drew on the theories of a life-force and the ideas of Brunonianism to argue the presence of a "secret bond" that ties the human spirit to nature in an "absolute identity." Nature, he summarizes in the famous concluding sentences, "aspires to be the visible spirit and spirit the invisible nature."[29] A year later, in his "hypothesis of the higher physics in explanation of the universal organism," entitled *On the World-Soul* (*Von der Weltseele,* 1798), Schelling adduced the phenomena of galvanic electricity as introduced by his Jena friend and colleague Ritter—the stimulation of a frog's leg (visible nature) by an electrical current (invisible spirit)—to argue that "one and the same principle links anorganic and organic nature."[30] The world-soul permeates all realms of nature: dormant in the mineral world, it begins to stir in the lower organisms and finally achieves full consciousness in the human mind—a progressive process in time and history.

Schelling begins with the assumption that nature consists of two conflicting forces: a positive force that continually strives forward and a negative one that seeks to return in an eternal cycle (the counterpart in nature, it will be noted, to the linear and cyclical theories of history). These two conflicting forces yield the idea of an organizing principle that shapes the world into a system—the world-soul.[31] From this virtually electrical polarity in the world as a whole, Schelling moves to consider the origin of organisms. Arguing that the basis of life is found neither solely within nor outside animal matter, he concludes that life results from opposing principles analogous to those in nature as a whole—Life as a continuous process functioning in time. "Since this principle of continuity maintains the anorganic and the organic world," he concludes, "and ties together all of nature in one general organism, we recognize in it once again that being which the most ancient philosophy welcomed as the common soul of nature. . . ."[32]

Schelling offered the most thorough account of his thought in his *First*

Draft of a System of Nature Philosophy (*Erster Entwurf eines Systems der Naturphilosophie,* 1799), which he published as the text for his lectures at the University of Jena. In the separately published *Introduction,* he first distinguishes between a (Fichtean) transcendental philosophy, whose task it is to subordinate the real to the ideal, and the philosophy of nature, which seeks to explain the ideal on the basis of the real.[33] Both aspects, he continues, constitute one unified science and differ only in the contrary thrust of their projects. The philosophy of nature is identical with "speculative physics" ("physics" in the generous sense of the study of nature as a whole). At present, Schelling maintains, physics is a jumble of empiricism—the collection of facts, the description of observations— and science (283). It is the task of *Naturphilosophie* to separate empiricism and science after the analogy of body and soul. Empiricism is concerned with the object in its Being as something already complete; science, in contrast, observes the object in its Becoming and as something yet to be achieved. "Nature as a mere product (*natura naturata*) is called Nature as Object (with which all empiricism is concerned). Nature as productivity (*natura naturans*) is called Nature as Subject (with which all theory is concerned)" (284). In sum: the philosophy of nature focuses on a temporalized nature in its state of productivity, genesis, and development.

Following this theoretical introduction, the *Draft* proper, bringing into play all the key words of recent science, begins with a "proof that nature in its most fundamental products is organic" (section one).[34] If life, as Schelling had argued in *Von der Weltseele,* results from the productive activity of two forces, it can achieve reality (i.e., become a product) only by being slowed down ("retarded"). But this process that Schelling calls *Bildung* "occurs through epigenesis (through metamorphosis or dynamic evolution)" (61). The force in the organism that cancels out the chemical forces and laws of the material world—here Schelling sounds very much like Humboldt—must be an "immaterial principle that is rightfully called Life-Force" (79–80) and that is stimulated through its irritability (excitability) and sensibility.

Nature, then, is basically organic and only secondarily anorganic (section two). But a fundamental correspondence can be established among these two aspects. For instance, the tendency to assume a form ("Bildungstrieb") in the organic world corresponds to chemical processes in the anorganic world; excitability (irritability) to electrical processes; and sensibility to magnetism. In this manner, by using the most recent scientific findings, Schelling overcomes the perceived difference between spirit and nature and between organic and anorganic nature. "There is therefore One Organization that gradually moves through all these stages down into the plant, and One uninterruptedly efficient cause that moves from the sensibility of the highest animal down to the reproductive power of the lowliest plant" (206). Schelling concludes with observations on illness, which with his own variation of Brunonianism he divides into those of heightened sensibility and diminished irritability, on the one hand, and illnesses of diminished sensibility and heightened irritability, on the other (236). "The concept of disease, like that of life, compels us necessarily to assume a physical cause which, external to the organism, contains the reason for its excitability and indirectly through it of all the transformations that take place within it" (238).

Having thus defined the realm, scope, and task of philosophy of nature, Schelling effectively turned his back on *Naturphilosophie* and devoted his next major work to his *System des transzendentalen Idealismus* (1800) and, only two years later, moved on to the theory of aesthetics in his *Philosophy of Art* (*Philosophie der Kunst*, 1802). In the meantime, his personal life had been anything but serene. In 1798, on the recommendation of Goethe, who was greatly taken by his conception of the world-soul and his *Naturphilosophie* altogether, Schelling—now only twenty-three—was called to Jena as a professor *extraordinarius* and the younger colleague of Fichte. As a member of the lively Romantic circle in Jena, he met the literary scholar-critic August Wilhelm Schlegel and his fascinating wife Caroline, with whom he promptly fell in love. In the course of the winter 1799–1800, the circle began to fall apart. In the summer of 1799, Fichte had been compelled to leave the university because of accusations of atheism, and gradually most of the others moved away. In May 1800 Caroline decided to leave Schlegel in order to join Schelling in Bamberg, where he had taken a leave to pursue his medical studies with Marcus and Röschlaub. When Caroline's fifteen-year-old daughter Auguste suddenly died, a scandal erupted and it was (incorrectly) rumored that Schelling had caused her death by (mis)treating her according to principles of Brunonian medicine. In October, Schelling returned to Jena where he assumed Fichte's professorship. At the beginning of 1801, he was joined by his old friend Hegel, who came to Jena as a *Privatdozent* and, with Schelling, founded a new *Kritisches Journal der Philosophie*.

In the spring of 1803, Caroline obtained her divorce and married Schelling. Schelling, whose *Naturphilosophie* had undergone sharp attacks by faculty colleagues at Jena and whose marital affairs had scan-

dalized the town, decided to leave the university and accept a professorship at the University of Würzburg, from which he resigned in 1806 to become a member of the Academy of Sciences in Munich. By 1809, when
Caroline's death left him at age thirty-four in a profound depression,
Schelling's star, which had blazed so brilliantly across the academic sky,
was already in decline, almost wholly effaced by the glory of Hegel's *Phenomenology of Spirit* (1807). For the next thirty years, and in a second
marriage, he withered away, lecturing on the philosophy of mythology
and the philosophy of revelation and opening the public sessions of the
Academy with semiannual lectures. His call to the University of Berlin in
1841, where it was hoped by many conservative thinkers that he would be
able to offset the perceived baleful influence of Hegelianism, was a pa-
thetic anticlimax to his career. Although his opening lecture, almost ten
years to the day after Hegel's death, was attended by crowds including
such young intellectuals as Friedrich Engels, Søren Kierkegaard, and
Mikhail Bakunin, as well as the luminaries of city, court, and university,
it was soon apparent to all that Schelling's former oratorical flames were
extinct. Attendance rapidly dwindled, and in 1846 Schelling resigned his
professorship. When he died in 1854 in Switzerland, the death of this once
leading philosopher was barely noted.

Between Science and Medicine

This preliminary discussion of the life sciences and the philosophy of
nature is relevant for at least two reasons. In the first place, the majority
of physicians and naturalists in Germany for the next few decades were
profoundly, often passionately, committed to the notions of *Naturphilosophie.*[35] Typical of these early followers was the young Norwegian
geologist Henrik Steffens (1773–1845), who read Schelling's *Ideas toward
a Philosophy of Nature* at the time of its publication. "The introduction
to this work elevated my entire existence resiliently; it was the decisive
turning point in my life."[36] In it, he said, he sensed the first pulse-beat of
the new unified life. When Schelling's *World Soul* appeared the following
year, "the most profound hope of my whole life, to grasp nature spiritually in all its diversity, seized me and determined my activity for the rest of
my life." Steffens was in the audience when Schelling delivered his inaugural lecture at Jena in 1798 and heard the young professor speak "about
the idea of a philosophy of nature, about the necessity of grasping nature
in its unity" (104). So taken was he by Schelling's brilliance that he sought

him out the next day and spent an hour discussing science, and in particular the currently exciting ideas of galvanism—the union of electricity
and chemical process in a higher unity. Most importantly for Steffens,
"Nature and history had taken on a new significance; sounds from the
past, events and theories, poetry and art yielded up secrets to me that I
had not previously suspected" (109). It was under such immediate intellectual and personal impressions that the young geologist took it upon
himself to introduce a new element into the philosophy of nature with his
Contributions to the Inner Natural History of the Earth (*Beiträge zur in-
neren Naturgeschichte der Erde,* 1799). "All existence should become history; I called it the inner natural history of the earth. It dealt not simply
with the influence of natural objects on human affairs, through which, as
Schelling put it, they took on a genuinely historical character, speech. Man
himself should be wholly a product of nature-development. Only to the
extent that he emerged as such not merely in part but wholly, could nature
concentrate its innermost mystery in humankind" (176). Steffens concluded that "history itself had to become wholly nature if it wanted to as-
sert itself as history by means of nature, that is, in all the directions of its
existence."

While these were the sounds issuing from the new generation of German naturalists, scientists following more empirical trends in France, England, and the United States regarded those developments with suspicion
and contempt, though often without taking the trouble to understand
them. "The so-called 'Nature Philosophy' of Schelling," complained one
historian of medicine, "which aimed to establish the subjective and objective identity of all things, and the system of Hegel, which, like evolution today, regarded everything as in a state of becoming something else
(*Werden*), exerted a very baneful effect on German medicine by diverting
mental activity away from the investigation of concrete facts into the
realm of fanciful speculation."[37] But German scholars of medical history
believed at the time that the teachings of *Naturphilosophie,* "inspired by
the great and happy idea of finding all nature effective as an organic whole
. . . fertilized the art of healing with the most fortunate ideas, which bore
the most splendid fruit in disciples striving, as a natural reaction, for ex-
perimental results."[38] And following a century of neglect, the productive
aspects of *Naturphilosophie* in such diverse fields as genetics, field theory
in physics, the psychology of Freud and Jung, transcranial magnetic stimulation in psychiatry, and the *Lebensphilosophie* of Nietzsche and Hei-
degger are once again coming to be appreciated.[39]

In the second place, as Goethe observed in 1794, "all these sciences are practiced almost exclusively by physicians."[40] Obviously, Goethe himself, along with Alexander von Humboldt, represented conspicuous exceptions, but as a generalization the statement was otherwise quite valid. German medicine up to this point had been either empirical-pragmatic or, to the extent that it had any theoretical basis, determined by the ancient theory of the humors, which had been handed down ever since Hippocrates.[41] As a result, physicians in this emerging age of *Wissenschaft* responded eagerly to any approach that promised to elevate medicine to a true science. In this effort to enhance its standing, medicine began to be regarded by many of its younger practitioners as an art rather than a mere trade, and the term "Heilkunst" ("the healing art") was employed with symbolic frequency. Treviranus, for instance, maintained that biology is "the basis of the healing art."[42] The argument is founded, on the one hand, on the fact that botany, which belonged to the medical faculty, traditionally provided the materials—the so-called *materia medica*—for most pharmaceutical remedies.[43] (Certain chemotherapeutical remedies were known—e.g., mercury against syphilis; but most of the common specifics, such as quinine for malaria, tended to be herbals.) On the other hand, zoology—and increasingly the long neglected discipline (since Vesalius) of comparative anatomy—provided valuable clues to the morphology and physiology of human beings. For these reasons many aspiring young scientists, like Carl Gustav Carus, enrolled in medical faculties "because that offered the richest opportunity to remain in the most intimate contact with all the branches of nature study."[44] Similarly, Karl Ernst von Baer reports in his *Autobiography* that he decided on medicine because that faculty provided the best opportunity for an academic career in science.[45] The well-known physiologist Johann Bernhard Wilbrand wrote, in his *Human Physiology* (*Physiologie des Menschen,* 1815), that "the scientific physician [der wissenschaftliche Arzt] should always draw on experience, but he should assimilate it in the spirit of science in one and the same scientific structure."[46] Johannes Müller, one of the greatest naturalists of the era, delivered his inaugural lecture at the University of Bonn in 1822 on the topic "Physiology's Need for a Philosophical Contemplation of Nature" ("Von dem Bedürfnis der Physiologie nach einer philosophischen Naturbetrachtung"), concluding with the assertion that "physiology is no science without the intimate connection with philosophy. Medicine is no science without the beginning and end of physiology."[47] It is no accident, finally, that Lorenz Oken, one of the most influential physicians of the Romantic age and himself a professor of medicine and of natural history, founded in 1822 the joint Society of German Naturalists and Physicians (Gesellschaft Deutscher Naturforscher und Ärzte), an organization that still exists today. German medicine of the early nineteenth century simply cannot be understood without an appreciation of its close connection to the natural sciences and to Schelling's *Naturphilosophie*.[48]

No one exemplifies this synthesis better than Lorenz Oken (1779–1851).[49] The son of peasants in the Black Forest, Oken obtained a scholarship to study medicine at the University of Freiburg, where he was soon attracted to *Naturphilosophie* and was awarded his medical degree in 1804. After continuing his studies at Würzburg, where he met his idol Schelling, in 1805 he became a *Privatdozent* at Göttingen. In 1807 he was called to Jena, where the Schellingian Steffens became his colleague, as professor *extraordinarius* of medicine and, five years later, professor of natural history. In 1816 he founded the international scholarly journal *Isis,* which published articles from every field of research except theology and law—and especially on anatomy, physiology, and zoology. But in 1819, the fateful year of political reaction in Germany, because of liberal articles that he had written for *Isis,* Oken was given the option by his government of giving up either the journal or his professorship. Choosing the latter alternative, he practiced medicine privately for a time in Jena and founded the Society of Naturalists and Physicians. After a stint at the University of Basel and further five years as professor of physiology in Munich (1827–32), he returned to Switzerland and became a professor of natural history and the first rector of the newly established University of Zurich, where he taught until his death.

Oken was the leading exponent of *Naturphilosophie* in German medicine, a factor evident in his early publication on procreation, *Die Zeugung* (1805). (The obsession with genetics, a fundamentally evolutionary field, is typical of *Naturphilosophie* and its belief in the temporal development of life.) Rejecting the theory of pre-formation, Oken argued that "pregnancy is not an analytical process (of seeds or a seedling-animalcule present in the mother) but a pure synthesis of the primal animals ["Urthiere"] (the seedling-animalcules) produced by the act of procreation by means of the mother's blood.—All animals by synthesis, none by evolution."[50] It was Oken's belief, developed in this early treatise and elaborated in many subsequent works, that the entire organic world—in short, all life—is produced by primary vesicles that he calls "infusoria":

galvanic points capable of nutrition, digestion, and respiration. The coming together of such infusoria (synthesis) generates organisms epigenetically; putrefaction, by way of contrast, is simply the reduction of complex organisms to their constitutive infusoria. Accordingly, Oken ends his book with the exclamation: "Nullum Vivum ex Ovo! Omne Vivum e Vivo!" ("No life from the egg! All life from something living!")

Oken's most representative work, and the exemplary elaboration of his *Naturphilosophie,* was his three-volume *Textbook of Natural History* (*Lehrbuch der Naturgeschichte,* 1809–11), dedicated to his friends Schelling and Steffens, which displays the same bold intellectual ambition that we have seen in Herder's *Ideas* and Hegel's *Phenomenology.* (The later editions, as well as the English translation, tone down the characteristic exuberance of this product of his initial enthusiasm.) In the preface Oken expresses his hope that he will be able to reconcile its opponents with *Naturphilosophie.* Conceding that its adherents have sometimes generated a good deal of nonsense, he urges sensible naturalists to consider with respectful attentiveness the solid science underlying the theory.[51] The philosophy of nature, he explains, "is the science of the eternal transformation of God in the world" (1:vii). Its task is to display the development of the world from its initial nothingness on, showing how the elements arose and were transmuted into higher forms, eventually becoming organic and finally attaining reason in humankind.

Accordingly *Naturphilosophie* falls into three parts: "Mathesis," or the theory of the whole; "Ontology," or the theory of the parts; and "Pneumatology," or the theory of the whole in its parts. "The highest mathematical idea," he begins, "or the basic principle of all mathematics, is zero = o" (§1). "God," he continues, "is the self-conscious nothingness [das selbstbewußte Nichts]" (§3). The philosophy of nature, "insofar as it represents the genesis of the world, represents the genesis of God's thoughts. It must seek out the forms in which God thinks, and as it does this, it represents the forms of the world. The philosophy of nature is therefore in its loftiest principles theosophy" (§38). Whereas theosophy concerns the immaterial whole of being, the material whole—the nature, entelechy, and form of the aether—is the realm of what Oken calls "hylogeny." Ontology, in turn, embraces cosmogeny (the cosmic bodies), "stoechiogeny" (the characteristics and number of the elements; from Greek *stoichion,* "element"), stoechiology (the qualities of fire, air, water, and earth), geology (ore, salt, earth) and geogeny (the shape of the planets and the earth at their earliest stages of formation). "Pneumatology," finally, deals with the origins of organic life: organogeny (the origins of the organic), phytosophy (the origins of plants), and zoosophy (the origins of animals).

As the enormously prolific Oken later explained in his seven-volume *General History of Nature for All Classes* (*Allgemeine Naturgeschichte für alle Stände,* 1833–42), all life consists of the "earth-element" ("Erd-Element") mixed in various proportions with water, fire, and air through a galvanic process (magnetic, electrical, or chemical). If only one property is added to the earth-element, the result is mineral; if water and air are conjoined, plants result; and if water, air, and aether are together combined with the earth-element, the result is animal.[52] In his various works Oken exemplified the productive union of biology and medicine in the age of Romantic *Naturphilosophie*—a union that emphasized both the essential unity of all natural phenomena and the belief in development—of the cosmos, the planet earth, organic life, and humankind.[53]

Oken was far from alone in his application of *Naturphilosophie* to medicine. A work with the telling title *Elemente der Biosophie* (1807) was published by the Swiss physician with the telling name Ignaz Paul *Vital* Troxler (1780–1866).[54] Troxler, trained in the typically Romantic combination of philosophy and medicine, believed that all earlier philosophy had suffered from separating those aspects that in the childhood of humankind were one: body and soul, existence and consciousness, life and thought. In the new field of biosophy, he claimed, "science and history, which in philosophy still stand apart from each other, are brought together."[55] Another prominent scholar and teacher was Ignaz von Döllinger (1770–1841), born in Bamberg, the center of Brunonian medicine in Germany, and the son of a professor in the medical school.[56] Following medical studies at his home university where he received his doctorate in 1794, Döllinger continued his studies in Vienna and Pavia, returning to Bamberg in 1796 where he taught anatomy, physiology, and pathology until 1803. When the University of Bamberg was closed down, he moved to Würzburg as professor of anatomy and physiology and for several years was closely associated with Schelling. In 1823 Döllinger was called to Munich where he finished his career.

Döllinger's brief essay on "the history of human reproduction" ("Versuch einer Geschichte der menschlichen Zeugung," 1816) represents an attempt to synthesize the contending theories of pre-formation and epigenesis. "The assumption of a pre-existing form to which an impulse comes is the principle of evolution. The view that the impulse also gives the form is the principle of epigenesis. But both are there: before procreation, as potentiality, and at the moment of procreation, as act" (§2).[57] Otherwise his ideas are essentially compatible with those of Oken and demonstrate the fascination of German naturalist-physicians of the age with embryology. The finest statement of Döllinger's views can be found in his fragmentary *Elements of Physiology* (*Grundzüge der Physiologie,* 1836), which views life as a process of constant development from the embryo to death. As he states in the introduction, "Physiology should be a history of what happens and how it happens in the course of man's individual process of life, according to his generic character."[58]

An additional factor should be mentioned. Hitherto medicine had been taught and practiced in strict distinction from surgery, which, though it had advanced beyond the guild companies of poorly esteemed barber-surgeons of early modern times, was still taught only in military-surgical schools. (It was not until 1794 that medical schools in France were reorganized to include both medicine and surgery.) This situation began to change as physicians realized that medicine could advance only through a knowledge of the human body that was available by means of surgery, dissection, and pathology. This shift is exemplified by a close contemporary of Döllinger, Karl Friedrich Burdach (1776–1847), whose *Naturphilosophie* was focused on neuroanatomy, rather than embryology and physiology.[59] Like Döllinger, the son of a physician, Burdach began his studies at the university in his hometown of Leipzig, which he left in 1798 with a doctorate of philosophy, since Leipzig did not offer the clinical training required for a medical degree. Following further studies in Vienna with a clinician who adhered to Brunonian principles, he received his medical degree from Leipzig in 1799 and engaged in private practice for the next twelve years while writing a series of works guided by the principles of *Naturphilosophie*—notably that particular aspects of the natural world must be understood "as integral parts of a coherent whole."[60] Called in 1811 to the remote University of Dorpat as professor of anatomy, physiology, and forensic medicine, Burdach moved in 1814 to the University of Königsberg and established a Royal Institute of Anatomy, which published the results of its research in annual reports (*Berichte*).

The first of these *Berichte* (1818) contained the initial findings of Burdach's neurological studies, which were more fully and systematically treated in his three volumes "on the structure and life of the brain" (*Vom Baue und Leben des Gehirns,* 1819–20).[61] In accordance with the principles of *Naturphilosophie*—and consistent with Schelling's identity of nature and spirit—Burdach argued that only an understanding of formation and the life-force can provide knowledge of any natural entity, including the human mind. Such understanding will necessarily involve both empirical examination and theoretical reflection or, in Burdach's words, "contemplating ideas in their necessity and demonstrating them in their reality." Accordingly, he sought to prove that the nervous system is a unity and not simply "a conglomerate of various anatomical structures." Burdach neatly summed up his views in the talk "On the Task of Morphology" ("Über die Aufgabe der Morphologie") that he wrote in 1817 for the opening of the Royal Anatomical Institute in Königsberg. "This theory [the morphology of the human body] is the main pillar of the art of healing, inasmuch as otherwise it is impossible to recognize the location and nature of the disease, to understand its course, and the treat it in a manner most beneficial for the total organism."[62]

We can conclude this representative sample with Karl Ernst von Baer (1792–1876), who studied with both Döllinger and Burdach.[63] Baer was born in Estonia, the son of a modest landholder whose ancestors had emigrated from Prussia two centuries earlier. In 1810 he enrolled at the new and undistinguished University of Dorpat as a student of medicine, planning on a career in the natural sciences. When he received his medical degree in 1814, he was so dissatisfied with his training that he advised patients seeking his advice to find a qualified physician. Baer himself continued his studies at Berlin, Vienna, and Würzburg where he pursued comparative anatomy with Döllinger. In 1817 he was invited by Burdach to join his Royal Institute of Anatomy, becoming in 1819 a professor *extraordinarius*, in 1826 a full professor of zoology, and in 1828 dean of the medical faculty. While the first half of Baer's career was devoted principally to embryology, he moved to St. Petersburg in 1834 as a member of the Academy of Sciences and devoted his energies increasingly to comparative anatomy, which he also taught at the Medico-Chirurgical Academy in St. Petersburg, and to anthropology.

Despite his considerable accomplishments in anatomy, anthropology, ethnographic geography, and an astonishing variety of other fields, Baer's reputation in the history of science and medicine rests principally on his contributions to embryology, which began with his famous "epistle" on mammalian eggs and human genesis (*De ovo mammalium et hominis genesi, 1827*). Essentially, it reports on his discovery of the egg of the mammal in the ovary, a search that had begun two centuries earlier. As he explains in his German "Commentar" on the Latin original, the discovery resulted from a "lucky accident."[64] While dissecting the ovary of a bitch (actually Burdach's household pet!) with the aim of comparing its structure with the ovaries of other animals, "I saw quite by chance and with unaided eyes a little yellow body in each Graafian vesicula in this ovary which under the microscope showed itself to be an ovulum" (91). Gratified that his investigation "harmonized the contending views and the apparently contradictory observations" of other naturalists, and encouraged by his accidental finding, Baer went on to study the ovaries of sows, where he was also able to detect eggs. His studies resulted in the conclusion that "the egg of mammals is formed in the Graafian vesicula long before fertilization" (123) and that, accordingly, every animal resulting from the union of male and female is developed epigenetically from an ovum, and not from any pre-formation—a conclusion that effectively laid to rest the controversy between the pre-formationists and epigeneticists that had been raging for two centuries. He elaborated these ideas more fully in his treatise *On the Developmental History of Animals* (*Über die Entwickelungsgeschichte der Thiere*, 1828, 1837), in which he sought to explain the course of vertebrate development from conception to birth and beyond. The extent of Baer's indebtedness to *Naturphilosophie,* to which he was introduced both by Döllinger and by Burdach, has been debated.[65] Certainly the centrality of "Entwicklung" or development to his thoughts on embryology, specifically, and physiology, generally, reflects the fundamental belief in temporalization that characterizes natural philosophy and natural history after Schelling.[66] As Baer summarized in a late work (1866), "the process of life can be apprehended only in a visualization of time."[67] Indeed, what has been called "the peculiar relationship between the concepts of history and ontogeny in German Romanticism" can be traced back to Herder, whose *Ideas* are quoted by Schelling in his *Draft* and cited frequently by the naturalists of the period.[68]

Schubert: Physician as *Naturphilosoph*

When Mme de Staël passed through Dresden in June 1808 on her second journey to Germany, she was greatly impressed by a twenty-eight-year-old physician who had just achieved a spectacular popular success with a series of lectures entitled "Aspects of the Nightside of the Natural Sciences" (*Ansichten von der Nachtseite der Naturwissenschaft,* 1808). In her classic work *De l'Allemagne* (1810), the indefatigable Frenchwoman subsequently reported that "Schubert has written a book about nature which one never tires of reading, so full is it of ideas that stimulate meditation. . . . He imagines nature as an ascending metempsychosis in which, from stone to human existence, a continual escalation takes place, whereby the life-principle is elevated step by step to the highest perfection."[69] Schubert believes, she explained, that there were earlier epochs when human beings enjoyed a vital relationship to nature and understood its innermost secrets—an ability that has given way to a sickly irritability of the nerves. "The works of the philosophers, scholars, and poets in Germany have the goal of reducing the arid power of reason without in the least obscuring enlightenment. And in this way the power of imagination of the ancient world can be reborn like the phoenix from the ashes of all errors."

The object of this fulsome praise, Gotthilf Heinrich Schubert (1780–1860), was born at Hohenstein in the Saxon Erzgebirge as the youngest son of a devout but impecunious pastor.[70] Growing up close to nature, he enthusiastically collected stones, plants, and animals and liked nothing better than to descend into the bowels of the earth with the local miners. When he had exhausted the possibilities of the nearby schools, his father sent him to Weimar, at that time the center of cultural life in Germany. There he came under the influence of Herder, the superintendent and chief examiner of the Gymnasium, in whose home Schubert's Christian religiosity was strengthened.

When he graduated from the Gymnasium in 1799 and entered the University of Leipzig, he enrolled, in compliance with his father's wishes, in the faculty of theology. But the youth, whose favorite reading had long been books of science and travel, soon tired of theology and asked his father's permission to study medicine—not for its own sake but in order to be able to concern himself more intensively with the natural sciences. After a further semester in Leipzig, Schubert moved to Jena, where he became acquainted with the physicist Ritter. Above all, Schelling's lectures made an indelible impression on him and determined his future as the leading promulgator and popularizer of *Naturphilosophie*. (Schubert later dedicated his autobiography to Schelling.) In 1803 Schubert received his medical degree and, infatuated with Alexander von Humboldt's accounts of his travels, tentatively planned to accept a position in South Africa. But when he returned home to seek his father's permission, he became engaged to one of his sister's friends. Renouncing his travel plans, he became a practicing physician and settled down in nearby Altenburg, where he soon developed a thriving practice, wrote a potboiler entitled

The Church and the Gods (*Die Kirche und die Götter*), and became co-editor of the *Medicinische Annalen,* an occupation that not only provided an additional income but also kept him in touch with the most recent professional publications.

Rapidly disenchanted with his life as a small-town doctor and eager to prepare himself for a teaching position in the sciences, he gave up his practice in 1805 and relocated his family to Freiberg, where he studied at the world-famous mining academy with the mineralogist and "Neptunist" Abraham Gottlob Werner and published the first volume of his "premonitions of a general history of life" (*Ahndungen einer allgemeinen Geschichte des Lebens,* 1805).[71] In this ambitious undertaking, which he had been planning ever since his studies at Jena, he proposed to solve the major problems of life by means of *Naturphilosophie.* Because he required a larger library to continue his work (which was never completed), he moved his family again—this time to Dresden, where he lived in the house of the artist Gerhard von Kügelgen (today the Museum of Dresden Romanticism). In this center of Romanticism, where such figures as the artist Caspar David Friedrich and the dramatist Heinrich von Kleist were living and working, Schubert was invited to participate in a series of lectures for a general audience. He agreed to speak on various para-scientific topics that currently engaged public interest: e.g., animal magnetism, clairvoyance, dreams, and similar matters—fourteen lectures held by candlelight in the Palais Carlowitz in the winter of 1807–1808. His topic—"the nocturnal aspects of the natural sciences"—was clearly a play on the title of Humboldt's recent *Aspects of Nature* (1807), and the resulting book, which was enthusiastically received and required a number of editions, became one of the classics of German Romanticism.

In his introductory lecture, Schubert sets forth his intention to deal with "those nocturnal aspects of the natural sciences, which hitherto have often been neglected" (2).[72] He does so not simply in order to expose curiosities of nature, but rather in the belief that the compilation of often misunderstood phenomena can cast a light on other aspects of natural science. Accordingly, he continues, the principal objects of his presentation will be "the oldest relationship of man to nature, the living harmony of the individual with the whole, the connection of a present existence with a future higher one, and how the seed of the new future life gradually unfolds in the midst of the present one" (3). Schubert does not immediately address the "nocturnal aspects." Indeed, in its early chapters, his book bears more than a superficial resemblance to the *Ideas* of his mentor Herder.

The first lectures (lectures 2–4) deal with "the history of that period when man was still at one with nature and when the eternal harmonies and laws of nature are expressed more clearly than otherwise ever in his own being"—a childhood period that we know as the Golden Age (7). It is only at the point when man ceased to be at one with nature and when nature emerged as something external, as an object, that the history of science ceased to be inseparably linked with the history of the human race (11). The new age of dissociation began with Christianity and continued through the Middle Ages. Then, at the moment when a new art was being brought forth in pious simplicity in Italy, by Raphael and his contemporaries, "the spirit of the new nature-lore first stirred in Germany" (13). Copernicus first inspired the dormant natural sciences with the lofty spirit and sense of the new age, and then Kepler, "the greatest astronomer of all time," discovered the eternal law of the heavens and exposed the innermost sanctuary of the natural sciences (14). In the fifth and sixth lectures, accordingly, Schubert discusses the cosmos and the laws of the planetary system (physics). Returning to our planet (lecture 7), Schubert portrays the creation of the earth (following Werner's theory of Neptunism) and its chemistry. The eighth lecture deals with the origins of organic life "on the border between the animal and plant world" (17). The next three evenings are devoted to the kingdom of the plants (lecture 9), the proximations of the plant to the animal kingdom (lecture 10), and the classes of mammals (lecture 11). "Finally, when the general history of life, insofar as we are able to understand it, has been presented in a few of its aspects, it will be tentatively succeeded, in the full consciousness of its deficiencies, by an investigation into the destiny of man, the meaning of his abilities, and his past and future" (18–19).

It is not until the thirteenth lecture—"On animal magnetism and several related phenomena"—that Schubert arrives at the announced "nocturnal" aspect of his lecture-series and the medical implications of the preceding discussions. Schubert knows perfectly well, he states, "that the topics of today's lecture belong to the most objectionable and misunderstood ones and, because they are not easily explained with the usual theories, are customarily wholly denied" (326). He is referring to animal magnetism, the term applied by Anton Mesmer (1734–1815) to designate a universal force that enhanced life and that he claimed to be able to manipulate by the movement of his hands and by the influence known, since James Braid's coinage in the 1840s, as hypnotism.[73] Greeted enthusiastically at first for the sensational cures that he seemingly effected in Vienna and Paris by means of his baquets (battery-like tubs of magnetic fluid), and even the elm trees that he magnetized for larger crowds, Mesmer's treatments were discredited by the medical profession in Vienna (1778) and later by a royal commission in France (1784). Giving up his enormously lucrative practice, Mesmer eventually retired to Switzerland where he lived in seclusion, even as his teachings enjoyed a revival in Germany.

Mesmer's theory, as he stated it in his *Memoir on the Discovery of Animal Magnetism* (*Mémoire sur la découverte du magnétisme animal,* 1779), is based on the belief that there exists a mutual influence among celestial bodies, the earth, and living bodies (§1) that is controlled by a universal and continuous fluid of incomparable subtlety (§2).[74] The action and power of animal magnetism can be communicated to other animate and inanimate bodies depending on their susceptibility (§11). Both magnetism and electricity obtain their power from animal magnetism (§22). With this new knowledge physicians can determine the origin, the nature, and the progress of even the most complicated maladies (§26). Thereby the art of healing will at last reach its final perfection (§27).

Schubert acknowledges the "ridiculous exaggerations" of mesmerism's earliest disciples, but asks his audience to consider seriously the writings of "one of the most worthy magnetisers of those times" (327), J. F. R. Gmelin. He could hardly have cited a more persuasive example than that scion of the distinguished family of Swabian intellectuals. Schubert dismisses the absurd claims of mesmerism to answer metaphysical questions, to prophesy future political events, or to diagnose the illnesses of unexamined persons. But he proposes to demonstrate the valid merits of "magnetism." He reminds his listeners of the enthusiasm with which galvanism had recently been received—as "the mediator between soul and body, between nerves and muscles, and the means of healing of most diseases considered unhealable" (329). Today, even though the initial enthusiasm has dissipated, the basic phenomenon of electricity still remains. Similarly animal magnetism should not be dismissed because of the exaggerations of its early disciples.

Drawing on recent experiments, Schubert recapitulates the principal findings of animal magnetism. Sensitive and sickly persons of the other sex, especially those suffering from nervous afflictions, are especially susceptible to magnetism (hypnotism). During the period of somnambulism, which can last minutes or even hours, the patient answers questions with an unaccustomed clarity and liveliness. Upon awakening "all pains are eased, the digestion and nourishment is uncommonly heightened and improved" (333). And with longer hypnotism the patient's strength increases daily, the nervous attacks cease, and very often magnetism accomplishes what no other medical means was able to achieve. "These are the uncommonly positive effects of organic magnetism on health that have made it one of the most effective remedies" (334).

But Schubert wants to go beyond the medical effects to discuss unusual aspects of human nature that are awakened by animal magnetism. At this point he reports on various hypnotic effects—the difference between somnambulism and normal dreams, the recovery of the past, the identification with the hypnotist, and other phenomena familiar to modern psychoanalysis. The notion of identification or "sympathy" leads Schubert to speculate on the "intimate union of two human beings" made possible by means of animal magnetism—a profoundly Romantic notion (350). From this he goes on to discuss the relationship between organic and unorganic that is exposed in the somnambulist's sensitivity to various metals. He concludes with speculations on the similarity between animal magnetism and death. "Nature heals such otherwise untreatable diseases, which respond only to magnetism, through death and thus, through a total transformation, restores the lost inner harmony to the diseased human nature" (357).

In the fourteenth and final lecture, Schubert returns to the Romantic notion of the fundamental unity of all being that is unconsciously present in all of us. The facts presented, he argues, prove "that all individual, independently inspirited beings are connected among themselves and with the Whole in precisely such an intimate pre-established harmony, where the same life is completed simultaneously in all, without the need for one to be determined by another, like the separate parts of a living organic body" (367). When the greater whole is threatened by disease or some other significant alteration of its nature, the disposition to the malady develops simultaneously in all its individual parts—sooner in some and later in others; in some as a minor symptom and in others as the main character of the disease. "In this manner certain natural changes, which manifest themselves to the senses mainly in the atmosphere and changes in the weather, are independently prepared in all living beings." The same "life spirit" that produces alterations in external nature also inhabits all individual organic beings and produces in them, according to the same laws of succession, corresponding changes. Less perfect, and hence more sensitive organs experience such changes sooner, a fact that accounts for the remarkable precognitive dreams experienced by certain somnambulists

(369). "The lofty ideal of human nature is not wholly expressed in any single individual but is perfected only through all individuals—indeed through the separate ages of the world, in the great work of history. Only the genius who watches over the destinies of individuals as well as the history of the entire race, will bring together into spiritual harmony the manifold and often conflicting efforts of the different times" (380). Eventually the human race will return to "the sacred innocence and lofty perfection of all its powers" that it enjoyed at the beginning of its history (384).

Schubert's lectures, which trace the history of humankind in a grand Romantic arc from unity through alienation and back again, mark the high point of his career, which continued productively for fifty more years. In 1809 he moved to Nürnberg as director of a newly established secondary school and remained there—despite a call to the University of Berlin—until the school was suspended in 1816. Following a period as tutor to the family of the duke of Mecklenburg-Schwerin, he accepted an appointment as professor of natural history at the University of Erlangen, where he taught the traditional triplicity—mineralogy, zoology, and botany—until 1827, when he moved to Munich. There, apart from frequent journeys throughout Europe and the Middle East, he remained for the rest of his life. The prolific author wrote many more volumes, including works on mining, mineralogy, cosmology, and psychology as well as accounts of his travels and a three-volume autobiography. But only one further work after his *Aspects* had a lasting influence: *The Symbolism of Dreams* (*Die Symbolik des Traumes,* 1814), in which he elaborated his ideas concerning the patient's access to past and future and to distant realms while in the hypnotic state. (Schubert's work was cited appreciatively almost a century later, in 1900, by Freud in his *Interpretation of Dreams*).

Unlike Oken, von Baer, Döllinger, and other Romantic physicians, Schubert had little influence on the sciences of his day. He was not a specialist who contributed through his own research, but a generalist whose strength lay in the synthesizing assimilation and skillful popularization of others' work. But his *Aspects of the Nightside of the Natural Sciences* had a profound and lasting impact on his Romantic contemporaries and throughout the nineteenth century. His ideas on animal magnetism provided the theory motivating the heroines of Kleist's drama *Käthchen von Heilbronn* as well as Wagner's *The Flying Dutchman.* And his examples provided the material for E. T. A. Hoffmann's tale "Die Bergwerke zu Falun: ("The Mines of Falun," 1819) as well as Hugo von Hofmannsthal's drama on the same theme (1899). For our purposes, however, the main significance of the work lies in its effort to link the theories of *Naturphilosophie* and animal magnetism to medical diagnosis and healing.

Carus and Medical Studies around 1810

One of the most remarkable heirs of German Romanticism and one of the last "Universalgenies" in a century of increasing specialization was Carl Gustav Carus (1789–1869). Known in literary history as a friend, correspondent, and biographer of the older Goethe (*Göthe,* 1843) and acquainted with many of the leading writers and scholars of his day— among them Alexander von Humboldt and Ludwig Tieck—Carus also has a place in every history of German Romantic art as a companion of Caspar David Friedrich, as an accomplished painter of Romantic landscapes, and as a theoretician in his *Nine Letters on Landscape Painting* (*Neun Briefe über Landschaftsmalerei,* 1831). As a natural scientist and physician, he wrote an epoch-making textbook of comparative anatomy (*Lehrbuch der Zootomie,* 1818), the first systematic textbook of gynecology (1820), and many other scientific and medical works. His *Psyche* (1846)—which begins with the statement that "The key to the understanding of the nature of the conscious life of the soul lies in the region of the unconscious"—constitutes a landmark in the history of psychology, whose significance is repeatedly cited by C. G. Jung.[75] For our purposes, however, it is his autobiography (*Lebenserinnerungen und Denkwürdigkeiten,* 1865–66), a veritable cultural history of the era, that is relevant for its account of medical studies in the first decade of the nineteenth century in Germany. Carus's education very precisely reflects the development of the various ideas that we have been discussing.

Carus, the son of a master dyer, was born in Leipzig in the Revolutionary year and precisely at the moment when "the natural sciences and especially chemistry were awakened to new life in France and, along with the first storms of the Revolution, transported to other lands and specifically to Germany" (18).[76] Exposed at an early age by various family members to these sciences, he became an ardent botanist. His artistic talent showed up while he was a student in the Thomas Gymnasium in Leipzig, and he received private drawing lessons from Julius Dietz and later from Veit Hans Schnorr, the father of the Romantic artist Julius Schnorr von Carolsfeld, and from Johann Friedrich Tischbein, the director of the Leipzig Art Academy.

In 1804 he began his studies at the University of Leipzig, initially in the sciences—chemistry, physics, and especially botany. It was his father's plan that his son would eventually take over the family dye-works, but the idea of deserting "the forecourts of science" for factory work failed to appeal to the ambitious young man, who devoted himself increasingly to his scientific studies and to his art, which provided him with a useful tool for the required drawings of plants, animals, and geological formations. Two years passed happily in this manner, as Carus added to his herbaria and explored the countryside for his drawings. Only chemistry, which was taught in a shallow and wholly pharmaceutical manner, attracted him less and less. When his parents pressed him to make a decision regarding his future, he concluded that the profession of physician was the most desirable, because it offered the best opportunity to remain in touch with all branches of the natural sciences. He was also impressed, when he consulted his relative Friedrich August Carus, who was a professor of philosophy and psychology at the university, by the consideration that "This science is still so little closed off and completed that one may entertain considerable hope that it will be possible to discover much that is new, to improve much that is old, and to expose many an undiscovered truth" (52).

In order to compensate for deficiencies in his preparation—he had neglected the humanities in school—Carus had to devote himself to the classical languages and mathematics before he was qualified in 1806 to undertake the medical curriculum and begin the study of anatomy, a field that instantly appealed to him. "I dissected animals eagerly and sought to acquire them in any way possible" (61), carrying home the bodies of smaller dead animals or having larger ones brought along by servants. It was with a particular *frisson* of excitement, he recalls, that he entered the anatomical hall in the winter of 1807–08 and first dissected human corpses—an occupation that he pursued at every possible opportunity, filling pages of his notebooks with detailed drawings of his dissections. He was less attracted by physiology, "the theory of life itself" (62), which was abominably taught. While continuing his work in botany, mineralogy, and chemistry, he was introduced to the medical subjects of pathology, theory of medicaments, and therapy. In this connection, he singles out two of his teachers: Burdach, whose writings more than his lectures gave him an insight into the possibilities of physiology at its best; and J. C. F. A. Heinroth, professor of anthropology and psychiatry, whose personality exposed the philosophical dimensions of medical science.

Carus is frank about the deficiencies of medical education during his student years. "The inadequacy and the half hazily crude, half dryly abstract nature of physiology at that time was felt with full force also in pathology" (64). Instead of satisfying young minds with concrete details, the teachers preferred to construct abstract concepts. "We were tormented with irritability, sensibility, and reproduction [that is, Brunonian theory] and the division of diseases according to these factors, long before we knew how a cell arose, how a nerve reacted, and how a fibre constricted" (64). The natural sciences, he continues, would not have engaged his mind to such an extent had they not been revitalized at the time by a new movement and principle. "It was the principle of *a higher unity,* emerging in the light of *Naturphilosophie* that was just asserting its validity" (64). Earlier science, he reminds us, had been content with such encyclopedic compendia as Jan Swammerdam's seventeenth-century *Bible of Nature,* a history of insect life translated into German in 1752. Linné sought to create a certain order from this diversity and to organize it in a manner comprehensible to the thoughtful mind. Yet Linné's system lacked a higher intellectual principle—a principle ordering the universe into a single organic whole that was first provided by Schelling's conception of the world-soul. "In a remarkable manner this thought resounded simultaneously in many spirits, as often happens when humanity lies in labor and a great new idea is summoned to be born" (66). Like Schubert before him, Carus is fully aware of the exaggerations and distortions to which Schelling's ideas were subjected. "But among those who stepped up to the altar of Isis as worthy priests of the new era one man towered above with regard to the natural sciences: Oken." Carus met him in person twenty years later but Oken's spirit gripped and stimulated the young student already at that time. "He was the first who dared to introduce a single center-point into the chaotic diversity of natural forms and facts, a single new enlivening principle, and this principle was *genetic,* the principle of development" (66–67).

Years later Carus reflected: "What contemplation of the soul is more fruitful than the genetic? What is more instructive than the history of the development of man?" (127). For the moment, however, he completed his medical studies and in 1809 served as an intern in St.-Jacobs-Hospital in Leipzig, where he worked under the supervision of J. C. G. Joerg, one of the founders of modern gynecology. In the spring of 1811 he received the degrees of Magister liberalium artium and Doctor philosophiae from the University of Leipzig. The following fall he presented himself for the Magister legens (authorization to lecture at the university) with a dissertation under the title of "Specimen biologiae generalis" ("Draft of a general theory of life")—a clear reference to the *vis vitalis* of *Naturphilosophie*. That semester he began giving lectures on comparative anatomy, a subject not hitherto taught at Leipzig. And in December of 1811, he received his medical degree with a thesis on rheumatic inflammations of the musculature of the womb—an outcome of his studies in genetics and obstetrics. Recapitulating his medical education, then, we see that Carus experienced the critical moment when Brunonian theory and empiricism gave way to a medicine inspired by life-force and genetics and when "pure" medicine was supplemented by comparative anatomy, surgery, and obstetrics.

In 1814 Carus moved his young family to Dresden where he was appointed professor of obstetrics and where, for all his travels and growing fame, he remained until his death in 1869. Despite his many literary, artistic, and scientific interests and undertakings, Carus, unlike Schubert, remained throughout his entire life a dedicated physician, becoming personal physician to the king of Saxony, and an active and widely honored member of the medical profession in Germany. From the beginning, he writes, he regarded the calling of physician in a lofty sense: "the approximation of the art of healing ["Heilkunst"] to the priesthood" in the classical Greek sense (78).

If Carus's early career reflects the gradually shifting nature of medical education in Germany during the first decade of the nineteenth century in response to new developments—notably *Naturphilosophie* and the concept of genetic evolution— those developments are evident in a more formal-academic manner in the medical curriculum of the new University of Berlin, which opened in 1810 and to which Humboldt had succeeded in attracting a large and distinguished medical faculty.[77] In order to appreciate how well-rounded it was, we must remind ourselves that earlier faculties had been not only smaller; they also tended to be either wholly empirical or single-mindedly theoretical, like Bamberg with its Brunonian focus. As we have seen, medicine around 1800 was occasionally viewed as so theoretical a subject that it was practiced by philosophers with no formal medical training or degree, such as Schelling and Steffens. In addition, most medical schools taught nothing but "pure" medicine with no surgery, which was left either to the barbers or to military surgeons, who in turn were not permitted to practice medicine; and no obstetrics, which was left to the midwives.[78] In Berlin the university was able to draw on the strengths both of the Charité Hospital and of the special schools of military and even veterinary surgery.

Among the six *ordinarii* or full professors active in that first semester of 1810, Christoph Wilhelm Hufeland (1762–1836) taught *materia medica*— a subject for which he was well equipped from his first years as a physician in Weimar, when he had to prepare his own potions, powders, and pills[79]—and basic medicine (*practicam medendi artem*). (Hufeland, who as chief physician at the Charité first instituted a polyclinic for medical instruction and introduced public vaccination into Prussia, also became the first dean of the medical faculty.) Johann Christian Reil (1759–1813) arrived from Halle to teach pathology and psychology. Karl Ferdinand von Graefe (1787–1840), professor of surgery and ophthalmology—and the first plastic surgeon in Germany—lectured on surgery and obstetrics. Professor of physiology Horkel offered physiology and "metamorphoses" (that is, transformations and degeneration) of the heart. Christoph Knape (1747–1831), a professor of anatomy who came from the Collegium Medico-Chirurgicum in Berlin, taught osteology, "syndesmology" (medicine of the ligaments), and "splanchnology" (medicine of the viscera). Karl Asmund Rudolphi (1771–1832), a professor of anatomy and director of the Anatomical Institute (with substantial accomplishments in botany [the Leguminosae "Rudolphia"], veterinary medicine, and the history of medicine), taught the basic survey and methodology of medicine, as well as anatomy: human (in the anatomical theater), comparative, and pathological. All the professors, in addition, conducted clinical exercises in their specialties in the clinic of Charité Hospital.

In addition to the full professors, Gottfried Christian Reich (1769–1848), professor *extraordinarius* of pathology and therapy and known especially for his work on scarlet fever and cholera, taught "pyretology" or the principles of fever, which was still considered a disease in itself and not a symptom. (The prevalence of typhus and other febrile conditions— e.g., the European epidemics of yellow fever in 1803–04 and of typhus in 1805–06—accounted for the lively interest.) And seven *Privatim docentes* supplemented these offerings with courses on surgical instruments, obstetrics, veterinary medicine, and toxicology. Two of these are especially noteworthy. A. L. E. Horn (1774–1848) was a neurologist who first taught systematic psychiatry in Germany; in his function as director of the clinical institute at Charité Hospital as well as professor at the Pépinière (medical training institute for the military) he was notorious for his purely physiological diagnoses and treatments, which frequently involved him in disputes with colleagues; he taught clinical medicine and nosology. Karl Christian Wolfart (1778–1832), an enthusiastic disciple of Mesmer and animal magnetism, taught "semiotics" (symptomology) and *formulare* (medical prescriptions). (Since Wolfart was a personal friend of Schleiermacher, Savigny, and Wilhelm von Humboldt, in 1817 and over the objections of the medical faculty, he was appointed to the newly established chair of "Healing Magnetism." Carus witnessed—with a certain ambivalence—some of his treatments.)

If we pause to summarize this rich variety, supplemented in following semesters by other courses, we note immediately that almost every facet of contemporary medical practice and theory is represented. The faculty, comprising physicians at the peak of their careers, combined traditional medicine with the surgical, pharmaceutical, and obstetrical skills that had traditionally been practiced separately. Both *Naturphilosophie* and mesmerism were represented, respectively, by Hufeland and Wolfart. Physiology in the modern sense as a science of life was paralleled by the new field of comparative anatomy. In sum, the students enrolled in the medical faculty—and in that first semester they accounted for almost half of the 256 registered students—were exposed to the full spectrum of contemporary medical knowledge, most of it (physiology, obstetrics/genetics, psychology, comparative anatomy) informed by the new sense of temporalization generated by *Naturphilosophie* and professed by several of the leaders of modern medical science. This was consistent with the convictions of Hufeland, who as dean of the medical faculty insisted on a well-rounded education for medical students—a *Bildung* including philosophy and ethics.[80] It should be mentioned, finally, that Hufeland's initiatives in pediatrics and gerontology reflect his Romantic awareness of human development through time, from childhood to old age, and the accompanying belief in new needs and approaches to human health and medical treatment.

One further symptom of the early nineteenth-century temporalization-historicization of medicine needs to be mentioned. In that first semester at the University of Berlin, professor *extraordinarius* Reich offered "to those who wished it" (*desiderantibus*) a course on the history of medicine (*historiam medicinae*)—a subject not customarily provided by medical faculties. There had of course been earlier treatments, such as the five-volume *Pragmatic History of Medicine* (*Versuch einer pragmatis-*

chen Geschichte der Arzneikunde, 1792–99) by Kurt Sprengel (1766–1833), known as the father of medical history (who subsequently turned away from medicine to botany to write his *Historia rei herbariae,* 1807–08). But Sprengel's pragmatic history was vitiated by its critical impatience with divergent approaches. It was only in response to the new sense of history that coherent histories of medicine began to be written.[81] One rather idiosyncratic system was developed by K. J. H. Windischmann (1775–1839), who after studying medicine and philosophy—that typical Romantic combination—became a professor at Aschaffenburg and, after its founding in 1818, at the University of Bonn. Influenced first by Schelling's *Naturphilosophie* and then by Hegelianism, which he accommodated to his devout Catholicism, he argued in a series of books—e.g., *On the Self-Destruction of Time and the Hope of Rebirth* (*Von der Selbstvernichtung der Zeit und der Hoffnung der Wiedergeburt,* 1807), *Essay on the Progress of Education in the Healing Art* (*Versuch über den Gang der Bildung in der heilenden Kunst,* 1809), and *Some Needs of the Art of Healing: An Attempt to Combine this Art with Philosophy* (*Über Etwas, das der Heilkunst noththut,* 1824)—that human spiritual development is tantamount to the healing process of fallen humanity. Diseases are living organisms that change in the course of time along with the phylum in which they thrive and on which they are dependent. Just as there are diseases characteristic of childhood, youth, maturity, and old age, so too there are diseases of humanity in its various epochs.[82] If one better understood the history of the diseases, the progress and age of the human race could be precisely determined. Windischmann believed that humanity was presently entering the dangerous period of maturity, for its diseases distinguished themselves generally from those of earlier ages by their frequently irritable character, which produces diseases of the brain and nervous system. "The history of human suffering enters more profoundly into the depths of life, and so the art of healing must also go more into the inner being." Another Schellingian, the Jena psychiatrist Dietrich Georg Kieser, published a general *System der Medizin* (1817) to which he prefaced a brief survey of the history of medicine.[83] Hufeland, who had included a brief history of "the science of the life-power" in his *Makrobiotik,* later published a short *History of Health* (*Geschichte der Gesundheit,* 1813), which is based on the ideas of Herder, whom he had known during his boyhood and early professional life in Weimar. "Like every individual, so too the life of humanity as a whole has its striving and its destiny, its development, periods, blossoms, and transformations produced from within."[84] And Friedrich Schnurrer's well-regarded two-volume *Worldwide Chronicle of the Plagues* (*Chronik der Seuchen*) was published in 1823–24.

While all these works show the influence of the new sense of history, the first proper—that is, non-chronicling—*Universal History of Medicine* (*Allgemeine Geschichte der Heilkunde*, 1827) was published by J. M. Leupoldt, professor at the University of Erlangen, who sought to bring together the two prevailing trends in medicine, empiricism and theory, without rejecting the useful contributions of either.[85] According to Leupoldt, what was lacking in earlier histories of medicine was precisely any understanding of the idea of development—of the human race as well as nature generally. Thoughtful people will soon be persuaded, he argues, that no aspect of the history of medicine can be excluded from general history—not only the systems of schools and sects of medicine and of individual physicians of every age, but also the diseases peculiar to the various ages and regions of the earth, along with their causes and origin. "All this is vitally connected and made fertile by the disclosure of the idea of an organically systematic development of the human race and the external nature nurturing it."[86]

Four years later, Heinrich Damerow, Hegel's colleague in Berlin, published his *Elements of the Immediate Future of Medicine* (*Elemente der nächsten Zukunft der Medizin*, 1829), in which he argued: "The more scientific the history of medicine becomes, the more closely connected it is with nature, where alone it finds its truth. The philosophy of the history of medicine is its harmony with the laws of natural development. The history of medicine's scientific development is the true natural history of medicine. One law prevails in both."[87] He continues, "the scientific history of medicine does not seek to force a spirit into itself; rather, it seeks to fetch forth the inherent spirit and become aware of it." Ludwig Hermann Friedländer also proceeds from *Naturphilosophie* and its theory of development in his lectures on the history of medicine at the University of Halle, which were published in 1839. He portrays the art of healing as "a science that shapes itself organically and periodically and in which especially the human spirit strives to reveal its agreement with nature."[88]

By 1848, when Eduard Morwitz brought out his *History of Medicine* (*Geschichte der Medicin*), which surveys the art of healing from its primal beginnings by way of its first scientific grounding by the Greeks and down to the end of the eighteenth century, the history of medicine had emerged in a recognizably modern form. This development, based on the understanding of nature as evolution and human growth as genetic, was made possible only by the new sense of history that emerged with Herder, that was elaborated by *Naturphilosophie,* that was placed at the center of intellectual endeavors by Hegel, and that made its way into medical science thanks to the efforts of many Romantic scientists and physicians.

CONCLUSION

Connections

Personal relations among the advocates of the new sense of history at the University of Berlin, at least during the first few years, were cordial. Niebuhr, Schleiermacher, Savigny, and Hufeland were all among the thirty-some members of the Academy of Sciences and participated actively in its programs and events. Niebuhr and Schleiermacher both belonged to several other societies, notably the "Graeca," a small group that met weekly to share their interests in classical studies, and "The Lawless Club," a biweekly social gathering that came together in a local restaurant to discuss scientific and intellectual topics.[1] Savigny, a highly reserved and private person, held himself aloof from the purely social groups. But he maintained friendly relations with Schleiermacher and most of his university colleagues, with many of whom he worked closely on various committees and commissions—and whose respect motivated them to elect him, following Fichte, as the second rector of the university. He enjoyed a collegial and reciprocally productive relationship in the faculty of law with Eichhorn. He was particularly close to Niebuhr, as we have noted, and the two families usually visited each other every week.[2] In addition, Savigny was familiar with the works of Schubert, saying that there was no other contemporary writer "whom on the basis of his writings I have come to like so well personally without ever having seen him."[3] (In the course of a trip to Hamburg in 1817 Savigny made a point of visiting Schubert, who had recently declined an appointment to the University of Berlin and was now tutor to the family of the Duke of Mecklenburg-Schwerin in the residence at Ludwigslust.) In sum, there is every reason to imagine that a lively and productive exchange of ideas took place initially among the leading representatives of historicization.

This had changed by the time Hegel arrived in 1818. Reil had died in the typhus epidemic of 1813–14. Niebuhr had left in 1816 to become special envoy to the Vatican in Rome where he spent the next six years. And in 1817 Eichhorn followed the call to Göttingen. Hegel, the most prominent living philosopher in Germany, was called to the University of Berlin without prior faculty consultation by the Prussian minister of education, Karl von Altenstein, to assume the chair vacant since Fichte died of typhus in 1814. Schleiermacher, a skeptic regarding all "speculative philosophy," was lukewarm about Hegel's appointment from the start,[4] and the philosopher's behavior succeeded further in antagonizing even the normally sociable theologian. Hegel disparaged Schleiermacher publicly in his lectures, going so far as to call the popular preacher a "demagogue."[5] Hegel went even further in the "Preface" (1822) that he wrote for the history of religion by H. F. W. Hinrichs, Hegel's student. Criticizing Schleiermacher's notion of religion as a feeling of dependence upon God, Hegel reasoned that in that case a dog would be the best Christian, because it feels so keenly dependent upon its master and experiences redemption whenever its hunger is satisfied by a bone.[6] As a result, until Hegel's death in 1831, Schleiermacher succeeded in blocking his appointment to the Academy of Sciences—even at the end, when Hegel was rector of the university.

Savigny was also opposed to Hegel's appointment and joined Schleiermacher in blackballing the philosopher in the Academy. Hegel paid him back in kind when, in his lectures, he accused Savigny of insulting both the German people and the legal profession by saying they were not yet mature enough to codify their own laws. Savigny soon came to lament what he regarded as the pernicious influence of the mushrooming school of Hegelian philosophy, saying that the conceit and arrogance of his disciples were worse even than formerly among Fichte's followers, who were at least restrained to a degree by the vigorous spirit of the man himself.[7]

> What I object to about Hegel is not merely his high-handed and superficial condemnation of many fields of knowledge unknown to him . . . but that the same conceit extends to everything in the world, so that his zealous students even renounce all religious connections . . . ; further, his thoroughly distorted, wrong-headed, confused conduct and speech in all non-scholarly matters, especially in the rather complicated relations of the university to the government, about which all the other professors are of one voice.[8]

It was this deteriorating situation at the university that eventually prompted Savigny to give up the teaching to which he had hitherto committed himself so wholeheartedly.

Common Themes

The unfortunate personal dissensions are all the more regrettable since, in hindsight at least, the generational similarities among Hegel and his colleagues in Berlin are conspicuous enough to outweigh such differences as Hegel's rejection of positivism in religion and law. We have already noted the striking parallels between Hegel's *Phenomenology* and the works of his Romantic contemporaries, as well as their common source in Herder. All of them were aware that the French Revolution and the equally consequential industrial and epistemological revolutions had brought Germany to a turning point in its history. Hegel, in his farewell lecture to the students at Jena in 1806 and in the preface to the *Phenomenology,* advised them that the age was a time of rebirth and transition to a new era. Niebuhr's keen awareness of Prussia's humiliation gave him a feeling of kinship in his historical project with Tacitus. A few years earlier Schleiermacher had concluded his addresses *On Religion* with the observation that the present-day marked the boundary between two different orders of things. Savigny opened his pamphlet on codification with the remark that "the historical sense has awakened everywhere" in the wake of the Napoleonic wars. Eichhorn prefaced his history of German law with an appeal to history in the face of moral and legal uncertainties. And Schubert began his Dresden lectures in 1807–08 with a reference to "this significant condition of the natural sciences today, the looking-forth on every side from their midst of a new age" (15). This idea, as we have seen, belonged to the shared convictions of the day, transcending any difference of opinion regarding the transforming power: e.g., Hegel's belief in the "great man" (the "world-soul on horseback") versus Savigny's faith in the *Volksgeist.*

The belief that they were living in a new epoch was by no means limited to the political realm. The age required a reappraisal of all human knowledge, which was now understood to constitute a unified whole in contrast to the discrete taxonomies of the earlier polymath encyclopedism. It was this conviction that inspired the awesomely ambitious projects undertaken between Herder's *Ideas* (1784) and Savigny's *History of Roman Law in the Middle Ages* (1815) and including Hegel's *Phenomenology,* Schleiermacher's *On Religion,* Oken's *Textbook of Natural History,* and Schubert's

Aspects of the Nightside of the Natural Sciences—vast projects that aspired to encompass all human knowledge extending, in some cases, from the creation of the universe to current events and in all cases embracing the breadth of human culture. The same impulse manifested itself in the new passion for comparison in such emerging fields as "comparative" anatomy, literature, philology, religion, sociology, and others.[9]

Whether the individual author believed that the unifying center of this entity was philosophy, religion, law, or biology receded in significance before the shared view that human knowledge constitutes a vital whole. That whole, in turn, could be grasped in its totality only through a twofold approach employing both history and system, diachrony and synchrony. Hegel's *Phenomenology* is based implicitly on this premise: the systematic analysis of developments within each of his three historical braids. Oken's *Textbook* and Schubert's *Aspects* trace the history of humankind through a systematic analysis of the relationship between man and nature in each historical phase. Savigny in his early "methodology" instructed his students that any proper approach to law used both "history" and "system" to organize texts made accessible by "interpretation." His life-work, culminating in his *history* of Roman law in the Middle Ages and his later *system* of Roman law, exemplified that theory. Schleiermacher had a similar message for his students in his *Brief Outline,* which divided theology into the trilogy of philosophical, historical, and practical theology, a combination underlying his Christological *magnum opus, The Christian Faith according to the Principles of the Evangelical Church* (*Der christliche Glaube nach den Grundsätzen der evangelischen Kirche,* 1821–22), which justifies the *dogma* of the Christian *community* on the basis of the life of the *historical* Jesus.

"History" did not have for these Romantic historicizers the same meaning that it had held for earlier generations—the "elegant" and "universal" and "pragmatic" historians. Indeed, they regarded it as their principal challenge to rid history of the accretions that in their opinion had obscured and deformed it over the course of time. Niebuhr impressed his contemporaries by the then novel approach of going directly to the sources, rather than to secondary accounts, in order to get back to the origins of Roman history. Savigny found it imperative to separate the original Roman law from the *usus modernus pandectarum* that had arisen around it since the late Middle Ages through the assimilation of bits and pieces from canon law, Germanic common law, and the commentaries of the Italian *glossatores.* Schleiermacher informed his skeptical audience of modern intellectuals that the "religion" of which they were so contemptuous was not true religion at all but the product of almost two thousand years of (mis)interpretation for the benefit of various churches and sects; he proposed to acquaint them with religion in its original, pre-institutionalized form. Hegel believed that no one before him had understood and properly analyzed the history of human consciousness and spirit. Schubert proposed to get back past the analytical detachment of Enlightenment science to the original unity binding man with nature.

The means by which they sought to accomplish this return to the past was hermeneutics. As Schleiermacher defined it for his students in 1810, every text must be understood in the context from which it emerged and in the circumstances governing the lives of its authors and their audiences. "All understanding of the specific is qualified by an understanding of the whole." This is precisely identical with "interpretation" as Savigny expounded it in his "methodology": "Interpretation = reconstruction of the law." The exegete must put himself into the place of the original legislator and imagine all the factors that qualified the promulgation of the law in the first place. While Niebuhr never made such an explicit methodological statement, his approach is clearly identical with that of his friends. In his demythification of Roman history, he went back to the sources—documents, institutions, songs, annals—and sought to understand them in the context of early Roman life even in its most mundane aspects. Hegel's history of spirit is based on an analysis of the different "phenomena" it manifests over time in response to historical circumstances and stimuli.

Once the ground has been cleared and the sources exposed, the next step is to retrace the history of the various subjects—philosophy, theology, law, nature, or humankind—within the context of a unified knowledge and employing the method adumbrated by the new mode-word "genetic." The concept had been known since at least 1651 when Harvey coined the term "epigenesis." The vocable "genetic" (*genetisch*) was first naturalized in the field of embryology, in which German science was pre-eminent during the late eighteenth and early nineteenth century. It was quickly adopted by colleagues in other disciplines who appreciated its appropriateness for their own projects: e.g., Herder, who labeled one of the chapters of his *Ideas* "Genetic Power as the Mother of All Formations on Earth" (bk. 7, chap. 4); Savigny, who in 1802–03 introduced the term "genetic" into his lectures on methodology; and Carus, who advocated a "genetic" contemplation of the human soul. But whether a particular writer used the term or not, the method was clearly genetic and evolutionary when Hegel was tracing the history of spirit, Schleiermacher the growth of religion, Savigny the development of law, or such *Naturphilosophen* as Oken, Burdach, Baer, and Schubert the genesis of the earth, of humankind, and the individual embryo.

The historicization of the faculties proceeded apace, notably after 1815, as new chairs for history began to be established at most universities.[10] The same impetus produced the first history of historiography, Ludwig Wachler's two-volume *History of the Art of History and its Investigation since the Reestablishment of Literary Culture in Europe* (*Geschichte der historischen Forschung und Kunst seit der Wiederherstellung der literarischen Cultur in Europa,* 1812–20).[11] Another academic outgrowth of the turn to history was the vast project of the *Monumenta Germaniae Historica.* Already in 1814 Savigny had broached to Jakob Grimm his dream of "a large German society for the investigation of German history."[12] Savigny was keenly aware of the importance of documentary evidence as the result of the ten years he had spent collecting material for his history of Roman law. He realized that the Academy of Sciences, which had already committed itself to the edition of all Greek inscriptions from classical antiquity—the *Corpus Inscriptionum Graecarum,* edited by August Boeckh (1828–77)—, would be the appropriate body to organize and fund such a huge and necessarily cooperative undertaking. Among his Berlin colleagues he gained the immediate agreement of Eichhorn, Niebuhr, and others including the influential minister Karl von Altenstein. Knowing that such a long-term national project required the support of a major public figure, he submitted his proposal through an intermediary to the former Prussian chancellor, the respected Baron Karl von Stein, who was easily persuaded of its validity. When Eichhorn and Niebuhr left Berlin, taking with them much of the enthusiasm that had motivated the Academy, Stein took over the initiative and the financial leadership, establishing in 1819 a Society for Older German Historiography (*Gesellschaft für ältere deutsche Geschichtskunde*). Under its auspices the first volume of the monumental project, edited by G. H. Pertz (1795–1876), appeared in 1826. Even the tyranny of positivism in the second half of the nineteenth century could not eradicate the awareness of history that had by now gained a firm place in every faculty.

Extracurricular Activities

In addition to developments within the universities and academies, the process of historicizing went on in fields not yet included within the four faculties. In art history, Carl Friedrich von Rumohr (1785–1843)—renowned to a large international audience for his speculative study of the culinary arts *The Spirit of Cooking (Der Geist der Kochkunst,* 1823)— published a three-volume account of the first-hand research he had carried out in Italy, *Italienische Forschungen* (1827–31). This landmark oeuvre, while in one sense the last of the great amateur-aestheticizing works in the tradition of the post-Winckelmann era, overcame the classicist disdain of medieval art and opened the era of modern art histories.[13]

Rumohr, in turn, was chief consultant for the Altes Museum, the architectural masterpiece that Karl Friedrich Schinkel (1781–1841) was erecting in the Lustgarten directly across from the palace and adjacent to the cathedral, thereby making an architectural statement about the equality of church, state, and culture.[14] Thanks to Rumohr, the Altes Museum, which opened in 1830, became the first museum to renounce the practice of other European collections, which arranged paintings according to such random principles as symmetry, date of acquisition, subject matter, and others. The Berlin museum, consistent with the new sense of history being expounded just a few steps away on Unter den Linden in the university and the Academy, organized its collection in a loosely historical sequence and in a manner intended to illustrate the development of art over the centuries. Schinkel's passion for history is manifested both in his architectural designs and in his paintings. The museum, according to admirers from Mies van der Rohe to Philip Johnson, is perhaps the principal monument of neoclassical architecture in Europe, featuring an imposing frontal colonnade of eighteen Ionic columns and a great domed central rotunda, a design widely imitated in Europe and the United States. Schinkel's paintings— e.g., the paired vistas of a Greek and a medieval German city, painted in 1815 to celebrate the end of the Napoleonic wars—are exemplary in their detailed and accurate representation of architectural detail from different ages, especially classical antiquity and the Middle Ages, which had only recently been rehabilitated by Savigny and others.

Around the same time, Felix Mendelssohn (1809–1847), who according to his French contemporary Hector Berlioz (in his *Memoirs*) was "a little too fond of the dead," introduced the sense of history into music. In 1829 the twenty-year-old musical prodigy, who was personally close to Schleiermacher through family ties and familiar with intellectual currents in the capital, established his position as a leader in German musical culture by producing and directing the first performance of the *St. Matthew Passion* since Bach's death. The Bach revival that was initiated by that epoch-making performance in a historicizing Berlin marked a turn away from the hitherto customary practice of performing only contemporary music and represented the introduction of older music—i.e. the historical dimension—into German concert halls.

The history of modern, and notably post-medieval literature, while not yet generally accepted within the universities, found an interested audience in the general reading public. The critic Friedrich Schlegel (1772–1829) was fascinated from his earliest youth by history. At the University of Göttingen in the years immediately after the French Revolution, he attended lectures by the historians Spittler and Heeren, read Gibbon and Herder, and occupied himself more with the history of Rome than with his legal studies. Later at the University of Leipzig, he was planning "a treatment of national history."[15] It is not an exaggeration to claim that Schlegel was in fact utterly historical in temperament and intellect. In his famous early essay "On the Study of Greek Poetry" ("Über das Studium der griechischen Poesie," 1797), Schlegel maintained that modern literature in all its seeming disparateness can be understood only if we seek its unity historically in two directions: "back to the first source of its origin and development and forwards toward the final goal of its progress."[16] A year later in his so-called "Athenaeum Fragments," written around the time he was sharing an apartment in Berlin with Schleiermacher, with whom his intellectual exchange was both specific and profound, he made clear his familiarity with contemporary trends. He characterized the history of states, using the new mode-word, as "a genetic definition of phenomena of the present political condition of a nation"—a purely scientific undertaking in contrast to universal history, which becomes "sophistic" as soon as it puts moral ideas ahead of the spirit of the general cultivation of humanity as a whole. For his part, Schlegel remarks, "history is a *becoming* philosophy and philosophy a *completed* history."[17]

Ten years later, responding to the spirit of the times, Schlegel delivered a set of public lectures in Vienna, *On Modern History* (*Über die neuere Geschichte,* 1810), which began with the claim that three topics above all attract and elevate the minds of educated individuals: "the philosophy of life, the appreciation of the fine arts, and the study of history."[18] All three are indispensable, he continues, but it is, in particular, the study of history, through its reference to man's destinies and powers that gives "a firm midpoint" to the striving for the cultivation of mind. "Without a knowledge of our great past the philosophy of life, no matter how much it captivates us with its wit and enraptures us with its rhetoric, is not capable of tearing us loose from the present, from the narrow circle of our habits and immediate environments." History, in contrast, if it goes beyond mere chronicle, is itself "a true philosophy," comprehensive and available and useful to all. "If philosophy occupies the understanding and the fine arts our feeling and imagination, then history demands the participation of the entire human being and all his powers of soul." Only our familiarity with the past can provide us with "a calm, firm overview of the present, a measure of its greatness or smallness, and a correct judgment about it." It is the great boon of our age, he concludes his opening remarks, to have reinvigorated the study of history.

While Schlegel was committed to history in general and lectured on the subject, his true originality and contribution lay more specifically in the field of literary history, which he regarded as the principal access to the wellsprings of every people. In the introduction to the lectures on the "History of Ancient and Modern Literature" that he delivered in Vienna in 1812, he justified his undertaking with the argument: "For the entire further development of a nation, indeed for its entire spiritual development, it seems important . . . that a people have grand national memories, which are still mostly lost in the dark periods of its first origins and which it is the foremost business of poetry to preserve and to glorify."[19] Needless to say, in his reading of poetic documents as the principal source for ancient history, Schlegel is echoing the principles of Niebuhr's *Roman History,* which he praises in his third lecture. And in his understanding of the history of literature as a genetic process of development, he translates Herder's ideas into another dimension. This approach to the history of literature represents something entirely different from the polyhistorical compendiums, such as Ludwig Wachler's *Tentative General History of Literature (Versuch einer allgemeinen Geschichte der Litteratur,* 1793), that had hitherto presented themselves as literary histories—works that encompassed printed matter from every field, including philosophy, history, and science, and that were based on a second-hand acquaintance with most of the mentioned works.[20] Schlegel's *History,* in contrast, derived its authority from the author's phenomenal familiarity with primary texts in the many languages, ancient and modern, that he had mastered with playful ease. For these reasons, as Hans Eichner has suggested, a new epoch in the writing of German literary history can be dated from Schlegel's accomplishment. It is unnecessary to discuss August Wilhelm Schlegel's 1801–02 Berlin lectures on the "history of classical literature" (*Geschichte der klassischen Literatur*) or his 1808–09 Vienna "lectures on dramatic art and literature" (*Vorlesungen über dramatische Kunst und*

Literatur), for they are based extensively on the ideas of his younger brother. However, through their huge popular success they contributed to the new era of literary history in Germany.

It was not only the literary aspect of language(s) that came under fresh scrutiny during these early decades of the nineteenth century. Language itself was for the first time subjected to historicizing in the new discipline of comparative philology. A tentative approach had already been made in 1786 when Sir William Jones, the distinguished English jurist and orientalist, gave an address before the Asiatic Society in which he suggested that Sanskrit, Greek, and Latin must all have shared a common source. But Jones's inspired hint had little further effect until, thirty years later, the idea was systematized by the young German scholar Franz Bopp (1791– 1867), who in 1816 published a monograph on the conjugational system of Sanskrit, Greek, Latin, Persian, and Germanic languages. This landmark study, showing that the verb forms shared essential characteristics that proved their membership in a common language group, was the first to establish in the study of linguistics the principles of historical development and genealogical connection among languages. In 1820, Bopp extended his study to include other grammatical elements, and he gradually added the Slavonic and Celtic languages to his analysis, as well as Armenian, Albanian, and others, thus creating the field of Indo-European comparative philology.[21] Yet it was not until 1821 that Bopp, who while pursuing independent studies in Paris and London had never paused to take a degree (and had only recently been awarded an honorary doctorate at Göttingen), was called to a chair at the University of Berlin. Up to that point comparative philology, in contrast to classical philology, was not regarded as a respectable academic discipline.

Meanwhile, others were pursuing similar investigations of specific language groups according to historical principles. Incorporating findings of the Danish scholar Rasmus Rask, who in 1818 published a study on Old Icelandic as the parent from which the modern Scandinavian languages had developed, Jakob Grimm brought out the first volume of the major scholarly work for which he is remembered and which is dedicated to Savigny, his *Deutsche Grammatik* (1819). The course of language, he wrote in his preface to the first edition, "is slow but inexorable. It can never actually come to a standstill, much less regress." In the second edition (1822), Grimm omitted that statement and others that he considered "immature speculations"; but he insisted that philology still lacked studies of the historical aspect of the vernacular (i.e., non-classical) languages (xii) and that "history warns historical grammar against outrageous reforms and reveals to us the virtues of the past, through the consideration of which we can moderate the arrogance of the present" (xviii). (Grimm is referring, among other things, to the capitalization of substantives in modern German, which he opposed and refused to observe.) One of the important historical principles of progressive linguistic transformation that he discovered can be found in any dictionary under the rubric "Grimm's law": it defines the specific changes that certain consonants underwent as the Germanic languages developed from their common Indo-European source (accounting for the differences, for instance, between Latin *pes, pedis* and English *foot* or Latin *dens, dentis* and English *tooth*). The great *Deutsches Wörterbuch* (1852), conceived and undertaken by Jakob Grimm and his brother Wilhelm, constitutes a remarkable, and still indispensable, example of the practical application of historical linguistics by providing etymologies and examples of historical changes in usage for every word. The brothers Grimm shared the belief of Niebuhr and Friedrich Schlegel that the earliest evidences of human culture are to be found in poetry—a belief that informed not only Jakob's early essay on "Poetry in the Law," but also the brothers' subsequent collections and studies of Germanic sagas (*Deutsche Sagen*, 1816–18) and myths (*Deutsche Mythologie*, 1835).

To round out this survey of developments in architecture, art, music, literature, and linguistics we should remind ourselves that the decade following 1810 also witnessed the birth of the historical novel as we know it today. Earlier "historical novels"—like the encyclopedic histories or the paintings that clothed historical figures in modern garb—were based on no real understanding or appreciation of the past. Sir Walter Scott was the first to write historical novels with a modern sense of history—that is, as he put it in the often cited postscript to *Waverley* (1814), an awareness of the changes wrought over time that have rendered "the present people of Scotland a class of beings as different from their grandfathers, as the existing English are from those of Queen Elizabeth's time." His model was rapidly followed in France and especially in Germany by novelists beginning with Savigny's brother-in-law Achim von Arnim in *Guardians of the Crown (Die Kronenwächter*, 1819) and Schubert's friend Ludwig Tieck in his *Revolt in the Cevennes (Der Aufruhr in den Cevennen*, 1826).

More generally, the new conception of *Bildung*—the idea that the cultivation of the individual is a continuing process of inner development that parallels not only the development of civilization as a whole but also the growth of the embryo and of the body from birth until death—is a direct product of and inconceivable without the new sense of history. It was reflected in Wilhelm von Humboldt's project for an altogether new kind of university: no longer the traditional *Gelehrten-universität,* where students were the passive recipients of knowledge communicated by their professors from standard textbooks, but an institution of "freedom and solitude" (*Freiheit und Einsamkeit*), in which professor and student were joined in a common search for truths that had not yet been discovered and set forth. But it also found its literary analogy in the genre of the German Bildungsroman—e.g., Goethe's *Wilhelm Meister's Apprenticeship* and Hölderlin's *Hyperion*—which revolves not around plot but around the spiritual growth of the hero through a series of experiences in time.

The sense of history had the effect of temporalizing every facet of human thought, within the faculties and without. In *Genesis and Geology,* Charles C. Gillispie demonstrated how modern geology, and especially its disturbing implications concerning the age and formation of the earth, came into conflict with the cosmogonical teachings of the Bible in England from 1790 to 1840. And the dispute was not limited to England. Writers from Herder to Schubert began their histories of human development with the formation of the earth. Karl Ritter (1779–1859), the founder of scientific geography, defined his topic with a typically Romantic analogy as a "physiology of the earth." Ritter's major work on "geography in its relationship to nature and the history of man" (*Erdkunde im Verhältnis zur Natur und Geschichte des Menschen,* 1816) is nothing less than the attempt to link geography and history by exposing the influence of the earth on the peoples that inhabit it.

Michel Foucault devotes the second half of *The Order of Things: An Archaeology of the Human Sciences* to the process of historicizing that took place in economics, biology, and philology as exemplified by the English economist David Ricardo, the French biologist Georges Cuvier, and the German philologist Franz Bopp. Wolf Lepenies, in his provocative book on *The End of Natural History* (*Das Ende der Naturgeschichte*), focuses on temporalization as the key factor separating the natural history of the eighteenth century from the modern sciences as they developed in the nineteenth century, and notably in France. But neither in England nor in France did this process have the same impact on the disciplines of philosophy, law, and theology as was the case in the faculties of German universities—first in Berlin and gradually elsewhere. The historicization of medicine and the natural sciences, while not unique to Germany, was more conspicuously evident there because of the prevalence of a historicizing *Naturphilosophie* that was generally ridiculed in France and England.

Lessons?

What, if anything, do Hegel, Schleiermacher, Savigny, and the other historicizers of the faculties in the early nineteenth century have to say to us, two hundred years later and standing at the beginning of our own new century? Can we contemplate the past, like Niebuhr and his audience, with any hope of understanding our own present?

Like those great forerunners, we are living in a period of crisis generated by political, economic, and intellectual disruptions. However, our crisis is not merely European but global in scope, brought on by the clash with revolutionary forces in other parts of the world, by economic globalization, and by rapid intellectual exchange facilitated by the Internet. We too have witnessed an epochal shift from a static politico-social world to a more dynamic one—from the stable postwar society of "The Lonely Crowd" and "The Man in the Gray Flannel Suit" to the global world of the present, unconstrained by traditional patterns and fluid in its movement. Our cosmologists and philosophers of science are again searching eagerly for a unified field theory that will prove the unity of all being. And that transition has been accompanied in our time, too, by a shift from thinking dominated by images from the "timeless" science of atomic physics (the mushroom cloud) to one inspired by a cosmology that thinks in billions of years (the Big Bang) and the progressive genetics of molecular biology (the double helix).

It is a natural response in periods of political, economic, and intellectual turmoil to turn to history. Livy undertook his history of Rome, as he confides in the preface to *Ab urbe condita,* in order to distract his mind from the evils of his era—the period of war and revolution preceding the Roman principate. Two millennia later and against the background of the tumultuous 1930s, Ronald Syme wrote his magisterial *Roman Revolution* (1939), which dealt precisely with the years during which Livy lived, with the explicit hope of understanding through historical analogy the civil strife and rise of dictatorships of his own era. Is it far-fetched to imagine that a rehistoricization of a Western civilization that increasingly lives for the present, and that a familiarity with an earlier society whose experience was strikingly analogous to our own, might provide both a model and a caution for our situation?

Dissatisfaction with the limitations of analytic philosophy, which dominated most of the twentieth century as rationalism dominated the eighteenth, has recently caused many young philosophers to turn, like Hegel, to a new historicization of their discipline and to a fresh consideration of Plato, Kant, and other seminal thinkers of the past. The intrusion into the Western Judeo-Christian consciousness of beliefs from other continents, along with compelling social issues in our own society, has opened debate on the meaning of religion that Schleiermacher would have found both familiar and congenial. In the United States, complex and problematical legal issues concerning civil rights, affirmative action, immigration policy, national security, business ethics, and others have sent the courts again and again back to the American Constitution in search of guiding principles and the matter of original intent—precisely the question faced by Savigny, Eichhorn, and their colleagues. The contemporary search for health and eternal youth has focused interest on matters·discussed by Hufeland in his *Makrobiotik,* while research on human subjects and the implications of genetic research has raised ethical issues confronted by the early embryologists and anatomists.

We have much to learn from the manner in which that generation of often brilliant thinkers confronted a cultural crisis remarkably analogous to our own. At the same time, we should also take a cautionary example from their experience so that any new turn to history will not result this time in the political and social conservatism that for much of the nineteenth century justified repressive governments and underlay an increasingly intolerant society. What Jakob Grimm observed in 1822 about history in grammar applies equally well to history in life: it warns us against outrageous reforms and reveals the virtues of the past, through the consideration of which we can moderate the arrogance of the present. Or as Cicero put it almost two thousand years earlier (in his *De oratore* II.9.36), history is not only the preceptress of life (*magistra vitae*) but also a messenger from the past (*nuntia vetustatis*) and a witness to the times (*testis temporum*)—in sum, the light of truth (*lux veritatis*).

NOTES

ONE: HISTORY

1. Rosenkranz, *Hegel's Leben,* 214–15.

2. Hegel to Niethammer, 13 Oct. 1806.

3. Wilhelm Dilthey, "Das achtzehnte Jahrhundert und die geschichtliche Welt" (1901), in *Gesammelte Schriften,* 3:207–75; and Peter Gay, *Science of Freedom,* 368–96.

4. In a letter of August 1770; quoted by Gay, *Science of Freedom,* 369.

5. Srbik, *Geist und Geschichte,* 121–28.

6. Breisach, *Historiography,* 217–21.

7. Karl Hillebrand, *Zwölf Briefe eines ästhetischen Ketzers* (1873), 11; quoted in Rothacker, *Einleitung in die Geisteswissenschaften,* 5. Hillebrand's pleiad consists of Winckelmann, Herder, F. A. Wolf, Friedrich Schlegel, Wilhelm von Humboldt, Niebuhr, and Savigny.

8. Meinecke, *Entstehung des Historismus,* 355–444, esp. 386ff.

9. *Historisches Wörterbuch der Philosophie,* 3:416–42; here 420.

10. Clark, *Herder,* 188–91; and the editors' notes in *Werke,* 4:821–32.

11. *Werke,* 4:22 and 36.

12. Ibid., 4:38.

13. Ibid., 4:34.

14. Ibid., 4:39.

15. Ibid., 4:45.

16. Ibid., 4:98.

17. *An Prediger. Fünfzehn Provinzialblätter,* 14; *Werke,* 9/1: 127–28.

18. See the discussion in Clark, *Herder,* 308–35.

19. Berlin, "Herder and the Enlightenment," in *Vico and Herder,* 147–52, summarizes Herder's debt to many earlier thinkers.

20. Dilthey, "Das achtzehnte Jahrhundert," 268.

21. Berlin, *Vico and Herder,* 187.

22. For a good summary of the opposition, see Wells, *Herder and After,* 149–67.

23. Acton, in his inaugural lecture "On the Study of History" (1895), in *Lectures on Modern History,* 29.

24. Droz, *L'Allemagne et la Révolution Française,* 483.

25. Kelley, *Historians and the Law,* 72.

26. Gollwitzer, *Ludwig I von Bayern,* 136.

27. Landes, *Unbound Prometheus,* 135–36.

28. Ibid., 142.

29. Ibid., 140.

30. Ziolkowski, *German Romanticism and Its Institutions,* 18–27.

31. Wackenroder, *Dichtung,* 20–21.

32. Holborn, *History of Modern Germany,* 366–80.

33. Ziolkowski, *Berlin . . . um 1810,* 27–44.

34. F. W. A. Bratring, *Statistisch-topographische Beschreibung der gesamten Mark Brandenburg* (Berlin, 1804), cited by Ziolkowski, *Berlin . . . um 1810,* 32.

35. Riedel, "Prometheus und Herakles: Fragen an Friedrich Schlegels 'Idylle über den Müßiggang,'" in *Literarische Antikerezeption,* 173–79.

36. Landes, *Unbound Prometheus,* 2.

37. Sauer, *Säculardichtungen,* vi.

38. Schleiermacher, *Reden über die Religion,* 207.

39. Krieger, *German Idea of Freedom,* 139–47; here 141.

40. Hattenhauer, *Thibaut und Savigny,* 100.

41. Rudolf Stadelmann, "Die Romantik und die Geschichte," in *Romantik,* ed. Steinbüchel, 151–75; here 157.

42. Rothacker, *Einleitung in die Geisteswissenschaften,* 74–75.

43. Foucault, *Order of Things,* xxii, 221.

44. Auden, "The Poet and the City," in *The Dyer's Hand,* 76.

45. Marrou, *History of Education in Antiquity,* xiv.

46. Engel, *Die deutschen Universitäten,* 237.

47. Marrou, *History of Education in Antiquity,* 192–93, 289–91, and 326–29.

48. Haskins, *Rise of Universities,* 5–15, 29.

49. At the University of Strasbourg, for instance, the percentage of students enrolled in the four faculties between 1621–30 and 1781–90 changed as follows: theology, from 19 to 6 percent; law, from 38 to 58 percent; medicine, from 8 to 19 percent; and philosophy, from 35 to 16 percent; and at Heidelberg between 1704–10 and 1821–30: theology, 12 to 9 percent; law, 12 to 55 percent; medicine, 1 to 20 percent, and philosophy 53 to 15 percent. See Eulenberg, *Frequenz,* 311.

50. Engel, "Die deutschen Universitäten," 248–49.

51. Machlup, *Branches of Learning,* provides a statistically based "taxonomy" of the branches of learning in the nineteenth and twentieth centuries, along with an overview of the various modes of organization in academies, libraries, and universities.

52. Rothacker, *Einleitung in die Geisteswissenschaften;* and Makkreel, *Dilthey,* 131–34.

53. Kant, *Werke,* 9:261–393, esp. 279–300; here 300.

54. Ziolkowski, *German Romanticism and Its Institutions,* 220–28; and Rothblatt, "Student Sub-culture . . . in Early 19th Century Oxbridge."

55. I have outlined this history more thoroughly in *German Romanticism and Its Institutions,* 237–52.

56. Schiller, *Sämtliche Werke,* 4:749–67.

57. Ibid., 751.

58. Ibid., 752.

59. Fichte, *Gesamtausgabe,* 1/3, 25–68.

60. Anrich, *Idee der deutschen Universität*, 1–123, esp. 1–6.

61. On the development of history generally see Koselleck, "Geschichte."

62. In the following paragraphs I take much of my information from Engel, "Die deutschen Universitäten und die Geschichtswissenschaft," esp. 242–94; here 245.

63. Koselleck, "Auflösung des Topos."

64. Srbik, *Geist und Geschichte*, 107–08.

65. Engel, "Die deutschen Universitäten," 266.

66. Ibid., 257 ("Enttheologisierung").

67. Srbik, *Geist und Geschichte*, 121–28.

68. Gooch, *History and Historians*, 10.

69. I take the terms from Troeltsch, "Die Krisis des Historismus," 578.

70. Engel, "Die deutschen Universitäten," 294–95; Breisach, *Historiography*, 229–32.

71. See Ziolkowski, *German Romanticism and Its Institutions*, 286–94; and Shaffer, "Romantic philosophy and the organization of the disciplines."

72. Genschorek, *Hufeland*, 145.

73. The most important of these proposals are reprinted in Müller, *Gelegentliche Gedanken*.

74. Schleiermacher's treatise is reprinted in Müller, *Gelegentliche Gedanken*, 159–253; see esp. 198–202.

75. Humboldt's writings on educational theory are conveniently available in vol. 4 of his *Werke*; here 31.

76. Humboldt, *Werke*, 4:115.

77. Srbik, *Geist und Geschichte*, 191.

78. Ziolkowski, *Berlin . . . um 1810*, 175–91.

79. Christ, *Römische Geschichte und deutsche Geschichtswissenschaft*, 15.

80. Savigny to Friedrich Creuzer, 14 Nov. 1810.

81. Niebuhr, *Briefe*, 2:163.

82. Niebuhr to Hardenberg, 12 June 1810.

83. I base my depiction largely on Witte's biography and Walther, *Niebuhrs Forschung*, 29–294.

84. Christ, *Römische Geschichte und deutsche Geschichtswissenschaft*, 39.

85. Niebuhr to Nicolovius, 11 Sept. 1810.

86. "Kunstwerk," xiii. Here and below I translate from vol. 1 of the first edition (1811).

87. Savigny to F. Creuzer, 14 Nov. 1810; Stoll, *Savigny*, 2: 59; and Savigny to L. Creuzer, 13 Dec. 1810; Stoll, *Savigny*, 2:61.

88. For such evaluations see Christ, *Römische Geschichte und deutsche Geschichtswissenschaft*; Wilamowitz, *History of Classical Scholarship*; and Srbik, *Geist und Geschichte*, 210–20.

89. Wilamowitz-Moellendorf, *History of Classical Scholarship*, 117–19. Niebuhr's terms occur in his *Römische Geschichte*, x.

90. Christ, *Römische Geschichte und moderne Geschichtswissenschaft*, 35–43.

91. Gooch, *History and Historians*, 14.

92. Niebuhr to Goethe, 8 Aug. 1812.

93. "Zauberstab der Analogie," in "Die Christenheit oder Europa"; *Schriften*, 3:518.

94. Niebuhr to Dore Hensler, 14 Sept. 1810.

95. Renker, *Niebuhr*, 53.

96. Srbik, *Geist und Geschichte,* 217.

97. See, for instance, the works cited above by Christ, Wilamowitz, Breisach, and Srbik.

TWO: PHILOSOPHY

1. The emblem books of the seventeenth and eighteenth centuries fashioned wholly new allegorical figures for both philosophy and history. In a 1779 English edition of Ripa's *Iconology* Philosophy is depicted as "a venerable matron . . . with a diadem on her head, gracefully sitting upon a throne of marble . . . holding two open books [*Naturalis* and *Moralis*]." History is represented as "a matron of a noble aspect, in a thoughtful attitude, with large wings at her shoulders, . . . and writing upon a book. . . . she is dressed in white, the symbolick colour of sincerity, which ought to guide the pen of historians."

2. On the difficulties of combining history and philosophy see the article on "Geschichtsphilosophie" in *Historisches Wörterbuch der Philosophie,* 3:416–42, esp. 418.

3. Vorländer, *Immanuel Kant,* 1:310–29; esp. 312.

4. Benjamin to Gershon Sholem, 6. Dec. 1917.

5. Kant, "Zu Johann Gottfried Herder: Ideen zur Philosophie der Geschichte der Menschheit," in *Werke,* 10:779–806; here 802–03. On Kant and Herder see Wells, *Herder and After,* 136–49.

6. "M. Immanuel Kants Nachricht von der Einrichtung seiner Vorlesungen in dem Winterhalbenjahre, von 1765–1766"; Kant, *Werke,* 2:905–17; here 908.

7. Kant, *Werke,* 2:916.

8. Ibid., 4:709.

9. Ibid., 9:31–50; here 45.

10. Ibid., 9:49.

11. Koselleck, "*Historia magistra vitae,*" 207.

12. Kant, *Werke,* 9:83–102.

13. Pöggeler, *Hegels Idee,* 323–27, speaks of their "transcendental history."

14. Srbik, *Geist und Geschichte,* 1:178.

15. Fichte, *Gesamtausgabe,* 3:53.

16. Pöggeler, "Philosophie und Geschichte," in *Hegels Idee,* 299–368; here 323–27.

17. Fichte, *Grundlage,* 141.

18. Rpt. in Anrich, *Die Idee der deutschen Universität,* 1–123; here 65.

19. Wilhelm G. Jacobs, "Geschichte als Prozess der Vernunft," in Baumgartner (ed.), *Schelling,* 39–44.

20. Schelling, *System,* 263; on history in Schelling's *System* see Marx, *Schelling,* 13–62.

21. Schelling, *System,* 265–66: "das allmähliche Entstehen der weltbürgerlichen Verfassung."

22. Hyppolite, *Genesis,* 27–30.

23. Schaeffler, *Einführung in die Geschichtsphilosophie,* 158–77.

24. Hegel to Schelling, Jan. 1795.

25. On Hegel's early life see Rosenkranz, *Hegel's Leben;* Pinkard, *Hegel;* and Harris, *Hegel's Development.*

26. Hegel's diary is reproduced in *Dokumente,* 6–41. Forty-five years later, when the University of Berlin celebrated the three-hundredth anniversary of the Augsburg Confession, Hegel as rector delivered—in Latin—one of the two main addresses. See Pinkard, *Hegel,* 627–28.

27. In "the character of . . . an entire nation" we sense an anticipation of Hegel's later concept of the world-spirit. Hegel's preference for "pragmatic" history resurfaces and is defined years later in the introduction to his lectures on the philosophy of history.

28. A sample of Hegel's *Exzerpte* is provided in *Dokumente*, 54–166; the reference to Meiners in Rosenkranz, *Hegel's Leben*, 14.

29. *Dokumente*, 37.

30. Rosenkranz, *Hegel's Leben*, 8.

31. Harris, "Hegel's Intellectual Development," 33.

32. Lukács, *Der junge Hegel*, 62–63; and Pinkard, *Hegel*, 47.

33. *Dokumente*, 171–72.

34. Pinkard, *Hegel*, 51.

35. Rosenkranz, *Hegel's Leben*, 60.

36. Hegel to Schelling, Christmas Eve 1794.

37. Hegel to Schelling, 16 April 1795.

38. *Dokumente*, 257–77.

39. Lukács, *Der junge Hegel*, 388–99.

40. *Dokumente*, 278–82.

41. Nohl, *Theologische Jugendschriften*, 237-240; here 215.

42. Lukács, *Der junge Hegel*, 385.

43. Rosenkranz, *Hegel's Leben*, 201.

44. Lukács, *Der junge Hegel*, 592.

45. Beiser, "Hegel's Historicism," 270–74.

46. Windelband, *Geschichte der Philosophie*, 482.

47. Barth, *Die protestantische Theologie*, 1:332.

48. Haym, *Hegel und seine Zeit*, 243.

49. On Hegel's history of philosophy, see Beiser, "Introduction."

50. Srbik, *Geist und Geschichte*, 1:188.

51. See Geldsetzer, "Der Methodenstreit," for a discussion of the principal participants.

52. Beiser, "Introduction," xxxv–xxxvi, n.8.

53. Ibid., xxviii.

54. Hegel, *Vorlesungen über die Geschichte der Philosophie*, 47–49.

55. Goethe, *Werke*, 13:319.

56. Rosenkranz, *Hegel's Leben*, 201–02.

57. The opening paragraphs of the "Preface" to the *Phenomenology* contain an extensive justification of this view, comparing the succession of philosophical systems to the growth of a plant, where the bud is replaced by the blossom and the blossom in turn by the fruit.

58. Geldsetzer, *Die Philosophenwelt*, 147.

59. Burckhardt, *Weltgeschichtliche Betrachtungen*, 4.

60. For a different line of development in the philosophy of history—one that leads from Novalis by way of Schelling, Friedrich Schlegel, and Görres to Ernst von Lasaulx, Burckhardt, and Spengler—see Rudolf Stadelmann, "Die Romantik in der Geschichte," in *Romantik*, ed. Steinbüchel, 151–75.

61. McCullagh, "Historical Explanation."

62. Hegel, *Vorlesungen über die Philosophie der Geschichte*, 134.

63. Ibid., 45.

64. Ibid., 20.

65. Ibid., 540.

66. Ibid., 86.

67. Ibid., 30.

68. Windelband, *Blüthezeit,* 315.

69. See Pöggeler, "Komposition," and Hoffmeister's introduction to his edition of the *Phänomenologie,* xxvii–xxxviii.

70. Kaufmann, *Hegel,* 152; see 363 for quotations from other admirers of the "preface."

71. Here I differ with Lukács, *Der junge Hegel,* who stresses precisely the differences distinguishing Hegel from his Romantic contemporaries.

72. Rosenkranz, *Hegel's Leben,* 181–85; here 184.

73. Royce, *Lectures on Modern Idealism,* 142.

74. Hegel, *Phänomenologie des Geistes,* 54.

75. Hegel to Knebel, 21 Nov. 1807.

76. Heckman, "Introduction," in Hyppolite, *Genesis,* xxvi.

77. Hegel, *Phänomenologie des Geistes,* 41. Windelband, *Geschichte der Philosophie,* 464ff., discusses "Triplizität" in various of Hegel's philosophical contemporaries.

78. Jaspers, *Schelling,* 131–48.

79. See his essays "Wechsel der Töne," "Über die Verfahrungsweise des poetischen Geistes," and "Über den Unterschied der Dichtarten" in *Sämtliche Werke,* 4:248–50 and 4:251–76, and 4:277–84. See Ziolkowski, *Classical German Elegy,* 119–22.

80. Ziolkowski, "Rhetoric der Revolution."

81. Royce, *Lectures on Modern Idealism,* 143; and Hirsch, "Die Beisetzung der Romantiker."

82. Rosenkranz, *Hegel's Leben,* 11.

83. Steiner, *Antigones,* 1–42.

84. Royce, *Lectures on Modern Idealism,* 64.

85. For my understanding of the *Phenomenology,* and specifically on the role of history, I have benefited most from Hyppolite, *Genesis,* 27–50; Lukács, *Der junge Hegel,* 594–99; and Beiser, "Hegel and History."

86. In an aphorism from his Jena period in *Dokumente,* 360.

87. Barth, *Die protestantische Theologie,* 1:320, 324, 329.

88. Here and in the following discussion all page numbers refer to *Phänomenologie des Geists,* which unless otherwise noted I cite in my own translation.

89. Hoffmeister's Introduction to *Phänomenologie des Geistes,* vii–xvii.

90. See, for instance, Lessing's *On the Education of Humankind (Über die Erziehung des Menschengeschlechts)* and Schiller's letters on *The Aesthetic Education of Man (Über die ästhetische Erziehung des Menschen).*

91. Lukács, *Der junge Hegel,* 599–679, uses this tripartite division in his discussion of the *Phenomenology.*

92. Hyppolite, *Genesis,* 11; Abrams, *Natural Supernaturalism,* 229–30. Indeed, so routine has the analogy become that recent scholars are apparently unaware of its source in Royce; e.g., Cutrofello, *Owl at Dawn,* 34, who attributes it to Judith Butler, *Subjects of Desire,* 17, who in turn credits Abrams. Kaufmann's attempt, in his *Hegel* (134–42), to find

an analogy to Goethe's *Faust* rather than to the Bildungsroman is more distracting than helpful, because Hegel himself adduces the Faustian analogy to define simply one among many specific forms in the evolution of the spirit.

93. Royce, *Lectures on Modern Idealism,* 149.

94. In much the same sense recent scholars have sometimes spoken of the Bible as "the mother of all *Entwicklungsromane*" ("novels of development") to the extent that it can be read as God's coming to historical consciousness. See Jan Ross, "Faust, Freud, Bach und Bibel," in *Die Zeit,* 27 March 2002: 1, in a discussion of Jack Miles, *God: A Biography* (New York: Knopf, 1995).

95. Hyppolite makes this point in his "Anmerkungen," 46.

96. See, for instance, Tieck's story *Die Gesellschaft auf dem Lande* (1825), in which the old hussar from the Seven Years' War still proudly sports his military pigtail.

97. Kojève, *Introduction,* consists essentially of a reading of this key passage.

98. Gay, *Enlightenment,* 1:299–304.

99. Hyppolite, *Genesis,* 285.

100. Pinkard, *Hegel,* 499.

101. See Norton, *Beautiful Soul,* 246–82, for a full discussion.

102. Pinkard, *Hegel,* 216.

THREE: THEOLOGY

1. Goethe, *Werke,* 9:43 (end of bk. 1).

2. Goethe, *Werke,* 9:288–92.

3. Hazard, *European Thought in the Eighteenth Century,* 3–129; Holborn, *History of Modern Germany,* 310–14; and Gay, *Rise of Modern Paganism,* 212–419.

4. See Aner, *Theologie der Lessingzeit*; Barth, *Protestantische Theologie im 19. Jahrhundert,* 112–46; and Hirsch, *Geschichte der neuern evangelischen Theologie,* 4:3–119. While Barth concedes appreciably less originality to the neologists than do Aner and Hirsch, they agree in most essentials regarding their achievements.

5. Tillich, *History of Christian Thought,* 276–319; here 308–09. Tillich is much more sympathetic to the achievements of Protestant orthodoxy than are most historians.

6. Barth, *Protestantische Theologie,* 64–112; here 82.

7. Aner, *Theologie der Lessingzeit,* 22–25; Barth, *Protestantische Theologie,* 131–32.

8. Aner, *Theologie der Lessingzeit,* 144–201; Barth, *Protestantische Theologie,* 137–46.

9. Quoted by Aner, *Theologie der Lessingzeit,* 162.

10. Ibid., 335n3.

11. Ibid., 229, 271.

12. Ibid., 335n3: "Ein Mann, dem man alle Ehre antut, wenn man glaubt, es habe ihm im Kopfe gefehlt."

13. Ibid., 298.

14. Barner, *Lessing,* 272.

15. From the preface to Nicolai's *Beschreibung einer Reise durch Deutschland und die Schweiz* (Berlin, 1786); quoted by Clark, *Herder,* 21.

16. Lessing, "Axiomata," *Werke,* 8:130.

17. Kant, *Werke,* 9:51–61; here 60.

18. Lessing, *Werke,* 7:35, 39.

19. Schweitzer, *Quest of the Historical Jesus,* 13–26; here 13, 23.

20. On Lessing's attack on neologism see Aner, *Theologie der Lessingzeit,* 343–61.

21. Lessing, *Werke,* 7:474. This volume contains the Reimarus-Fragments along with Lessing's earlier writings on the criticism of theology.

22. Ibid., 7:458.

23. See Barner, *Lessing,* 280–97, on the "Fragmentenstreit."

24. Lessing, *Werke,* 8:490. These early paragraphs of *The Education* (§§1–53) had already appeared three years earlier in Lessing's commentary to the Reimarus-Fragments (*Werke,* 7:476–88).

25. Kant, *Werke,* 7:645–879.

26. Ibid., 7:788–803; here 788.

27. Ibid., 9:300.

28. *Zerstreute Blätter 2,* in Herder, *Sämmtliche Werke,* 15: 506–07.

29. Ibid., 15:506.

30. Herder, *Werke,* 4:18.

31. Ibid., 4:22, 28, 31.

32. Ibid., 4:45.

33. Ibid., 4:101.

34. Ibid., 9/1:84–85, 101, 124.

35. Ibid., 9/1:110.

36. On the *Letters* see Frei, *Eclipse of Biblical Narrative,* 183–201.

37. Herder, *Werke,* 9/1:150.

38. On Herder's "ambiguity" regarding the historicity of the Old Testament see Frei, *Eclipse of Biblical Narrative,* 184–88.

39. Herder, *Werke,* 9/1:284.

40. Ibid., 9/1:416.

41. Ibid., 9/1:564.

42. Ibid., 7: bk.9,chap. 5.

43. Clark, *Herder,* 277.

44. Herder is not mentioned in the broad survey of Tillich's *History of Christian Thought*; and Barth, *Die protestantische Theologie,* concludes his chapter on Herder, which compares Herder rather disparagingly to Kant, with the statement that "the dawn of a new era, which many have wanted to see in Herder, was after all only a Bengal flare" (281).

45. On the influence of the two works, see the editor's notes in: Herder, *Werke,* 9/1:929–30 and 987–98.

46. Tillich, *History of Christian Thought,* 388.

47. I take the biographical information primarily from Dilthey, *Leben Schleiermachers,* in *Gesammelte Schriften,* 13/1:1–83 and 208–312; Redeker, *Schleiermacher: Life and Thought,* 6–33; Kantzenbach, *Schleiermacher,* 9–96; Nowak, *Schleiermacher,* 15–223; and Schleiermacher's letters in KGA, V/1–3.

48. Schleiermacher to Brinckmann, 22 July 1789.

49. Schleiermacher to Brinckmann, 9–10 Dec. 1789.

50. Schleiermacher to J.G.A. Schleyermacher, 23 Dec. 1789.

51. Schleiermacher to his sister, 12 Feb. 1801.

52. Ibid.

53. Friedrich Schlegel to A. W. Schlegel, 26. Aug. 1797; Schlegel's letters from this period (July 1797–August 1799) can be found in vol. 24 of the *Kritische Ausgabe.*

54. Friedrich Schlegel to Novalis, 26 Sept. 1797.

55. Schleiermacher to his sister, 22 Oct. 1797.

56. Schleiermacher to his sister, 31 Dec. 1797.

57. Schlegel to Brinkmann, Jan. 1798.

58. In his introduction to the 1926 edition.

59. For background see Moretto, *Etica e storia in Schleiermacher,* 49–156.

60. See the editor's note in Schleiermacher's KGA, 5/1: 29n.33.

61. KGA, 1/1: 489–97.

62. Quoted here and elsewhere in my own translation from the first edition of 1799 as reprinted by Reclam. Most English translations are based on the third edition of 1821, which is more systematic and complete, but lacks the energy and several of the key words and concepts of the first edition.

63. Ziolkowski, *German Romanticism and Its Institutions,* 252–55.

64. Hegel, *Theologische Jugendschriften,* 137–342; the quoted phrases—"Die Zufälligkeit" and "das Vergängliche"—are on 145.

65. Reardon, *Religion in the Age of Romanticism,* 54.

66. Redeker, *Schleiermacher,* 6.

67. KGA, 1/5:39–100; cited here according to Tice's translation of Schleiermacher, *Christmas Eve.*

68. Quoted by Wolfgang Trillhaus, "Der Berliner Prediger," in Lange, *Schleiermacher,* 14.

69. Scholz's introduction to his edition of the *Kurze Darstellung,* xxxii.

70. Redeker, *Schleiermacher,* 103.

71. Cited in Tice's preface to his translation of the *Brief Outline,* i. Also see Tice's "bibliographical note" in his translation of the *Brief Outline,* 215–24.

72. See Nowak, *Schleiermacher,* 223–34; here 228.

73. Barth, *Protestantische Theologie,* 596.

74. Schleiermacher is not mentioned in Gooch, *History and Historians in the Nineteenth Century,* or Breisach, *Historiography; On Religion* is mentioned several times in Srbik, *Geist und Geschichte,* but not the *Brief Outline;* and despite frequent allusions to Schleiermacher and other works in the eight volumes of the *Geschichtliche Grundbegriffe,* the *Brief Outline* does not occur there. Dilthey's *Leben Schleiermachers* does not go beyond 1807.

75. KGA, 1/6:243–315 and 317–46. For convenience I refer to the second edition, in which the paragraphs are numbered consecutively throughout; the numerous changes since the first edition are essentially stylistic and not substantive. In general, my paraphrases are based on the German text, but for direct quotations I have usually used Tice's translation of *Brief Outline,* which follows Scholz's standard edition of the *Kurze Darstellung* in presenting the second edition as the principal text and, beneath it in smaller type, the text of the first edition. The *Kritische Gesamtausgabe* prints both texts, but consecutively rather than diplomatically.

76. See Frank's edition of Schleiermacher's *Hermeneutik und Kritik.*

77. Kimmerle, *Hermeneutik,* 46.

FOUR: LAW

1. Savigny's preface to *System des heutigen Römischen Rechts,* xxix–xxx.

2. Bader, "Deutsches Recht"; and Watson, *Evolution of Law,* 43–65.

3. Koschaker, *Europa und das römische Recht.*

4. Watson, *Making of the Civil Law,* 53–61.

5. Ziolkowski, *Mirror of Justice,* 69–73.

6. On the "Reception" see Wieacker, *Private Law,* 71–155.

7. I discuss the disenchantment at length in *Mirror of Justice,* 74–143.

8. On *usus modernus* see Wieacker, *Private Law,* 159–95.

9. Watson, *Making of the Civil Law,* 83–98; Wieacker, *Private Law,* 199–256; and Hazard, *European Thought,* 145–59.

10. Wolf, *Große Rechtsdenker,* 464–65, distinguishes two main variants of *Naturrecht* in the second half of the century: a pragmatic-utilitarian form and an idealistic-literary-philosophical one. For examples of literary *Naturrecht* see Ziolkowski, *German Romanticism and Its Institutions,* 86–90.

11. On the codifications see Wieacker, *Private Law,* 257–75.

12. Stühler, *Diskussion um die Erneuerung,* 224–26 and passim; and Whitman, *Legacy of Roman Law,* 41–65.

13. Reitemeier, "Vorrede," in *Encyclopädie und Geschichte der Rechte in Deutschland,* xi–xii; quoted in Stühler, *Diskussion um die Erneuerung,* 119–20.

14. Feuerbach, "Blick auf die teutsche Rechtswissenschaft"; quoted in Stühler, *Diskussion um die Erneuerung,* 197–98.

15. Kleist, *Werke,* 2:503.

16. Savigny, "Der zehente Mai 1788. Beytrag zur Geschichte der Rechtswissenschaft," *Zeitschrift für geschichtliche Rechtswissenschaft* 9 (1838): 421–32; here 422.

17. Grimm, "Selbstbiographie" (1831), in *Kleinere Schriften,* 1–19; here 5–6.

18. Wieacker, *Private Law,* 300; Stühler, *Diskussion um Erneuerung,* 147; Stoll, *Savigny,* 1:172.

19. On this topic generally see Ziolkowski, *Mirror of Justice.*

20. Among legal historians Wieacker, in his distinguished *History of Private Law,* has most prominently made a principle of establishing "a relationship between the legal method of a period and the type of thinking generally prevalent at the time" (6). On "The Origins of the Historical School" see 279–99.

21. Savigny, "Der zehente Mai 1788," 423.

22. ADB, 13:321–28; Stühler, *Diskussion um die Erneuerung,* 134–50; Kleinheyer and Schröder, *Deutsche Juristen,* 131–34; Kelley, *Historians and the Law,* 76–77.

23. *Civilistisches Magazin* 2 (1797): 25; quoted in Stühler, *Diskussion um die Erneuerung,* 23.

24. *Civilistisches Magazin* 1 (1791): 10; quoted in Stühler, *Diskussion um die Erneuerung,* 134–35.

25. Savigny, "Recension des Lehrbuchs der Geschichte des Römischen Rechts von Gustav Hugo," in *Vermischte Schriften,* 5:1–36, here 2.

26. Kleinheyer/Schröder, *Deutsche Juristen,* 65–67; Wolf, *Große Rechtsdenker,* 217–51.

27. On the Göttingen school see especially Stühler, *Diskussion um die Erneuerung,* 114–51.

28. Reitemeier, *Encyclopädie und Geschichte der Rechte in Deutschland* (1785), xxiv; quoted in Stühler, *Diskussion um Erneuerung,* 123.

29. Hufeland, *Lehrbuch der Geschichte und Encyclopäedie aller in Deutschland gel-*

tenden positiven Rechte (1796), §1; quoted in Stühler, *Die Diskussion um die Erneuerung,* 129–30.

30. Stühler, *Diskussion um Erneuerung,* 151.

31. For biographical information I have relied on ADB 30: 425–52; Denneler, *Savigny;* Wolf, *Große Rechtsdenker,* 464–535; Marini, *Savigny,* and especially Stoll, *Savigny.*

32. Nörr, *Savignys philosophische Lehrjahre.*

33. See, for instance, Savigny's letter to Friedrich Creuzer, 14 July 1807; Stoll, *Savigny,* 1:304.

34. Quoted in Stoll, *Savigny,* 1:33.

35. Felgentraeger, "Briefe Savignys an Weis."

36. Stoll, *Savigny,* 1:70.

37. Ibid., 1:71.

38. Letter of Savigny's student friend Friedrich von Leonhardi to Leonhard Creuzer, 19 March 1799; Stoll, *Savigny,* 1:54.

39. Savigny's travel journal, 30 July—2 August, 1799; Stoll, *Savigny,* 1: 116–17.

40. In his preface to the 4th edition of 1822; *Recht des Besitzes,* iv.

41. Momigliano, "Friedrich Creuzer and Greek Historiography," in his *Studies in Historiography,* 75–90.

42. On the reception of the work see Stoll, *Savigny,* 1: 171–72.

43. *Recht des Besitzes,* 560 (§48).

44. Wolf, *Große Rechtsdenker,* 480–83.

45. I refer here to Savigny's own notes as recently reprinted in Mazzacane's edition, 86–131. Grimm's notes, long the only source, have been published by G. Wesenberg (ed.), *Juristische Methodenlehre, nach der Ausarbeitung des Jakob Grimm* (Stuttgart: Koehler, 1951). See also Marini, *Savigny,* 52–73.

46. Engel, *Die deutschen Universitäten,* 223.

47. Stoll, *Savigny,* 176.

48. Stoll, *Savigny,* 171–75, records several tributes from the Grimms and other students.

49. Savigny to Hans von Bostel, 4 February 1805; Stoll, *Savigny,* 244.

50. Savigny to Zentner, 28 April 1808; Stoll, *Savigny,* 1: 323.

51. Stoll, *Savigny,* 1:386.

52. Savigny to Bang, 13 April 1810; Stoll, *Savigny,* 1:415.

53. The period in Landshut is charmingly portrayed by Bettine, who was with the family, in her correspondence with Goethe: *Goethes Briefwechsel mit einem Kinde* (1835).

54. Quoted in ADB, 30:428.

55. Otto Lehmann, quoted by Stoll, *Savigny,* 3:191.

56. Wieacker, *Private Law,* 300–29.

57. I discuss the literary use of legal themes in *German Romanticism and Its Institutions,* 64–69 and 86–137.

58. Kleinheyer/Schröder, *Deutsche Juristen,* 75–78.

59. Eichhorn, *Rechtsgeschichte,* 1:xiii.

60. Stoll, *Savigny,* 2:25.

61. Ibid., 2:95. The German is ambiguous here: the bracketed phrase—"mit jeder Sammlung, die man lieb gewonnen hat"—could also be a reference to the various manuscript and book collections of which Savigny has grown fond.

62. See Hattenhauer's introduction to *Thibaut und Savigny*. I have discussed the controversy for other contexts in *German Romanticism and Its Institutions*, 78–86, and *The Mirror of Justice*, 191–94.

63. Quoted in Hattenhauer, *Thibaut und Savigny*, 40.

64. Translated from the text as reprinted in Hattenhauer, *Thibaut und Savigny*, 61–94.

65. Kleinheyer/Schröder, *Deutsche Juristen*, 297–300; Hattenhauer, *Thibaut und Savigny*, 10–20.

66. Translated from the text as reprinted in Hattenhauer, *Thibaut und Savigny*, 98–192.

67. See Hattenhauer, *Thibaut und Savigny*, 193–298, for a selection of representative documents.

68. Wolf, *Große Rechtsdenker*, 500, plays down the immediate effect of Savigny's *Vom Beruf*.

69. On the more general contributions of Savigny's *Vom Beruf* see Rothacker, *Einleitung in die Geisteswissenschaften*, 44–62.

70. Savigny, *Geschichte des Römischen Rechts*, v.

71. Savigny to the Grimm brothers, 5 Dec. 1813; Stoll, *Savigny*, 2:95.

72. Kantorowicz, "Savigny and the Historical School of Law," 337.

73. It is a mistake to assume, as is sometimes done, that Savigny was opposed to philosophy in law: his enemy was the trivialized rationalism of natural law. But already in his "methodology," as we noted, he maintained that jurisprudence is both a historical and a philosophical science—a lesson well learned by his students. In a drawing made and presented to him soon after 1815 by his student Moritz August von Bethmann-Hollweg, Savigny and his family are depicted within a framework presided over by the figure of Justitia, while putti on either side hold up signs respectively for *philosophia* and *historia*.

74. Whitman, *Legacy of Roman Law*, 92–150.

75. Reprinted in Hattenhauer, *Thibaut und Savigny*, 274–98; here 298.

76. Savigny, *System des heutigen Römischen Rechts*, xiv–xv.

77. Quoted by Stühler, *Diskussion um die Erneuerung*, 215; on Feuerbach's criticism, 214–21.

78. See Rothacker, *Einleitung in die Geisteswissenschaften*, 82–129.

79. *Grundlinien der Philosophie des Rechts* (1821), §211; *Werke* 7:363.

80. See Wieacker, *Wandlungen im Bilde der historischen Rechtsschule*; and Kantorowicz, "Savigny and the Historical School of Law."

81. Klenner, "Savigny's Research Program," 69.

82. Kantorowicz, "Savigny and the Historical School," 343.

83. John Macdonell, *Great Jurists of the World*, 581.

FIVE: MEDICINE

1. Conger, *Theories of Macrocosms and Microcosms*.

2. Herder, *Ideen*, 65.

3. Lepenies, *Ende der Naturgeschichte*, 78–87.

4. Lovejoy, *Great Chain of Being*, esp. 183.

5. Hans Querner, "Ordnungsprinzipien und Ordnungsmethoden in der Naturgeschichte der Romantik," in *Romantik in Deutschland*, ed. Brinkmann, 214–25.

6. See Lovejoy, *Great Chain of Being*, 242–87; and Gode-Von Aesch, *Natural Science in German Romanticism*, 7–8.

7. Lepenies, *Ende der Naturgeschichte*, 29. In fact, the vocable occurred as early as 1736 in its Latin form; but it was not used in its vernacular forms until the early nineteenth century. See Richards, *Romantic Conception of Life*, 4n8.

8. "Biology" in *DHS*, 43.

9. On the complex and controversial role of Kant, and notably his third Critique, in the scientific thought of the period see esp. the contributions of Ginsborg and Guyer in *Kant and the Sciences*; and Richards, *Romantic Conception of Life*, 229–37.

10. Gode Von Aesch, *Natural Science in German Romanticism*, 183–203.

11. Quoted by Genschorek, *Hufeland*, 85.

12. Hufeland, *Makrobiotik*; for the passage on "Lebenskraft," 30–48.

13. Gode-Von Aesch, *Natural Science in German Romanticism*, 199–201; Lenoir, *Strategy of Life*, 35–37; and Richards, *Romantic Conception of Life*, 255–61.

14. Wetzels, *Johann Wilhelm Ritter*, 18–29.

15. Included in Humboldt's own notes in *Ansichten der Natur*, 323.

16. Humboldt, *Ansichten der Natur*, 319–25.

17. Lepenies, *Ende der Naturgeschichte*, 9–114. See also the chapter titled "The Temporalizing of the Chain of Being," in Lovejoy, *Great Chain of Being*, 242–87; "Time and Eternity: The Problem of Evolution," in Gode-Von Aesch, *Natural Science in German Romanticism*, 74–92; and Engelhardt, "Historical Consciousness in the German Romantic *Naturforschung*."

18. "Epigenesis/preformation," in DHS, 127; see also Richards, *Romantic Conception of Life*, 211–16.

19. Temkin, "German concepts of Ontogeny and History around 1800," in *Double Face of Janus*, 373–89; here 380.

20. See Gode-Von Aesch, *Natural Science in German Romanticism*, 74–92.

21. Goethe, *Werke*, 13:120–27. This "Betrachtung über Morphologie" was published posthumously.

22. Engelhardt, "Historical Consciousness in the German Romantic *Naturforschung*."

23. Jaspers, *Schelling*, 48.

24. On Schelling's *Naturphilosophie* see Richards, *Romantic Conception of Life*, 114–92, 289–306.

25. "Brunonianism, in *DHS*, 47; see also Gode-Von Aesch, *Natural Science in German Romanticism*, 186–91; Leibbrand, *Die spekulative Medizin der Romantik*, 76–83; Neubauer, *Bifocal Vision*, 23–30; and Broman, *Transformation of German Academic Medicine*, 128–58.

26. On Marcus and Röschlaub see Neubauer, *Bifocal Vision*, 28, 104–10; and Leibbrand, *Die spekulative Medizin der Romantik*, 89–94.

27. Gode-Von Aesch, *Natural Science in German Romanticism*, 190.

28. See Karl E. Rothschuh, "Naturphilosophische Konzepte der Medizin aus der Zeit der deutschen Romantik," in *Romantik in Deutschland*, ed. Brinkmann, 245–66.

29. Schelling, *Schriften von 1794–1798*, 380.

30. Ibid., 404.

31. Ibid., 435.

32. Ibid., 623.

33. *Einleitung*, in vol. 3 of Schelling's *Sämmtliche Werke*, 269–326; here 272.

34. *Entwurf,* in vol. 3 of *Sämmtliche Werke,* 1–268.

35. Sudhoff, *Geschichte der Medizin,* 354–55.

36. Steffens, *Lebenserinnerungen,* 81.

37. Garrison, *History of Medicine,* 408. It is, of course, a mistake to assume that all German science of this period neglected empirical research for the sake of speculation. See Paul Walden, "Einfluß der Romantik auf die exakten Naturwissenschaften," and Alfred Kühn, "Biologie der Romantik," in *Romantik,* ed. Steinbüchel, 195–212, 213–34.

38. Morwitz, *Geschichte der Medicin,* 410.

39. Temkin, "Wunderlich, Schelling and the History of Medicine," in *Double Face of Janus,* 346–51; Leibbrand, *Die spekulative Medicin der Romantik,* 98–99; and Kirchhoff, *Schelling,* 52. Indeed, a thoughtful *apologia* for Romantic science is the principal theme of Richards, *Romantic Conception of Life.*

40. In his "Betrachtung über Morphologie überhaupt"; Goethe, *Werke,* 13:126.

41. Broman, *Transformation of German Academic Medicine,* 13–41.

42. Quoted by Leibbrand, *Die spekulative Medizin der Romantik,* 59.

43. Lepenies, *Ende der Naturgeschichte,* 78.

44. Carus, *Lebenserinnerungen,* 51.

45. Meyer, *Human Generation,* 52.

46. Quoted by Leibbrand, *Die spekulative Medizin der Romantik,* 119.

47. The entire address is reprinted in Meyer-Abich, *Biologie der Goethezeit,* 256–81; here 281.

48. See Dietrich Engelhardt, "Bibliographie der Sekundärliteratur zur romantischen Naturforschung und Medizin, 1950–1975," in *Romantik in Deutschland,* ed. Brinkmann, 307–30.

49. *NDB,* 19:498–99; *DSB,* 10:194–96; Leibbrand, *Die spekulative Medizin der Romantik,* 59–65; Querner, "Ordnungsprinzipien," in *Romantik in Deutschland,* ed. Brinkmann, 217–20; and Richards, *Romantic Conception of Life,* 492–501.

50. Oken, *Zeugung,* v.

51. On some of the more far-fetched excrescences of *Naturphilosophie,* see Brunschwig, *Enlightenment and Romanticism,* 190–204.

52. Oken, *Allgemeine Naturgeschichte,* vol. 1, p. 5.

53. On the importance of the term "Entwicklung" and "Entwicklungsgeschichte" see Temkin, "Ontogeny and History," in *Double Face of Janus,* 378–79.

54. *ADB* 38:667; Leibbrand, *Die spekulative Medizin der Romantik,* 133–37; and Rothschuh, "Naturphilosophische Konzepte der Medizin," in *Romantik in Deutschland,* ed. Brinkmann, 254–56.

55. Troxler's introduction is reprinted in Bietak, *Romantische Wissenschaft,* 243–47; here 247.

56. On Döllinger see Temkin, "Ontogeny and History," *Double Face of Janus,* 377–82; Meyer, *Human Generation,* 26–32; and Lenoir, *Strategy of Life,* 65–71.

57. Meyer, *Human Generation,* 41; note that Meyer's translation of this passage (33) is inaccurate.

58. Quoted from Temkin, *Double Face of Janus,* 379.

59. *DSB,* 2:594–97.

60. Alan S. Kay, "Burdach," in *DSB,* 2:594–97; here 595.

61. I follow Kay, *DSB,* 595, because I have not had access to the original.

62. Reprinted in Bietak, *Romantische Wissenschaft*, 266–68; here 268.

63. On Baer see Meyer, *Human Generation*, 49–58 and 124–38; Jane Oppenheimer in *DSB*, 1:385–89; and Lenoir, *Strategy of Life*, 72–95. Other Romantic physicians, whose work does not so explicitly exemplify the tendency toward temporalization, are discussed by Huch, *Romantik*, 590–617; and Leibbrand, *Die spekulative Medizin der Romantik*, 226–70.

64. I have seen only the English translation in Meyer, *Human Generation*, 90–123.

65. Meyer, *Human Generation*, 59–66, represents the most extreme denial. Most historians of science put him squarely in the tradition of *Naturphilosophie;* see Lenoir, *Strategy of Life*, 72; and Richards, *Romantic Conception of Life*, 191, 312.

66. On the frequency of "Entwicklung" see Temkin, "Ontogeny and History," in *Double Face of Janus*, 378.

67. Quoted by Gode-Von Aesch, *Natural Science in German Romanticism*, 78.

68. Temkin, "Ontogeny and History," in *Double Face of Janus*, 386–87.

69. De Staël, *De l'Allemagne*, 371. The complete text is also available in the German translation, *Über Deutschland*, 721ff.

70. *ADB* 23:631–35.

71. On the appeal of mining in Romanticism see Ziolkowski, *German Romanticism and Its Institutions*, 18–63.

72. Translated here and elsewhere from Schubert, *Ansichten*.

73. On Mesmer, see Tatar, *Spellbound*, 3–25; and on mesmerism in Germany, Gode-Von Aesch, *Natural Science in German Romanticism*, 158–66; and Leibbrand, *Die spekulative Medizin der Romantik*, 174–90.

74. Translated from the reprint in Tatar, *Spellbound*, 273–76.

75. Jung, *Archetypes and the Collective Unconscious*, 3, 152, and 276, as well as his autobiography.

76. Quoted here and below in my own translation from Carus's *Lebenserinnerungen*.

77. I base the following remarks on the official catalog of courses for the fall semester of 1810 published in Berlin by Friedrich Starck in 1810; and on the biographical information in Keune, *Gelehrtenbildnisse*.

78. On medical training in the eighteenth century see Bruford, *Germany in the Eighteenth Century*, 256–60; and Broman, *Transformation of German Academic Medicine*, 180–92.

79. Genschorek, *Hufeland*, 45.

80. Ibid., 144.

81. See Broman, *Transformation*, 136–43.

82. I have not seen Windischmann's works; I follow the discussion in Huch, *Romantik*, 611–12.

83. Gode-Von Aesch, *Natural Science*, 159.

84. Genschorek, *Hufeland*, 158.

85. I base my discussion in the following paragraphs on the chapter "Das Geschichtsbild" in Leibbrand, *Die spekulative Medizin der Romantik*, 271–89; here 272–73.

86. Translated from the quotation in Leibbrand, *Die spekulative Medizin der Romantik*, 276.

87. Ibid., 276–77.

88. Ibid., 282.

CONCLUSION

1. Ziolkowski, *Berlin . . . um 1810*, 222–25.

2. Stoll, *Savigny*, 2:61.

3. Savigny to the Grimms, 23 Nov. 1816; Stoll, *Savigny*, 2:212.

4. Pinkard, *Hegel*, 446.

5. Ibid., 515.

6. Hegel, *Werke*, 11:58.

7. Savigny to Leonhard Creuzer, 26 Nov. 1821; Stoll, *Savigny*, 2:278.

8. Savigny to Friedrich Creuzer, 6 April 1822; Stoll, *Savigny*, 2:288.

9. Comparative anatomy was discussed in the preceding chapter, and comparative philology will be taken up below. See also Jordan, *Comparative Religion*; Mayo, *Herder and the Beginnings of Comparative Literature*; and for sociology Wells, *Herder and After*.

10. Engel, *Die deutschen Universitäten*, 305–14.

11. Ibid., 232.

12. Savigny to Jakob Grimm, 8 Nov. 1814; Stoll, *Savigny*, 2: 126.

13. Waetzoldt, *Deutsche Kunsthistoriker*, 292–318.

14. On the Altes Museum see Ziolkowski, *German Romanticism and Its Institutions*, 309–21.

15. See Eichner's introduction to Schlegel's *Geschichte der alten und neuen Literatur*; *Kritische Ausgabe*, 6:xi.

16. Schlegel, *Kritische Schriften*, 123.

17. Ibid., 48, 62.

18. Schlegel, *Über die neuere Geschichte* (1811); *Kritische Ausgabe*, 7:127–28.

19. Schlegel, *Geschichte der alten und neuen Literatur* (1815); *Kritische Ausgabe*, 6:15.

20. See Eichner's introduction to Schlegel's *Geschichte*; *Kritische Ausgabe*, 6:xxxi–xxxiv.

21. See Foucault, *Order of Things*, 280–94.

BIBLIOGRAPHY

Abrams, M. H. *Natural Supernaturalism: Tradition and Revolution in Romantic Literature.* New York: Norton, 1973.

Acton, John Emerich Edward, Lord. *Lectures on Modern History.* 1906. New York: Meridian, 1961.

Allgemeine Deutsche Biographie (ADB). Edited by the Historische Commission bei der Königlichen Akademie der Wissenschaften. 56 vols. 2d ed. Berlin: Duncker & Humblot, 1967–71.

Aner, Karl. *Die Theologie der Lessingzeit.* Halle: Niemeyer, 1929.

Anrich, Ernst, ed. *Die Idee der deutschen Universität.* Darmstadt: Wissenschaftliche Buchgesellschaft, 1964.

Auden, W. H. *The Dyer's Hand and Other Essays.* New York: Random House, 1962.

Bader, Karl. "Deutsches Recht." In *Deutsche Philologie im Aufriß,* edited by Wolfgang Stammler, 3:1971–2023. 2d ed. Berlin: Erich Schmidt, 1962.

Barner, Wilfried, ed. *Lessing. Epoche-Werk-Wirkung.* 4th ed. Munich: Beck, 1981.

Barth, Karl. *Die protestantische Theologie im 19. Jahrhundert. Ihre Vorgeschichte und ihre Geschichte.* 2 vols. Hamburg: Siebenstern, 1975.

Baumgartner, Michael, ed. *Schelling. Einführung in seine Philosophie.* Freiburg: Alber, 1975.

Beiser, Frederick C. "Hegel's Historicism." In *The Cambridge Companion to Hegel,* edited by F. C. Beiser, 270–300. Cambridge: Cambridge University Press, 1993.

——. Introduction to *Lectures on the History of Philosophy,* by G. W. F. Hegel. Translated by E. S. Haldane. Lincoln: University of Nebraska Press, 1995.

Benjamin, Walter. *Gesammelte Briefe.* Edited by Theodor W. Adorno Archiv. 6 vols. Frankfurt am Main: Suhrkamp, 1995–2000.

Berlin, Isaiah. *Vico and Herder: Two Studies in the History of Ideas.* New York: Vintage, 1977.

Bietak, Wilhelm, ed. *Romantische Wissenschaft.* Deutsche Literatur in Entwicklungsreihen: Reihe Romantik 13. Leipzig: Reclam, 1940.

Breisach, Ernst. *Historiography. Ancient, Medieval, & Modern.* Chicago: University of Chicago Press, 1983.

Brinkmann, Richard, ed. *Romantik in Deutschland. Ein interdisziplinäres Symposion.* Stuttgart: Metzler, 1978.

Broman, Thomas H. *The Transformation of German Academic Medicine,* 1750–1820. Cambridge: Cambridge University Press, 1996.

Bruford, W. H. *Germany in the Eighteenth Century: The Social Background of the Literary Revival.* 1935. Cambridge: Cambridge University Press, 1971.

Brunschwig, Henri. *Enlightenment and Romanticism in Eighteenth-Century Prussia.* Translated by Frank Jellinek. Chicago: University of Chicago Press, 1974.

Burckhardt, Jacob. *Weltgeschichtliche Betrachtungen.* Edited by Rudolf Marx. 7th ed. Stuttgart: Kröner, 1949.

Butler, Judith. *Subjects of Desire: Hegelian Reflections in Twentieth-Century France.* New York: Columbia University Press, 1987.

The Cambridge Companion to Hegel. Edited by Frederick C. Beiser. Cambridge: Cambridge University Press, 1993.

Carus, Carl Gustav. *Lebenserinnerungen und Denkwürdigkeiten.* Edited by Elmar Jansen. 2 vols. Weimar: Kiepenheuer, 1966.

———. *Psyche.* Edited by Ludwig Klages. Jena: Diederichs, 1926.

Christ, Karl. *Römische Geschichte und deutsche Geschichtswissenschaft.* Munich: Beck, 1982.

Clark, Robert T., Jr. *Herder: His Life and Thought.* Berkeley: University of California Press, 1969.

Conger, George P. *Theories of Macrocosms and Microcosms in the History of Philosophy.* New York: Columbia University Press, 1922.

Cunningham, Andrew, and Nicholas Jardine, eds. *Romanticism and the Sciences.* Cambridge: Cambridge University Press, 1990.

Cutrofello, Andrew. *The Owl at Dawn: A Sequel to Hegel's Phenomenology of Spirit.* Albany: State University of New York Press, 1995.

Denneler, Iris. *Friedrich Karl von Savigny.* Berlin: Stapp, 1985.

Dictionary of the History of Science (DHS). Edited by W. F. Bynum, E. J. Browne, Roy Porter. Princeton: Princeton University Press, 1981.

Dictionary of Scientific Biography (DSB). Edited by Charles Coulston Gillispie. 18 vols. New York: Scribner, 1970–90.

Dilthey, Wilhelm. *Gesammelte Schriften.* 23 vols. Leipzig: Teubner, 1914–2000.

Dokumente zu Hegels Entwicklung. Edited by Johannes Hoffmeister. Stuttgart: Frommann, 1936.

Droz, Jacques. *L'Allemagne et la révolution française.* Paris: Presses universitaires de France, 1949.

———. *Le romantisme allemand et l'état. Résistance et collaboration dans l'Allemagne napoléonienne.* Paris: Payot, 1966.

Eichhorn, Karl Friedrich. *Deutsche Staats- und Rechtsgeschichte.* 4 vols. 5th ed. Göttingen: Vandenhoeck und Ruprecht, 1843–44.

Engel, Josef. "Die deutschen Universitäten und die Geschichtswissenschaft." *Historische Zeitschrift* 189 (1959): 223–378.

Engelhardt, Dietrich von. "Historical Consciousness in the German Romantic *Naturforschung.*" In *Romanticism and the Sciences,* edited by Andrew Cunningham and Nicholas Jardine, 55–68. Cambridge: Cambridge University Press, 1990.

Eulenberg, Franz. *Die Frequenz der deutschen Universitäten von ihrer Gründung bis zur*

Gegenwart. Abhandlungen der philologisch-historischen Klasse der Königl. Sächsischen Gesellschaft der Wissenschaften. Vol. 24, pt. 2. Leipzig: Teubner, 1904.

Felgentraeger, Wilhelm. "Briefe F. C. von Savignys an P. F. Weis (1804–1807)." *Zeitschrift der Savigny-Stiftung für Rechtsgeschichte,* Romanistische Abteilung 48 (1928):114–69.

Fichte, Johann Gottlieb. *Gesamtausgabe der Bayerischen Akademie der Wissenschaften.* Edited by Reinhard Lauth and Hans Jacob. Stuttgart: Frommann, 1962ff.

———. *Grundlage der gesamten Wissenschaftslehre.* Edited by Wilhelm G. Jacobs. Hamburg: Meiner, 1979.

———. *Reden an die deutsche Nation.* Edited by Reinhard Lauth. Hamburg: Meiner, 1978.

Foucault, Michel. *The Order of Things: An Archaeology of the Human Sciences.* New York: Vintage, 1994.

Frei, Hans W. *The Eclipse of Biblical Narrative: A Study in Eighteenth and Nineteenth Century Hermeneutics.* New Haven: Yale University Press, 1974.

Garrison, Fielding H. *An Introduction to the History of Medicine.* Philadelphia: Saunders, 1929.

Gay, Peter. *The Science of Freedom.* Vol. 2 of *The Enlightenment: An Interpretation.* New York: Knopf, 1969.

Geldsetzer, Lutz. "Der Methodenstreit in der Philosophiegeschichtsschreibung 1790–1820." *Kant-Studien* 56 (1966): 519–27.

———. *Die Philosophenwelt in Versen vorgestellt.* Stuttgart: Reclam, 1995.

Genschorek, Wolfgang. *Christoph Wilhelm Hufeland. Der Arzt, der das Leben verlängern half.* 2d ed. Leipzig: Hirzel, 1977.

———. *Geschichtliche Grundbegriffe. Historisches Lexikon zur politisch-sozialen Sprache in Deutschland.* Edited by Otto Brunner, Werner Conze, Reinhart Koselleck. 8 vols. Stuttgart: Klett-Cotta, 1972–97.

Gillispie, Charles Coulston. *Genesis and Geology. A Study in the Relations of Scientific Thought, Natural Theology, and Social Opinion in Great Britain, 1790–1850.* New York: Harper & Row, 1959.

Ginsborg, Hannah. "Kant on Understanding Organisms as Natural Purposes." In *Kant and the Sciences,* edited by Eric Watkins, 231–58. New York: Oxford University Press, 2001.

Gode-Von Aesch, Alexander. *Natural Science in German Romanticism.* New York: Columbia University Press, 1941.

Goethe, Johann Wolfgang. *Werke.* Edited by Erich Trunz. 14 vols. Hamburg: Wegner, 1956–60.

Gollwitzer, Heinz. *Ludwig I. von Bayern. Königtum im Vormärz. Eine politische Biographie.* Munich: Süddeutscher Verlag, 1986.

Gooch, G. P. *History and Historians in the Nineteenth Century.* 1913. Boston: Beacon, 1962.

Grimm, Jacob. *Deutsche Grammatik.* 4 vols. 2d ed. Göttingen: Dieterich, 1822.

———. *Kleinere Schriften.* 8 vols. Berlin: Dümmler, 1865–1890.

Guyer, Paul. "Organisms and the Unity of Science." In *Kant and the Sciences,* edited by Eric Watkins, 259–81. New York: Oxford University Press, 2001.

Harris, H. S. *Hegel's Development: Toward the Sunlight, 1770–1801.* Oxford: Clarendon, 1972.

———. "Hegel's Intellectual Development to 1807." In *The Cambridge Companion to Hegel,* edited by Frederick C. Beiser, 25–51. Cambridge: Cambridge University Press.

Haskins, Charles Homer. *The Rise of Universities.* 1923. Ithaca: Cornell University Press, 1979.

Hattenhauer, Hans. *Thibaut und Savigny. Ihre programmatischen Schriften.* Munich: Vahlen, 1973.

Haym, Rudolf. *Hegel und seine Zeit. Vorlesungen über Entstehung und Entwickelung, Wesen und Wert der Hegel'schen Philosophie.* 2d ed. Leipzig: Heims, 1927.

Hazard, Paul. *European Thought in the Eighteenth Century: From Montesquieu to Lessing.* Translated by J. Lewis May. Cleveland: Meridian, 1963.

Hegel, Georg Wilhelm Friedrich. *Briefe von und an Hegel.* Vol. 1. 1785–1812. Edited by Johannes Hoffmeister. Hamburg: Meiner, 1952.

——. *Encyclopedie der philosophischen Wissenschaften.* Vols. 8–10 of *Werke in zwanzig Bänden.* Edited by Eva Moldenhauer and Karl Markus Michel. Frankfurt am Main: Suhrkamp, 1970.

——. *Phänomenologie des Geistes.* Edited by Johannes Hoffmeister. Hamburg: Meiner, 1952.

——. *Phenomenology of Spirit.* Translated by A. V. Miller. New York: Oxford University Press, 1979.

——. *Theologische Jugendschriften.* Edited by Hermann Nohl. Tübingen: Mohr, 1907.

——. *Vorlesungen über die Geschichte der Philosophie.* Vol. 18 of *Werke in zwanzig Bänden.* Edited by Eva Moldenhauer and Karl Markus Frankfurt am Main: Suhrkamp, 1971.

——. *Vorlesungen über die Philosophie der Geschichte.* Vol. 12 of *Werke in zwanzig Bänden.* Edited by Eva Moldenhauer and Karl Markus Michel. Frankfurt am Main: Suhrkamp, 1986.

Herder, Johann Gottfried. *Sämmtliche Werke.* Edited by Bernhard Suphan. 33 vols. Berlin: Weidmann, 1877–1913.

——. *Schriften zu Philosophie, Literatur, Kunst und Altertum 1774–1787.* Vol. 4 of *Werke in zehn Bänden,* edited by Günter Arnold et al. Frankfurt am Main: Deutscher Klassiker Verlag, 1994.

——. *Theologische Schriften.* Vol. 9, pt. 1 of *Werke in zehn Bänden,* edited by Günter Arnold et al. Frankfurt am Main: Deutscher Klassiker Verlag, 1994.

Hirsch, Emanuel. "Die Beisetzung der Romantiker in Hegels Phänomenologie." *Deutsche Vierteljahresschrift für Literaturwissenschaft und Geistesgeschichte* 2 (1924): 510–32.

——. *Geschichte der neuern evangelischen Theologie im Zusammenhang mit den allgemeinen Bewegungen des europäischen Denkens.* 5 vols. Gütersloh: Bertelsmann, 1949–54.

Historisches Wörterbuch der Philosophie. Edited by Joachim Ritter. 11 vols. Basel: Schwabe, 1971–2001.

Holborn, Hajo. *A History of Modern Germany, 1648–1840.* Princeton: Princeton University Press, 1964.

Hölderlin, Friedrich: *Sämtliche Werke.* Edited by Friedrich Beissner. Kleine Stuttgarter Ausgabe. 6 vols. Stuttgart: Kohlhammer, 1944–62.

Huch, Ricarda. *Die Romantik.* 1899–1902. Tübingen: Wunderlich, 1951.

Hufeland, Christoph Wilhelm. *Makrobiotik oder Die Kunst das menschliche Leben zu verlängern.* 4th ed. Berlin: Witsch, 1805.

Humboldt, Alexander von. *Ansichten der Natur: erster und zweiter Band.* Edited by Hanno Beck. Vol. 5 of *Studienausgabe.* Darmstadt: Wissenschaftliche Buchgesellschaft, 1987.

Hyppolite, Jean. "Anmerkungen zur Vorrede der Phänomenologie des Geistes und zum

Thema: das Absolute ist Subject." In *Materialien zu Hegels "Phänomenologie des Geistes,"* edited by Hans Friedrich Fulda and Dieter Henrich, 45–53. Frankfurt am Main: Suhrkamp, 1973.

———. *Genesis and Structure of Hegel's Phenomenology of Spirit.* Translated by Samuel Cherniak and John Heckman. Evanston: Northwestern University Press, 1974.

Jaspers, Karl. *Schelling. Größe und Verhängnis.* 1955. Munich: Piper, 1986.

Jordan, Louis Henry. *Comparative Religion: Its Genesis and Growth.* New York: Scribner, 1905.

Jung, Carl Gustav. *The Archetypes and the Collective Unconscious.* Translated by R. F. C. Hull. Bollingen Series XX. 2d ed. Princeton: Princeton University Press, 1968.

Kant, Immanuel. *Werke in zehn Bänden.* Edited by Wilhelm Weischedel. 2d ed. Darmstadt: Wissenschaftliche Buchgesellschaft, 1968.

Kantorowicz, Hermann. "Savigny and the Historical School of Law." *The Law Review Quarterly* 53 (1937): 326–43.

Kantzenbach, Friedrich Wilhelm. *Friedrich Daniel Ernst Schleiermacher in Selbstzeugnissen und Bilddokumenten.* Reinbek bei Hamburg: Rowohlt, 1967.

Kaufmann, Walter. *Hegel: Reinterpretation, Texts, and Commentary.* Garden City: Doubleday, 1965.

Keune, Angelika. *Gelehrtenbildnisse der Humboldt-Universität zu Berlin. Denkmäler, Büsten, Reliefs, Gedenktafeln, Gemälde, Zeichnungen, Graphiken, Medaillen.* Berlin: Humboldt-Universität, 2000.

Kirchhoff, Jochen. *Friedrich Wilhelm Joseph von Schelling in Selbstzeugnissen und Bilddokumenten.* Reinbek bei Hamburg: Rowohlt, 1982.

Kleinheyer, Gerd, and Jan Schröder. *Deutsche Juristen aus fünf Jahrhunderten. Eine biographische Einführung in die Geschichte der Rechtswissenschaft.* 3d ed. Heidelberg: Müller, 1989.

Klenner, Hermann. "Savigny's Research Program of the Historical School of Law and Its Intellectual Impact in 19th Century Berlin." *The American Journal of Comparative Law* 37 (1989): 67–80.

Kluckhohn, Paul. *Das Ideengut der deutschen Romantik.* 2d ed. Halle: Niemeyer, 1942.

Kojève, Alexandre. *Introduction to the Reading of Hegel. Lectures on the Phenomenology of Spirit.* Edited by Allan Bloom. Translated by James H. Nichols, Jr. Ithaca: Cornell University Press, 1960.

Koselleck, Reinhart. "Geschichte." In *Geschichtliche Grundbegriffe: Historisches Lexikon zur politisch-sozialen Sprache in Deutschland.* 2:593–717.

———. "*Historia magistra vitae.* Über die Auflösung des Topos im Horizont neuzeitlich bewegter Geschichte." In *Natur und Geschichte,* edited by Hermann Braun and Manfred Riedel, 196–219. Stuttgart: Kohlhammer, 1967.

Koschaker, Paul. *Europa und das römische Recht.* Berlin: Biederstein, 1947.

Kuhn, Thomas S. *The Structure of Scientific Revolution.* 2d ed. Chicago: University of Chicago Press, 1970.

Landes, David S. *The Unbound Prometheus: Technological Change and Industrial Development in Western Europe from 1750 to the Present.* Cambridge: Cambridge University Press, 1969.

Lange, Dietz, ed. *Friedrich Schleiermacher 1769–1834. Theologe—Philosoph—Pädagoge.* Göttingen: Vandenhoeck & Ruprecht, 1985.

Lenoir, Timothy. *The Strategy of Life: Teleology and Mechanics in Nineteenth Century German Biology*. Dordrecht: Reidel, 1982.

Lepenies, Wolf. *Das Ende der Naturgeschichte. Wandel kultureller Selbstverständlichkeiten in den Wissenschaften des 18. und 19. Jahrhunderts*. Frankfurt am Main: Suhrkamp, 1978.

Lessing, Gotthold Ephraim. *Werke*. Edited by Herbert G. Göpfert. 8 vols. Munich: Hanser, 1970–1979.

Lovejoy, Arthur O. *The Great Chain of Being: A Study of the History of an Idea*. 1936. New York: Harper, 1960.

Lukács, Georg. *Der junge Hegel: Über die Beziehungen von Dialektik und Oekonomie*. Zürich: Europa Verlag, 1948.

Macdonell, John, ed. *Great Jurists of the World*. Boston: Little, Brown, 1914.

Machlup, Fritz. *The Branches of Learning*. Vol. 2 of *Knowledge: Its Creation, Distribution, and Economic Significance*. Princeton: Princeton University Press, 1982.

Makkreel, Rudolf A. *Dilthey: Philosopher of the Human Sciences*. Princeton: Princeton University Press, 1975.

Marini, Giuliano. *Friedrich Carl von Savigny*. Napoli: Guida, 1978.

Marrou, H. I. *A History of Education in Antiquity*. Translated by George Lamb. Madison: University of Wisconsin Press, 1982.

Marx, Werner. *Schelling: Geschichte, System, Freiheit*. Freiburg: Karl Alber, 1977.

Mayo, Robert S. *Herder and the Beginnings of Comparative Literature*. Chapel Hill: University of North Carolina Press, 1969.

McCullagh, C. B. "Historical Explanations, Theories of: Philosophical Aspects." In *International Encyclopedia of the Social and Behavioral Sciences*, edited by Neil J. Smelser and Paul B. Baltes, 10:6731–37. Amsterdam: Elsevier, 2001.

Meinecke, Friedrich. *Die Entstehung des Historismus*. Vol. 3 of *Werke*. Edited by Hans Herzfeld. Munich: Oldenbourg, 1959.

Meyer, Arthur William. *Human Generation: Conclusions of Burdach, Döllinger and von Baer*. Stanford: Stanford University Press, 1956.

Meyer-Abich, Adolf. *Biologie der Goethezeit: Klassische Abhandlungen über die Grundlagen und Hauptprobleme der Biologie von Goethe und den großen Naturforschern seiner Zeit*. Stuttgart: Hippokrates, 1949.

Momigliano, Arnaldo. *Studies in Historiography*. New York: Harper & Row, 1966.

Moretto, Giovanni. *Etica e storia in Schleiermacher*. Napoli: Bibliopolis, 1979.

Morwitz, Eduard. *Geschichte der Medicin*. 1848. Rpt. Wiesbaden: Sändig, 1966.

Müller, Ernst, ed. *Gelegentliche Gedanken über Universitäten*. Leipzig: Reclam, 1990.

Neubauer, John. *Bifocal Vision: Novalis' Philosophy of Nature and Disease*. Chapel Hill: University of North Carolina Press, 1971.

Neue Deutsche Biographie (NDB). Edited by Historische Kommission bei der Bayerischen Akademie der Wissenschaften. Berlin: Duncker & Humblot, 1953–.

Niebuhr, Barthold Georg. *Die Briefe*. Edited by Dietrich Gerhard and William Norvin. 2 vols. Berlin: De Gruyter, 1929.

——. *Römische Geschichte*. 2 vols. Berlin: Realschulbuchhandlung, 1811–12.

Nörr, Dieter. *Savignys philosophische Lehrjahre. Ein Versuch*. Frankfurt am Main: Klostermann, 1994.

Norton, Robert E. *The Beautiful Soul. Aesthetic Morality in the Eighteenth Century*. Ithaca: Cornell University Press, 1995.

Novalis (Friedrich von Hardenberg). *Schriften.* Edited by Richard Samuel et al. 4 vols. 2d ed. Darmstadt: Wissenschaftliche Buchgesellschaft, 1960–75.

Nowak, Kurt. *Schleiermacher: Leben, Werk und Wirkung.* Göttingen: Vandenhoeck & Ruprecht, 2001.

Oken, Lorenz. *Allgemeine Naturgeschichte für alle Stände.* 13 vols. Stuttgart: Hoffmann, 1833–42.

———. *Lehrbuch der Naturphilosophie.* 3 vols. Jena: Frommann, 1809–1811.

———. *Die Zeugung.* Bamberg: Goebhardt, 1805.

Pinkard, Terry. *Hegel: A Biography.* Cambridge: Cambridge University Press, 2001.

Pöggeler, Otto. *Hegels Idee einer Phänomenologie des Geistes.* Freiburg: Karl Alber, 1973.

———. "Die Komposition der Phänomenologie des Geistes." In *Hegel-Studien 1966.* Beiheft 3: 27–74.

Reardon, Bernard M. G. *Religion in the Age of Romanticism. Studies in Early Nineteenth Century Thought.* Cambridge: Cambridge University Press, 1985.

Redeker, Martin. *Schleiermacher: Life and Thought.* Translated by John Wallhausser. Philadelphia: Fortress, 1973.

Renker, Fritz. *Niebuhr und die Romantik.* Leipzig: Vogel, 1935.

Richards, Robert J. *The Romantic Conception of Life: Science and Philosophy in the Age of Goethe.* Chicago: University of Chicago Press, 2002.

Riedel, Volker. *Literarische Antikerezeption.* Aufsätze und Vorträge. Jena: Bussert, 1996.

Ripa, Cesare. *Iconology; or, a Collection of Emblematical Figures.* Selected and composed by George Richardson. 2 vols. London: Scott, 1779.

Rosenkranz, Karl. *Georg Wilhelm Friedrich Hegel's Leben.* Berlin: Duncker und Humblot, 1844.

Rottblatt, Sheldon. "The Student Sub-culture and the Examination System in Early 19th Century Oxbridge." In *The University in Society,* edited by Lawrence Stone, 1:247-303. Princeton: Princeton University Press, 1974.

Rothacker, Erich. *Einleitung in die Geisteswissenschaften.* 2d ed. Tübingen: Mohr, 1930.

Royce, Josiah. *Lectures on Modern Idealism.* New Haven: Yale University Press, 1919.

Sauer, August, ed. *Die deutschen Säculardichtungen an der Wende des 18. und 19. Jahrunderts.* Berlin: Behr, 1901.

Savigny, Friedrich Carl von. *Geschichte des Römischen Rechts im Mittelalter.* 2d ed. 7 vols. Heidelberg: Mohr, 1834–1851.

———. *Das Recht des Besitzes. Eine civilistische Abhandlung.* 5th ed. Stuttgart: Hausmann, 1937.

———. *System des heutigen Römischen Rechts.* 8 vols. Berlin: Veit, 1840–49.

———. *Vermischte Schriften.* 5 vols. Berlin: Veit, 1850.

———. *Vorlesungen über juristische Methodologie 1802–1842.* Edited by Aldo Mazzacane. Frankfurt am Main: Klostermann, 1993.

Schaeffler, Richard. *Einführung in die Geschichtsphilosophie.* Darmstadt: Wissenschaftliche Buchgesellschaft, 1980.

Schelling, Friedrich Wilhelm Joseph. *Sämmtliche Werke.* Stuttgart: Cotta, 1858.

———. *Schriften von 1794–98.* Darmstadt: Wissenschaftliche Buchgesellschaft, 1967.

———. *System des transzendentalen Idealismus.* Edited by Otto Weiß. Leipzig: Meiner, 1911.

Schiller, Friedrich. *Sämtliche Werke.* Edited by Gerhard Fricke, Herbert G. Göpfert, and Herbert Stubenrauch. 5 vols. 4th ed. Munich: Hanser, 1965–67.

Schlegel, Friedrich. *Kritische Friedrich-Schlegel-Ausgabe.* Edited by Ernst Behler with Jean-Jacques Anstett and Hans Eichner. 35 vols. Paderborn: Schöningh, 1958ff.

——. *Kritische Schriften.* Edited by Wolfdietrich Rasch. Munich: Hanser, 1956.

Schleiermacher, Friedrich. *Brief Outline of Theology as a Field of Study.* Translated by Terrence N. Tice. Lewiston, N.Y.: Edwin Mellen, 1988.

——. *Christmas Eve: Dialogue on the Incarnation.* Translated by Terrence N. Tice. Richmond: John Knox Press, 1967.

——. *Hermeneutik.* Nach den Handschriften neu herausgegeben und eingeleitet von Heinz Kimmerle. Abhandlungen der Heidelberger Akademie der Wissenschaften, Philosophisch-historische Klasse 1959/2. Heidelberg, 1959.

——. *Hermeneutik und Kritik.* Edited by Manfred Frank. Frankfurt am Main: Suhrkamp, 1977.

——. *Kritische Gesamtausgabe* (KGA). Edited by Hans-Joachim Birkner. Berlin: De Gruyter, 1980–.

——. *Kurze Darstellung des theologischen Studiums zum Behuf einleitender Vorlesungen.* 1810. Edited by Heinrich Scholz. 1910. Darmstadt: Wissenschaftliche Buchgesellschaft, 1993.

——. *Über die Religion.* Edited by Rudolf Otto. 5th ed. Göttingen: Vandenhoeck & Ruprecht, 1926.

——. *Über die Religion. Reden an die Gebildeten unter ihren Verächtern.* Edited by Carl Heinz Ratschow. Stuttgart: Reclam, 1969.

Schulz, Gerhard. *Die deutsche Literatur zwischen Französischer Revolution und Restauration.* 2 vols. Munich: Beck, 1983–89.

Schweitzer, Albert. *The Quest of the Historical Jesus. A Critical Study of Its Progress from Reimarus to Wrede.* Translated by W. Montgomery. New York: Macmillan, 1968.

Scott, Sir Walter. *Waverley; or, 'Tis Sixty Years Since.* Edited by Claire Lamont. Oxford: Clarendon, 1981.

Shaffer, Elinor S. "Romantic Philosophy and the Organization of the Disciplines: The Founding of the Humboldt University of Berlin." In *Romanticism and the Sciences,* edited by Andrew Cunningham and Nicholas Jardine, 38–54. Cambridge: Cambridge University Press, 1990.

Srbik, Heinrich Ritter von. *Geist und Geschichte vom deutschen Humanismus bis zur Gegenwart.* 2 vols. Munich: Bruckmann, 1950.

Staël, Anne-Louise-Germaine de. *De l'Allemagne.* Edited by André Monchoux. Nouvelle édition abrégée. Paris: Didier, 1956.

——. *Über Deutschland: Vollständige Ausgabe nach der deutschen Erstübertragung von 1814.* Edited by Monika Bosse. Frankfurt am Main: Insel, 1985.

Steffens, Henrik. *Lebenserinnerungen aus dem Kreis der Romantik.* Edited by Friedrich Gundelfinger. Jena: Diederichs, 1908.

Steinbüchel, Theodor, ed. *Romantik. Ein Zyklus Tübinger Vorlesungen.* Tübingen: Wunderlich, 1948.

Steiner, George. *Antigones.* Oxford: Clarendon, 1986.

Stoll, Adolf. *Der junge Savigny.* Vol. 1 of *Friedrich Karl von Savigny. Ein Bild seines Lebens mit Sammlungen seiner Briefe.* 3 vols. Berlin: Heymann, 1927–39.

——. *Ministerzeit und letzte Lebensjahre.* Vol. 3 of *Friedrich Karl von Savigny.*

——. *Professorenjahre in Berlin.* Vol. 2 of *Friedrich Karl von Savigny.*

Stühler, Hans-Ulrich. *Die Diskussion um die Erneuerung der Rechtswissenschaft von 1780–1815.* Berlin: Duncker & Humblot, 1978.

Sudhoff, Karl. *Kurzes Handbuch der Geschichte der Medizin.* Berlin: Karger, 1922.

Tatar, Maria M. *Spellbound: Studies on Mesmerism and Literature.* Princeton: Princeton University Press, 1978.

Temkin, Owsei. *The Double Face of Janus and Other Essays in the History of Medicine.* Baltimore: The Johns Hopkins University Press, 1977.

Tillich, Paul. *A History of Christian Thought: from Its Judaic and Hellenistic Origins to Existentialism.* Edited by Carl E. Braaten. New York: Simon and Schuster, 1972.

Toynbee, Arnold J. *A Study of History.* Vol. 4. London: Oxford University Press, 1939.

Troeltsch, Ernst. "Die Krisis der Historismus." *Neue Rundschau* 33 (1922): 572–90.

Vorländer, Karl. *Immanuel Kant: Der Mann und das Werk.* 2 vols. Leipzig: Meiner, 1924.

Wackenroder, Wilhelm. *Dichtung. Schriften. Briefe.* Edited by Gerda Heinrich. Munich: Hanser, 1984.

Waetzoldt, Wilhelm. *Deütsche Kunsthistoriker von Sandrart bis Rumohr.* Leipzig: Seemann, 1921.

Walther, Gerrit. *Niebuhrs Forschung.* Stuttgart: Steiner, 1993.

Watkins, Eric, ed. *Kant and the Sciences.* New York: Oxford University Press, 2001.

Watson, Alan. *The Evolution of Law.* Baltimore: Johns Hopkins University Press, 1985.

———. *The Making of the Civil Law.* Cambridge: Harvard University Press, 1981.

Wells, G. A. *Herder and After. A Study in the Development of Sociology.* 'S-Gravenhage: Mouton, 1959.

Wesenberg, G. *Juristische Methodenlehre, nach der Ausarbeitung des Jakob Grimm.* Stuttgart: Koehler, 1951.

Wetzels, Walter D. *Johann Wilhelm Ritter: Physik im Wirkungsfeld der deutschen Romantik.* Berlin: De Gruyter, 1973.

Whitman, James Q. *The Legacy of Roman Law in the German Romantic Era. Historical Vision and Legal Change.* Princeton: Princeton University Press, 1990.

Wieacker, Franz. *A History of Private Law in Europe with Particular Reference to Germany.* Translated by Tony Weir. Oxford: Clarendon, 1995.

———. *Wandlungen im Bilde der historischen Rechtsschule.* Juristische Studiengesellschaft Karlsruhe. Schriftenreihe, Heft 77. Karlsruhe: Müller, 1967.

Wilamowitz-Moellendorff, Ulrich von. *History of Classical Scholarship.* 1921. Translated by Alan Harris. Baltimore: Johns Hopkins University Press, 1982.

Windelband, Wilhelm. *Die Blüthezeit der deutschen Philosophie.* Vol. 2 of *Die Geschichte der neueren Philosophie.* 2d ed. Leipzig: Breitkopf und Härtel, 1899.

———. *Geschichte der Philosophie.* Freiburg im Breisgau: Mohr, 1892.

Witte, Barthold C. *Der preußische Tacitus. Aufstieg, Ruhm und Ende des Historikers Barthold Georg Niebuhr 1776–1831.* Düsseldorf: Droste, 1979.

Wolf, Erik. *Große Rechtsdenker der deutschen Geistesgeschichte.* 3d ed. Tübingen: Mohr, 1951.

Zeitschrift für geschichtliche Rechtswissenschaft. 15 vols. Berlin: Nicolai, 1815–50; continued from 1851 as *Zeitschrift für Rechtsgeschichte* and from 1880 to present as *Zeitschrift der Savigny-Stiftung für Rechtsgeschichte.*

Ziolkowski, Theodore. *Berlin. Aufstieg einer Kulturmetropole um 1810.* Stuttgart: Klett-Cotta, 2002.

——. *The Classical German Elegy, 1795–1950.* Princeton: Princeton University Press, 1980.

——. *German Romanticism and Its Institutions.* Princeton: Princeton University Press, 1990.

——. *The Mirror of Justice: Literary Reflections of Legal Crises.* Princeton: Princeton University Press, 1997.

——. "Rhetorik der Revolution in Jena: Schlegels drei Tendenzen." In *Geist und Gesellschaft. Zur deutschen Rezeption der Französischen Revolution,* edited by Eitel Timm, 83–97. Munich: Fink, 1990.

——. "Varieties of Experiencing Religion." *Journal of Religion* 67 (1987): 340–47.

INDEX

❧

ABOUT THE AUTHOR

THEODORE ZIOLKOWSKI is Class of 1900 Professor Emeritus of German and Comparative Literature at Princeton University. He is the author of many books, including *Virgil and the Moderns, The Mirror of Justice* (which received Phi Beta Kappa's Christian Gauss Award), and *The Sin of Knowledge: Ancient Themes and Modern Variations.*